THE BOOK ®

Yamaha XT & SR125 Singles
Service and Repair Manual

by Jeremy Churchill
with an additional Chapter on the 1991-on models by Penny Cox and Phil Mather

Models covered
XT125. 124cc. April 1982 to January 1985
SR125SE. 124cc. January 1982 to June 1985
SR125. 124cc. February 1991 onwards

(1021-192-7AB3)

© Haynes Publishing 2002

ABCDE
FGHIJ
KL

A book in the **Haynes Service and Repair Manual Series**

ISBN **1 85960 945 7**

British Library Cataloguing in Publication Data
A catalogue record for this book is available from the British Library

Printed in the USA

Haynes Publishing
Sparkford, Yeovil, Somerset BA22 7JJ, England

Haynes North America, Inc
861 Lawrence Drive, Newbury Park, California 91320, USA

Editions Haynes
4, Rue de l'Abreuvoir
92415 COURBEVOIE CEDEX, France

Haynes Publishing Nordiska AB
Box 1504, 751 45 UPPSALA, Sweden

Acknowledgements

Our thanks are due to Jim Patch of Yeovil Motorcycle Services Ltd, Yeovil, Somerset and to Fran Ridewood and Co of Wells, Somerset who supplied the two machines which feature in the photographs throughout this manual, and to Mitsui Machinery Sales (UK) Ltd who supplied the service information and gave permission to reproduce many of the line drawings.

We would like to thank the Avon Rubber Company, who kindly supplied information and technical assistance on tyre fitting, NGK Spark Plugs (UK) Ltd for information on spark plug maintenance and electrode conditions, and Reynold Ltd for advice on chain care and renewal.

About this manual

The purpose of this manual is to present the owner with a concise and graphic guide which will enable him to tackle any operation from basic routine maintenance to a major overhaul. It has been assumed that any work would be undertaken without the luxury of a well-equipped workshop and a range of manufacturer's service tools.

To this end, the machine featured in the manual was stripped and rebuilt in our own workshop, by a team comprising a mechanic, a photographer and the author. The resulting photographic sequence depicts events as they took place, the hands shown being those of the author and the mechanic.

The use of specialised, and expensive, service tools was avoided unless their use was considered to be essential due to the risk of breakage or injury. There is usually some way of improvising a method of removing a stubborn component, providing that a suitable degree of care is exercised.

The author learnt his motorcycle mechanics over a number of years, faced with the same difficulties and using similar facilities to those encountered by most owners. It is hoped that this practical experience can be passed on through the pages of this manual.

Where possible, a well-used example of the machine is chosen for the workshop project, as this highlights any areas which might be particularly prone to giving rise to problems. In this way, any such difficulties are encountered and resolved before the text is written, and the techniques used to deal with them can be incorporated in the relevant section. Armed with a working knowledge of the machine, the author undertakes a considerable amount of research in order that the maximum amount of data can be included in the manual.

A comprehensive section, preceding the main part of the manual, describes procedures for carrying out the routine maintenance of the machine at intervals of time and mileage. This section is included particularly for those owners who wish to ensure the efficient day-to-day running of their motorcycle, but who choose not to undertake overhaul or renovation work.

Each Chapter is divided into numbered sections. Within these sections are numbered paragraphs. Cross reference throughout the manual is quite straightforward and logical. When reference is made 'See Section 6.10' it means Section 6, paragraph 10 in the same Chapter. If another Chapter were intended, the reference would read, for example, 'See Chapter 2, Section 6.10'. All the photographs are captioned with a section/paragraph number to which they refer and are relevant to the Chapter text adjacent.

Figures (usually line illustrations) appear in a logical but numerical order, within a given Chapter. Fig. 1.1 therefore refers to the first figure in Chapter 1.

Left-hand and right-hand descriptions of the machines and their components refer to the left and right of a given machine when the rider is seated normally.

Motorcycle manufacturers continually make changes to specifications and recommendations, and these, when notified, are incorporated into our manuals at the earliest opportunity.

We take great pride in the accuracy of information given in the manual, but motorcycle manufacturers make alterations and design changes during the production run of a particular motorcycle of which they do not inform us. No liability can be accepted by the authors or publishers for loss, damage or injury caused by any errors in, or omissions from, the information given.

Contents

Left-hand view of 1982 SR125 SE

Engine/gearbox unit of 1982 SR125 SE

Left-hand view of 1983/84 XT125

Engine/gearbox unit of 1983/84 XT125

Introduction to the Yamaha SR125 SE and XT125 models

Before 1982 the 125cc capacity class of motorcycles was not particularly popular in the UK, since the machines were too slow to attract in large numbers the younger riders looking for performance above all else, and yet were too large to be attractive to the commuter, or non-enthusiast rider. With a few notable exceptions, principally in the trail bike class, their relatively dull specifications reflected the manufacturers natural lack of interest.

This situation was altered radically by the legislation that came into force during 1982 and early 1983; all learner motorcyclists were to be restricted to machines of a maximum engine size of 125cc, the power outputs being restricted to 9kW (12.2 bhp). Almost immediately the four Japanese manufacturers responded with a confusing mass of new models designed to attract the new captive market. Features formerly considered worthwhile only on machines of much larger engine capacity were included in the specification of the new models, many of which incorporated the latest ideas in suspension and styling.

Yamaha's new models were announced early in 1982, the SR125 SE becoming available almost immediately and the XT125 appearing by June. The two models share the same engine/gearbox unit which follows the now standard Japanese practice of using a single overhead camshaft for greater reliability at high engine speeds; indeed the whole unit is designed with economy, simplicity and ease of maintenance in mind. This is quite natural when one considers that Yamaha are also selling the two-stroke engined RD- and DT125 LC models in both restricted and unrestricted forms; with the performance-hungry section of the public well catered for, Yamaha did not need to produce a temperamental gimmick-loaded design. Given the performance restrictions imposed, a good four-stroke engine is at least the equal of any two-stroke and has much to commend it to the average owner. The traditional disadvantage of the four-stroke is its extra weight, but in this case it does not apply; a simple comparison between Yamaha's own models shows that the SR125 and XT125 are only very slightly heavier than their two-stroke counterparts.

The SR125 SE model, as the road version, has been given 'custom' styling of the sort that proved so popular on the factory's 250cc and 650cc machines; while this may not be to everyone's taste, there is no doubt that the feeling of extra control and security provided by the low seat height and wide handlebars make it very attractive to learners. There is also the attraction of electric starting, and it is interesting to see that the temptation has been resisted to fit alloy wheels and disc brakes; while more glamourous in some eyes, these are more difficult and expensive to service and repair than the wire-spoked wheels and drum brakes actually fitted.

The XT125 model comes equipped with all the features expected of a current trail bike, its cycle parts being very similar to those of the DT125 LC, the most popular machine in its class. Long-travel suspension, a high level exhaust system and 'enduro' styling all add up to a machine which is at least as good as those of the rival factories. As with all other motorcycle manufacturers, Yamaha pursue a policy of constant development during a model's life, ensuring that improvements and modifications reach the purchaser as soon as possible; for example the 1983 model XT125 was fitted with a tachometer and front fork gaiters, features that are missing from 1982 models. This policy can lead to some confusion when ordering replacement parts. Since it is not sufficient to identify a machine by giving its date of registration, it being quite possible for a 1982 model to be sold in 1983 and therefore wrongly identified by the owner as a '1983' machine, the following information is given to assist owners in identifying correctly their machines.

Model	Year	Frame Number
SR125 SE	1982	10F-000101
SR125 SE	1983	10F-010101
XT125	1982	12V-000101
XT125	1983	12V-050101

The frame numbers given are those with which each year's production run commenced, and are the only accurate means of identifying a particular machine. Owners of 1984 and 1985 models should note that there are no significant differences from 1983 models.

Refer to Chapter 7 for details of 1991-on SR125 models.

Model dimensions and weights

	SR125 SE	XT125
Overall length	1915 mm (75.4 in)	2155 mm (84.8 in)
Overall width	785 mm (30.9 in)	845 mm (33.3 in)
Overall height	1105 mm (43.5 in)	1160 mm (45.7 in)
Seat height	740 mm (29.1 in)	835 mm (32.9 in)
Wheelbase	1280 mm (50.4 in)	1330 mm (52.4 in)
Ground clearance	160 mm (6.3 in)	265 mm (10.4 in)
Dry weight	104 kg (229 lb)	98 kg (216 lb)
Kerb weight	111 kg (245 lb)	107 kg (236 lb)

Ordering spare parts

Before attempting any overhaul or maintenance work it is important to ensure that any parts likely to be required are to hand. Many of the more common parts such as gaskets and seals will be available off the shelf from the local Yamaha dealer, but often it will prove necessary to order more specialised parts well in advance. It is worthwhile running through the operation to be undertaken, referring to the appropriate Chapter and Section of this book, so that a note can be made of the items most likely to be required. In some instances it will of course be necessary to dismantle the assembly in question so that the various components can be examined and measured for wear and in these instances, it must be remembered that the machine may have to be left dismantled while the replacement parts are obtained.

It is advisable to purchase almost all new parts from an official Yamaha dealer. Almost any motorcycle dealer should be able to obtain the parts in time, but this may take longer than it would through the official factory spares arrangement. It is quite in order to purchase expendable items such as spark plugs, bulbs, tyres, oil and grease form the nearest convenient source.

Owners should be very wary of some of the pattern parts that might be offered at a lower price than the Yamaha originals. Whilst in most cases these will be of an adequate standard, some of the more important parts have been known to fail suddenly and cause extensive damage in the process. A particular danger in recent years is the growing number of counterfeit parts from Taiwan. These include items such as oil filters and brake pads and are often sold in packaging which is almost indistinguishable from the manufacturer's own. Again, these are often quite serviceable parts, but can sometimes be dangerously inadequate in materials or construction. Apart form rendering the manufacturer's warranty invalid, use of sub-standard parts may put the life of the rider (or the machine) at risk. In short, where there are any doubts on safety grounds purchase parts **only** from a reputable Yamaha dealer. The extra cost involved pays for a high standard of quality and the parts will be guaranteed to work effectively.

Most machines are subject to continuous detail modifications throughout their production run in addition to annual model changes. In most cases these changes will be known to the dealer but not to the general public, so it is essential to quote the engine and frame numbers in full when ordering parts. The engine number is embossed in a rectangular section of the crankcase just below the carburettor, and the frame number is stamped on the right-hand side of the steering head.

Location of engine number

Location of frame number

Safety first!

Professional motor mechanics are trained in safe working procedures. However enthusiastic you may be about getting on with the job in hand, do take the time to ensure that your safety is not put at risk. A moment's lack of attention can result in an accident, as can failure to observe certain elementary precautions.

There will always be new ways of having accidents, and the following points do not pretend to be a comprehensive list of all dangers; they are intended rather to make you aware of the risks and to encourage a safety-conscious approach to all work you carry out on your vehicle.

Essential DOs and DON'Ts

DON'T rely on a single jack when working underneath the vehicle. Always use reliable additional means of support, such as axle stands, securely placed under a part of the vehicle that you know will not give way.

DON'T attempt to loosen or tighten high-torque nuts (e.g. wheel hub nuts) while the vehicle is on a jack; it may be pulled off.

DON'T start the engine without first ascertaining that the transmission is in neutral (or 'Park' where applicable) and the parking brake applied.

DON'T suddenly remove the filler cap from a hot cooling system – cover it with a cloth and release the pressure gradually first, or you may get scalded by escaping coolant.

DON'T attempt to drain oil until you are sure it has cooled sufficiently to avoid scalding you.

DON'T grasp any part of the engine, exhaust or catalytic converter without first ascertaining that it is sufficiently cool to avoid burning you.

DON'T allow brake fluid or antifreeze to contact vehicle paintwork.

DON'T syphon toxic liquids such as fuel, brake fluid or antifreeze by mouth, or allow them to remain on your skin.

DON'T inhale dust – it may be injurious to health (see *Asbestos* below).

DON'T allow any spilt oil or grease to remain on the floor – wipe it up straight away, before someone slips on it.

DON'T use ill-fitting spanners or other tools which may slip and cause injury.

DON'T attempt to lift a heavy component which may be beyond your capability – get assistance.

DON'T rush to finish a job, or take unverified short cuts.

DON'T allow children or animals in or around an unattended vehicle.

DO wear eye protection when using power tools such as drill, sander, bench grinder etc, and when working under the vehicle.

DO use a barrier cream on your hands prior to undertaking dirty jobs – it will protect your skin from infection as well as making the dirt easier to remove afterwards; but make sure your hands aren't left slippery. Note that long-term contact with used engine oil can be a health hazard.

DO keep loose clothing (cuffs, tie etc) and long hair well out of the way of moving mechanical parts.

DO remove rings, wristwatch etc, before working on the vehicle – especially the electrical system.

DO ensure that any lifting tackle used has a safe working load rating adequate for the job.

DO keep your work area tidy – it is only too easy to fall over articles left lying around.

DO get someone to check periodically that all is well, when working alone on the vehicle.

DO carry out work in a logical sequence and check that everything is correctly assembled and tightened afterwards.

DO remember that your vehicle's safety affects that of yourself and others. If in doubt on any point, get specialist advice.

IF, in spite of following these precautions, you are unfortunate enough to injure yourself, seek medical attention as soon as possible.

Asbestos

Certain friction, insulating, sealing, and other products – such as brake linings, brake bands, clutch linings, torque converters, gaskets, etc – contain asbestos. *Extreme care must be taken to avoid inhalation of dust from such products since it is hazardous to health.* If in doubt, assume that they *do* contain asbestos.

Fire

Remember at all times that petrol (gasoline) is highly flammable. Never smoke, or have any kind of naked flame around, when working on the vehicle. But the risk does not end there – a spark caused by an electrical short-circuit, by two metal surfaces contacting each other, by careless use of tools, or even by static electricity built up in your body under certain conditions, can ignite petrol vapour, which in a confined space is highly explosive.

Always disconnect the battery earth (ground) terminal before working on any part of the fuel or electrical system, and never risk spilling fuel on to a hot engine or exhaust.

It is recommended that a fire extinguisher of a type suitable for fuel and electrical fires is kept handy in the garage or workplace at all times. Never try to extinguish a fuel or electrical fire with water.

Note: *Any reference to a 'torch' appearing in this manual should always be taken to mean a hand-held battery-operated electric lamp or flashlight. It does NOT mean a welding/gas torch or blowlamp.*

Fumes

Certain fumes are highly toxic and can quickly cause unconsciousness and even death if inhaled to any extent. Petrol (gasoline) vapour comes into this category, as do the vapours from certain solvents such as trichloroethylene. Any draining or pouring of such volatile fluids should be done in a well ventilated area.

When using cleaning fluids and solvents, read the instructions carefully. Never use materials from unmarked containers – they may give off poisonous vapours.

Never run the engine of a motor vehicle in an enclosed space such as a garage. Exhaust fumes contain carbon monoxide which is extremely poisonous; if you need to run the engine, always do so in the open air or at least have the rear of the vehicle outside the workplace.

If you are fortunate enough to have the use of an inspection pit, never drain or pour petrol, and never run the engine, while the vehicle is standing over it; the fumes, being heavier than air, will concentrate in the pit with possibly lethal results.

The battery

Never cause a spark, or allow a naked light, near the vehicle's battery. It will normally be giving off a certain amount of hydrogen gas, which is highly explosive.

Always disconnect the battery earth (ground) terminal before working on the fuel or electrical systems.

If possible, loosen the filler plugs or cover when charging the battery from an external source. Do not charge at an excessive rate or the battery may burst.

Take care when topping up and when carrying the battery. The acid electrolyte, even when diluted, is very corrosive and should not be allowed to contact the eyes or skin.

If you ever need to prepare electrolyte yourself, always add the acid slowly to the water, and never the other way round. Protect against splashes by wearing rubber gloves and goggles.

When jump starting a car using a booster battery, for negative earth (ground) vehicles, connect the jump leads in the following sequence: First connect one jump lead between the positive (+) terminals of the two batteries. Then connect the other jump lead first to the negative (–) terminal of the booster battery, and then to a good earthing (ground) point on the vehicle to be started, at least 18 in (45 cm) from the battery if possible. Ensure that hands and jump leads are clear of any moving parts, and that the two vehicles do not touch. Disconnect the leads in the reverse order.

Mains electricity and electrical equipment

When using an electric power tool, inspection light etc, always ensure that the appliance is correctly connected to its plug and that, where necessary, it is properly earthed (grounded). Do not use such appliances in damp conditions and, again, beware of creating a spark or applying excessive heat in the vicinity of fuel or fuel vapour. Also ensure that the appliances meet the relevant national safety standards.

Ignition HT voltage

A severe electric shock can result from touching certain parts of the ignition system, such as the HT leads, when the engine is running or being cranked, particularly if components are damp or the insulation is defective. Where an electronic ignition system is fitted, the HT voltage is much higher and could prove fatal.

Tools and working facilities

The first priority when undertaking maintenance or repair work of any sort on a motorcycle is to have a clean, dry, well-lit working area. Work carried out in peace and quiet in a well-ordered atmosphere of a good workshop will give more satisfaction and much better results than can usually be achieved in poor working conditions. A good workshop must have a clean flat workbench or a solidly constructed table of convenient working height. The workbench or table should be equipped with a vice which has a jaw opening of at least 4 in (100 mm). A set of jaw covers should be made from soft metal such as aluminium alloy or copper, or from wood. These covers will minimise the marking or damaging of soft or delicate components which may be clamped in the vice. Some clean, dry, storage space will be required for tools, lubricants and dismantled components. It will be necessary during a major overhaul to lay out engine/gearbox components for examination and to keep them where they will remain undisturbed for as long as necessary. To this end it is recommended that a supply of metal or plastic containers of suitable size is collected. A supply of clean, lint-free, rags for cleaning purposes and some newspapers, other rags, or paper towels for mopping up spillages should also be kept. If working on a hard concrete floor note that both the floor and one's knees can be protected from oil spillages and wear by cutting open a large cardboard box and spreading it flat on the floor under the machine or workbench. This also helps to provide some warmth in winter and to prevent the loss of nuts, washers, and other tiny components which have a tendency to disappear when dropped on anything other than a perfectly clean, flat, surface.

Unfortunately, such working conditions are not always available to the home mechanic. When working in poor conditions it is essential to take extra time and care to ensure that the components being worked on are kept scrupulously clean and to ensure that no components or tools are lost or damaged.

A selection of good tools is a fundamental requirement for anyone contemplating the maintenance and repair of a motor vehicle. For the owner who does not possess any, their purchase will prove a considerable expense, offsetting some of the savings made by doing-it-yourself. However, provided that the tools purchased meet the relevant national safety standards and are of good quality, they will last for many years and prove an extremely worthwhile investment.

To help the average owner to decide which tools are needed to carry out the various tasks detailed in this manual, we have compiled three lists of tools under the following headings: *Maintenance and minor repair*, *Repair and overhaul*, and *Specialized*. The newcomer to practical mechanics should start off with the simpler jobs around the vehicle. Then, as his confidence and experience grow, he can undertake more difficult tasks, buying extra tools as and when they are needed. In this way, a *Maintenance and minor repair* tool kit can be built-up into a *Repair and overhaul* tool kit over a considerable period of time without any major cash outlays. The experienced home mechanic will have a tool kit good enough for most repairs and overhaul procedures and will add tools from the specialized category when he feels the expense is justified by the amount of use these tools will be put to.

It is obvious not possible to cover the subject of tools fully here. For those who wish to learn more about tools and their use there is a book entitled Motorcycle Workshop Practice Manual (Book No. 1454) available from the publishers of this manual.

As a general rule, it is better to buy the more expensive, good quality tools. Given reasonable use, such tools will last for a very long time, whereas the cheaper, poor quality, item will wear out faster and need to be renewed more often, thus nullifying the original saving. There is also the risk of a poor quality tool breaking while in use, causing personal injury or expensive damage to the component being worked on.

For practically all tools, a tool factor is the best source since he will have a very comprehensive range compared with the average garage or accessory shop. Having said that, accessory shops often offer excellent quality tools at discount prices, so it pays to shop around. There are plenty of tools around at reasonable prices, but always aim to purchase items which meet the relevant safety standards. If in doubt, seek the advice of the shop proprietor or manager before making a purchase.

The basis of any toolkit is a set of spanners. While open-ended spanners with their slim jaws, are useful for working on awkwardly-positioned nuts, ring spanners have advantages in that they grip the nut far more positively. There is less risk of the spanner slipping off the nut and damaging it, for this reason alone ring spanners are to be preferred. Ideally, the home mechanic should acquire a set of each, but if expense rules this out a set of combination spanners (open-ended at one end and with a ring of the same size at the other) will provide a good compromise. Another item which is so useful it should be considered an essential requirement for any home mechanic is a set of socket spanners. These are available in a variety of drive sizes. It is recommended that the $\frac{1}{2}$-inch drive type is purchased to begin with as although bulkier and more expensive than the $\frac{3}{8}$-inch type, the larger size is far more common and will accept a greater variety of torque wrenches, extension pieces and socket sizes. The socket set should comprise sockets of sizes between 8 and 24 mm, a reversible ratchet drive, an extension bar of about 10 inches in length, a spark plug socket with a rubber insert, and a universal joint. Other attachments can be added to the set at a later date.

Maintenance and minor repair tool kit

Set of spanners 8 – 24 mm
Set of sockets and attachments
Spark plug spanner with rubber insert – 10, 12, or 14 mm
as appropriate
Adjustable spanner
C-spanner/pin spanner
Torque wrench (same size drive as sockets)
Set of screwdrivers (flat blade)
Set of screwdrivers (cross-head)
Set of Allen keys 4 – 10 mm
Impact screwdriver and bits
Ball pein hammer – 2 lb
Hacksaw (junior)
Self-locking pliers – Mole grips or vice grips
Pliers – combination
Pliers – needle nose
Wire brush (small)
Soft-bristled brush
Tyre pump
Tyre pressure gauge
Tyre tread depth gauge
Oil can
Fine emery cloth
Funnel (medium size)
Drip tray
Grease gun
Set of feeler gauges
Brake bleeding kit
Strobe timing light
Continuity tester (dry battery and bulb)
Soldering iron and solder
Wire stripper or craft knife
PVC insulating tape
Assortment of split pins, nuts, bolts, and washers

Repair and overhaul toolkit

The tools in this list are virtually essential for anyone undertaking major repairs to a motorcycle and are additional to the tools listed above. Concerning Torx driver bits, Torx screws are encountered on some of the more modern machines where their use is restricted to fastening certain components inside the engine/gearbox unit. It is therefore recommended that if Torx bits cannot be borrowed from a local dealer, they are purchased individually as the need arises. They are not in regular use in the motor trade and will therefore only be available in specialist tool shops.

Plastic or rubber soft-faced mallet
Torx driver bits
Pliers – electrician's side cutters
Circlip pliers – internal (straight or right-angled tips are
available)
Circlip pliers – external
Cold chisel
Centre punch
Pin punch
Scriber
Scraper (made from soft metal such as aluminium
or copper)
Soft metal drift
Steel rule/straight edge
Assortment of files

Electric drill and bits
Wire brush (large)
Soft wire brush (similar to those used for cleaning suede
shoes)
Sheet of plate glass
Hacksaw (large)
Valve grinding tool
Valve grinding compound (coarse and fine)
Stud extractor set (E-Z out)

Specialized tools

This is not a list of the tools made by the machine's manufacturer to carry out a specific task on a limited range of models. Occasional references are made to such tools in the text of this manual and, in general, an alternative method of carrying out the task without the manufacturer's tool is given where possible. The tools mentioned in this list are those which are not used regularly and are expensive to buy in view of their infrequent use. Where this is the case it may be possible to hire or borrow the tools against a deposit from a local dealer or tool hire shop. An alternative is for a group of friends or a motorcycle club to join in the purchase.

Valve spring compressor
Piston ring compressor
Universal bearing puller
Cylinder bore honing attachment (for electric drill)
Micrometer set
Vernier calipers
Dial gauge set
Cylinder compression gauge
Vacuum gauge set
Multimeter
Dwell meter/tachometer

Care and maintenance of tools

Whatever the quality of the tools purchased, they will last much longer if cared for. This means in practice ensuring that a tool is used for its intended purpose; for example screwdrivers should not be used as a substitute for a centre punch, or as chisels. Always remove dirt or grease and any metal particles but remember that a light film of oil will prevent rusting if the tools are infrequently used. The common tools can be kept together in a large box or tray but the more delicate, and more expensive, items should be stored separately where they cannot be damaged. When a tool is damaged or worn out, be sure to renew it immediately. It is false economy to continue to use a worn spanner or screwdriver which may slip and cause expensive damage to the component being worked on.

Fastening systems

Fasteners, basically, are nuts, bolts and screws used to hold two or more parts together. There are a few things to keep in mind when working with fasteners. Almost all of them use a locking device of some type; either a lock washer, lock nut, locking tab or thread adhesive. All threaded fasteners should be clean, straight, have undamaged threads and undamaged corners on the hexagon head where the spanner fits. Develop the habit of replacing all damaged nuts and bolts with new ones.

Rusted nuts and bolts should be treated with a rust penetrating fluid to ease removal and prevent breakage. After applying the rust penetrant, let it 'work' for a few minutes before trying to loosen the nut or bolt. Badly rusted fasteners may have to be chiseled off or removed with a special nut breaker, available at tool shops.

Flat washers and lock washers, when removed from an assembly should always be replaced exactly as removed. Replace any damaged washers with new ones. Always use a flat washer between a lock washer and any soft metal surface (such as aluminium), thin sheet metal or plastic. Special lock nuts can only be used once or twice before they lose their locking ability and must be renewed.

If a bolt or stud breaks off in an assembly, it can be drilled out and removed with a special tool called an E-Z out. Most dealer service departments and motorcycle repair shops can perform this task, as well as others (such as the repair of threaded holes that have been stripped out).

Spanner size comparison

Jaw gap (in)	Spanner size	Jaw gap (in)	Spanner size
0.250	$\frac{1}{4}$ in AF	0.945	24 mm
0.276	7 mm	1.000	1 in AF
0.313	$\frac{5}{16}$ in AF	1.010	$\frac{9}{16}$ in Whitworth; $\frac{5}{8}$ in BSF
0.315	8 mm	1.024	26 mm
0.344	$\frac{11}{32}$ in AF; $\frac{1}{8}$ in Whitworth	1.063	$1\frac{1}{16}$ in AF; 27 mm
0.354	9 mm	1.100	$\frac{5}{16}$ in Whitworth; $\frac{11}{16}$ in BSF
0.375	$\frac{3}{8}$ in AF	1.125	$1\frac{1}{8}$ in AF
0.394	10 mm	1.181	30 mm
0.433	11 mm	1.200	$\frac{11}{16}$ in Whitworth; $\frac{3}{4}$ in BSF
0.438	$\frac{7}{16}$ in AF	1.250	$1\frac{1}{4}$ in AF
0.445	$\frac{3}{16}$ in Whitworth; $\frac{1}{4}$ in BSF	1.260	32 mm
0.472	12 mm	1.300	$\frac{3}{4}$ in Whitworth; $\frac{7}{8}$ in BSF
0.500	$\frac{1}{2}$ in AF	1.313	$1\frac{5}{16}$ in AF
0.512	13 mm	1.390	$\frac{13}{16}$ in Whitworth; $\frac{15}{16}$ in BSF
0.525	$\frac{1}{4}$ in Whitworth; $\frac{5}{16}$ in BSF	1.417	36 mm
0.551	14 mm	1.438	$1\frac{7}{16}$ in AF
0.563	$\frac{9}{16}$ in AF	1.480	$\frac{7}{8}$ in Whitworth; 1 in BSF
0.591	15 mm	1.500	$1\frac{1}{2}$ in AF
0.600	$\frac{5}{16}$ in Whitworth; $\frac{3}{8}$ in BSF	1.575	40 mm; $\frac{15}{16}$ in Whitworth
0.625	$\frac{5}{8}$ in AF	1.614	41 mm
0.630	16 mm	1.625	$1\frac{5}{8}$ in AF
0.669	17 mm	1.670	1 in Whitworth; $1\frac{1}{8}$ in BSF
0.686	$\frac{11}{16}$ in AF	1.688	$1\frac{11}{16}$ in AF
0.709	18 mm	1.811	46 mm
0.710	$\frac{3}{8}$ in Whitworth; $\frac{7}{16}$ in BSF	1.813	$1\frac{13}{16}$ in AF
0.748	19 mm	1.860	$1\frac{1}{8}$ in Whitworth; $1\frac{1}{4}$ in BSF
0.750	$\frac{3}{4}$ in AF	1.875	$1\frac{7}{8}$ in AF
0.813	$\frac{13}{16}$ in AF	1.969	50 mm
0.820	$\frac{7}{16}$ in Whitworth; $\frac{1}{2}$ in BSF	2.000	2 in AF
0.866	22 mm	2.050	$1\frac{1}{4}$ in Whitworth; $1\frac{3}{8}$ in BSF
0.875	$\frac{7}{8}$ in AF	2.165	55 mm
0.920	$\frac{1}{2}$ in Whitworth; $\frac{9}{16}$ in BSF	2.362	60 mm
0.938	$\frac{15}{16}$ in AF		

Standard torque settings

Specific torque settings will be found at the end of the specifications section of each chapter. Where no figure is given, bolts should be secured according to the table below.

Fastener type (thread diameter)	kgf m	lbf ft
5mm bolt or nut	0.45 – 0.6	3.5 – 4.5
6 mm bolt or nut	0.8 – 1.2	6 – 9
8 mm bolt or nut	1.8 – 2.5	13 – 18
10 mm bolt or nut	3.0 – 4.0	22 – 29
12 mm bolt or nut	5.0 – 6.0	36 – 43
5 mm screw	0.35 – 0.5	2.5 – 3.6
6 mm screw	0.7 – 1.1	5 – 8
6 mm flange bolt	1.0 – 1.4	7 – 10
8 mm flange bolt	2.4 – 3.0	17 – 22
10 mm flange bolt	3.0 – 4.0	22 – 29

Choosing and fitting accessories

The range of accessories available to the modern motorcyclist is almost as varied and bewildering as the range of motorcycles. This Section is intended to help the owner in choosing the correct equipment for his needs and to avoid some of the mistakes made by many riders when adding accessories to their machines. It will be evident that the Section can only cover the subject in the most general terms and so it is recommended that the owner, having decided that he wants to fit, for example, a luggage rack or carrier, seeks the advice of several local dealers and the owners of similar machines. This will give a good idea of what makes of carrier are easily available, and at what price. Talking to other owners will give some insight into the drawbacks or good points of any one make. A walk round the motorcycles in car parks or outside a dealer will often reveal the same sort of information.

The first priority when choosing accessories is to assess exactly what one needs. It is, for example, pointless to buy a large heavy-duty carrier which is designed to take the weight of fully laden panniers and topbox when all you need is a place to strap on a set of waterproofs and a lunchbox when going to work. Many accessory manufacturers have ranges of equipment to cater for the individual needs of different riders and this point should be borne in mind when looking through a dealer's catalogues. Having decided exactly what is required and the use to which the accessories are going to be put, the owner will need a few hints on what to look for when making the final choice. To this end the Section is now sub-divided to cover the more popular accessories fitted. Note that it is in no way a customizing guide, but merely seeks to outline the practical considerations to be taken into account when adding aftermarket equipment to a motorcycle.

Fairings and windscreens

A fairing is possibly the single, most expensive, aftermarket item to be fitted to any motorcycle and, therefore, requires the most thought before purchase. Fairings can be divided into two main groups: front fork mounted handlebar fairings and windscreens, and frame mounted fairings.

The first group, the front fork mounted fairings, are becoming far more popular than was once the case, as they offer several advantages over the second group. Front fork mounted fairings generally are much easier and quicker to fit, involve less modification to the motorcycle, do not as a rule restrict the steering lock, permit a wider selection of handlebar styles to be used, and offer adequate protection for much less money than the frame mounted type. They are also lighter, can be swapped easily between different motorcycles, and are available in a much greater variety of styles. Their main disadvantages are that they do not offer as much weather protection as the frame mounted types, rarely offer any storage space, and, if poorly fitted or naturally incompatible, can have an adverse effect on the stability of the motorcycle.

The second group, the frame mounted fairings, are secured so rigidly to the main frame of the motorcycle that they can offer a substantial amount of protection to motorcycle and rider in the event of a crash. They offer almost complete protection from the weather and, if double-skinned in construction, can provide a great deal of useful storage space. The feeling of peace, quiet and complete relaxation encountered when riding behind a good full fairing has to be experienced to be believed. For this reason full fairings are considered essential by most touring motorcyclists and by many people who ride all year round. The main disadvantages of this type are that fitting can take a long time, often involving removal or modification of standard motorcycle components, they restrict the steering lock and they can add up to about 40 lb to the weight of the machine. They do not usually affect the stability of the machine to any great extent once the front tyre pressure and suspension have been adjusted to compensate for the extra weight, but can be affected by sidewinds.

The first thing to look for when purchasing a fairing is the quality of the fittings. A good fairing will have strong, substantial brackets constructed from heavy-gauge tubing; the brackets must be shaped to fit the frame or forks evenly so that the minimum of stress is imposed on the assembly when it is bolted down. The brackets should be properly painted or finished – a nylon coating being the favourite of the better manufacturers – the nuts and bolts provided should be of the same thread and size standard as is used on the motorcycle and be properly plated. Look also for shakeproof locking nuts or locking washers to ensure that everything remains securely tightened down. The fairing shell is generally made from one of two materials: fibreglass or ABS plastic. Both have their advantages and disadvantages, but the main consideration for the owner is that fibreglass is much easier to repair in the event of damage occurring to the fairing. Whichever material is used, check that it is properly finished inside as well as out, that the edges are protected by beading and that the fairing shell is insulated from vibration by the use of rubber grommets at all mounting points. Also be careful to check that the windscreen is retained by plastic bolts which will snap on impact so that the windscreen will break away and not cause personal injury in the event of an accident.

Having purchased your fairing or windscreen, read the manufacturer's fitting instructions very carefully and check that you have all the necessary brackets and fittings. Ensure that the mounting brackets are located correctly and bolted down securely. Note that some manufacturers use hose clamps to retain the mounting brackets; these should be discarded as they are convenient to use but not strong enough for the task. Stronger clamps should be substituted; car exhaust pipe clamps of suitable size would be a good alternative. Ensure that the front forks can turn through the full steering lock available without fouling the fairing. With many types of frame-mounted fairing the handlebars will have to be altered or a different type fitted and the steering lock will be restricted by stops provided with the fittings. Also check that the fairing does not foul the front wheel or mudguard, in any steering position, under full fork compression. Re-route any cables, brake pipes or electrical wiring which may snag on the fairing and take great care to protect all electrical connections, using insulating tape. If the manufacturer's instructions are followed carefully at every stage no serious problems should be encountered. Remember that hydraulic pipes that have been disconnected must be carefully re-tightened and the hydraulic system purged of air bubbles by bleeding.

Two things will become immediately apparent when taking a motorcycle on the road for the first time with a fairing – the first is the tendency to underestimate the road speed because of the lack of wind pressure on the body. This must be very carefully watched until one has grown accustomed to riding behind the fairing. The second thing is the alarming increase in engine noise which is an unfortunate but inevitable by-product of fitting any type of fairing or windscreen, and is caused by normal engine noise being reflected, and in some cases amplified, by the flat surface of the fairing.

Luggage racks or carriers

Carriers are possibly the commonest item to be fitted to modern motorcycles. They vary enormously in size, carrying capacity, and durability. When selecting a carrier, always look for one which is made specifically for your machine and which is bolted on with as few separate brackets as possible. The universal-type carrier, with its mass of brackets and adaptor pieces, will generally prove too weak to be of any real use. A good carrier should bolt to the main frame, generally using the two suspension unit top mountings and a mudguard mounting bolt as attachment points, and have its luggage platform as low and as far forward as possible to minimise the effect of any load on the machine's stability. Look for good quality, heavy gauge tubing, good welding and good finish. Also ensure that the carrier does not prevent opening of the seat, sidepanels or tail compartment, as appropriate. When using a carrier, be very careful not to overload it. Excessive weight placed so high and so far to the rear of any motorcycle will have an adverse effect on the machine's steering and stability.

Luggage

Motorcycle luggage can be grouped under two headings: soft and hard. Both types are available in many sizes and styles and have advantages and disadvantages in use.

Soft luggage is now becoming very popular because of its lower cost and its versatility. Whether in the form of tankbags, panniers, or strap-on bags, soft luggage requires in general no brackets and no modification to the motorcycle. Equipment can be swapped easily from one motorcycle to another and can be fitted and removed in seconds. Awkwardly shaped loads can easily be carried. The disadvantages of soft luggage are that the contents cannot be secure against the casual thief, very little protection is afforded in the event of a crash, and waterproofing is generally poor. Also, in the case of panniers, carrying capacity is restricted to approximately 10 lb, although this amount will vary considerably depending on the manufacturer's recommendation. When purchasing soft luggage, look for good quality material, generally vinyl or nylon, with strong, well-stitched attachment points. It is always useful to have separate pockets, especially on tank bags, for items which will be needed on the journey. When purchasing a tank bag, look for one which has a separate, well-padded, base. This will protect the tank's paintwork and permit easy access to the filler cap at petrol stations.

Hard luggage is confined to two types: panniers, and top boxes or tail trunks. Most hard luggage manufacturers produce matching sets of these items, the basis of which is generally that manufacturer's own heavy-duty luggage rack. Variations on this theme occur in the form of separate frames for the better quality panniers, fixed or quickly-detachable luggage, and in size and carrying capacity. Hard luggage offers a reasonable degree of security against theft and good protection against weather and accident damage. Carrying capacity is greater than that of soft luggage, around 15 – 20 lb in the case of panniers, although top boxes should never be loaded as much as their apparent capacity might imply. A top box should only be used for lightweight items, because one that is heavily laden can have a serious effect on the stability of the machine. When purchasing hard luggage look for the same good points as mentioned under fairings and windscreens, ie good quality mounting brackets and fittings, and well-finished fibreglass or ABS plastic cases. Again as with fairings, always purchase luggage made specifically for your motorcycle, using as few separate brackets as possible, to ensure that everything remains securely bolted in place. When fitting hard luggage, be careful to check that the rear suspension and brake operation will not be impaired in any way and remember that many pannier kits require re-siting of the indicators. Remember also that a non-standard exhaust system may make fitting extremely difficult.

Handlebars

The occupation of fitting alternative types of handlebar is extremely popular with modern motorcyclists, whose motives may vary from the purely practical, wishing to improve the comfort of their machines, to the purely aesthetic, where form is more important than function. Whatever the reason, there are several considerations to be borne in mind when changing the handlebars of your machine. If fitting lower bars, check carefully that the switches and cables do not foul the petrol tank on full lock and that the surplus length of cable, brake pipe,

and electrical wiring are smoothly and tidily disposed of. Avoid tight kinks in cable or brake pipes which will produce stiff controls or the premature and disastrous failure of an overstressed component. If necessary, remove the petrol tank and re-route the cable from the engine/gearbox unit upwards, ensuring smooth gentle curves are produced. In extreme cases, it will be necessary to purchase a shorter brake pipe to overcome this problem. In the case of higher handlebars than standard it will almost certainly be necessary to purchase extended cables and brake pipes. Fortunately, many standard motorcycles have a custom version which will be equipped with higher handlebars and, therefore, factory-built extended components will be available from your local dealer. It is not usually necessary to extend electrical wiring, as switch clusters may be used on several different motorcycles, some being custom versions. This point should be borne in mind however when fitting extremely high or wide handlebars.

When fitting different types of handlebar, ensure that the mounting clamps are correctly tightened to the manufacturer's specifications and that cables and wiring, as previously mentioned, have smooth easy runs and do not snag on any part of the motorcycle throughout the full steering lock. Ensure that the fluid level in the front brake master cylinder remains level to avoid any chance of air entering the hydraulic system. Also check that the cables are adjusted correctly and that all handlebar controls operate correctly and can be easily reached when riding.

Crashbars

Crashbars, also known as engine protector bars, engine guards, or case savers, are extremely useful items of equipment which can contribute protection to the machine's structure if a crash occurs. They do not, as has been inferred in the US, prevent the rider from crashing, or necessarily prevent rider injury should a crash occur.

It is recommended that only the smaller, neater, engine protector type of crashbar is considered. This type will offer protection while restricting, as little as is possible, access to the engine and the machine's ground clearance. The crashbars should be designed for use specifically on your machine, and should be constructed of heavy-gauge tubing with strong, integral mounting brackets. Where possible, they should bolt to a strong lug on the frame, usually at the engine mounting bolts.

The alternative type of crashbar is the larger cage type. This type is not recommended in spite of their appearance which promises some protection to the rider as well as to the machine. The larger amount of leverage imposed by the size of this type of crashbar increases the risk of severe frame damage in the event of an accident. This type also decreases the machine's ground clearance and restricts access to the engine. The amount of protection afforded the rider is open to some doubt as the design is based on the premise that the rider will stay in the normally seated position during an accident, and the crash bar structure will not itself fail. Neither result can in any way be guaranteed.

As a general rule, always purchase the best, ie usually the most expensive, set of crashbars you an afford. The investment will be repaid by minimising the amount of damage incurred, should the machine be involved in an accident. Finally, avoid the universal type of crashbar. This should be regarded only as a last resort to be used if no alternative exists. With its usual multitude of separate brackets and spacers, the universal crashbar is far too weak in design and construction to be of any practical value.

Exhaust systems

The fitting of aftermarket exhaust systems is another extremely popular pastime amongst motorcyclists. The usual motive is to gain more performance from the engine but other considerations are to gain more ground clearance, to lose weight from the motorcycle, to obtain a more distinctive exhaust note or to find a cheaper alternative to the manufacturer's original equipment exhaust system. Original equipment exhaust systems often cost more and may well have a relatively short life. It should be noted that it is rare for an aftermarket exhaust system alone to give a noticeable increase in the engine's power output. Modern motorcycles are designed to give the highest power output possible allowing for factors such as quietness, fuel economy, spread of power, and long-term reliability. If there were a magic formula which allowed the exhaust system to produce more power without affecting these other considerations you can be sure that the manufacturers, with their large research and development facilities, would have found it and made use of it. Performance increases of a worthwhile and noticeable nature only come from well-tried and properly matched modifications to the entire engine, from the air filter, through the carburettors, port timing or camshaft and valve design, combustion chamber shape, compression ratio, and the exhaust system. Such modifications are well outside the scope of this manual but interested owners might refer to specialist titles produced by the publisher of this manual.

Whatever your motive for wishing to fit an alternative exhaust system, be sure to seek expert advice before doing so. Changes to the carburettor jetting will almost certainly be required for which you must consult the exhaust system manufacturer. If he cannot supply adequate specific information it is reasonable to assume that insufficient development work has been carried out, and that particular make should be avoided. Other factors to be borne in mind are whether the exhaust system allows the use of both centre and side stands, whether it allows sufficient access to permit oil and filter changing and whether modifications are necessary to the standard exhaust system. Many two-stroke expansion chamber systems require the use of the standard exhaust pipe; this is all very well if the standard exhaust pipe and silencer are separate units but can cause problems if the two, as with so many modern two-strokes, are a one-piece unit. While the exhaust pipe can be removed easily by means of a hacksaw it is not so easy to refit the original silencer should you at any time wish to return the machine to standard trim. The same applies to several four-stroke systems.

On the subject of the finish of aftermarket exhausts, avoid black-painted systems unless you enjoy painting. As any trail-bike owner will tell you, rust has a great affinity for black exhausts and re-painting or rust removal becomes a task which must be carried out with monotonous regularity. A bright chrome finish is, as a general rule, a far better proposition as it is much easier to keep clean and to prevent rusting. Although the general finish of aftermarket exhaust systems is not always up to the standard of the original equipment the lower cost of such systems does at least reflect this fact.

When fitting an alternative system always purchase a full set of new exhaust gaskets, to prevent leaks. Fit the exhaust first to the cylinder head or barrel, as appropriate, tightening the retaining nuts or bolts by hand only and then line up the exhaust rear mountings. If the new system is a one-piece unit and the rear mountings do not line up exactly, spacers must be fabricated to take up the difference. Do not force the system into place as the stress thus imposed will rapidly cause cracks and splits to appear. Once all the mountings are loosely fixed, tighten the retaining nuts or bolts securely, being careful not to overtighten them. Where the motorcycle manufacturer's torque settings are available, these should be used. Do not forget to carry out any carburation changes recommended by the exhaust system's manufacturer.

Electrical equipment

The vast range of electrical equipment available to motorcyclists is so large and so diverse that only the most general outline can be given here. Electrical accessories vary from electric ignition kits fitted to replace contact breaker points, to additional lighting at the front and rear, more powerful horns, various instruments and gauges, clocks, anti-theft systems, heated clothing, CB radios, radio-cassette players, and intercom systems, to name but a few of the more popular items of equipment.

As will be evident, it would require a separate manual to cover this subject alone and this section is therefore restricted to outlining a few basic rules which must be borne in mind when fitting electrical equipment. The first consideration is whether your machine's electrical system has enough reserve capacity to cope with the added demand of the accessories you wish to fit. The motorcycle's manufacturer or importer should be able to furnish this sort of information and may also be able to offer advice on uprating the electrical system. Failing this, a good dealer or the accessory manufacturer may be able to help. In some cases, more powerful generator components may be available, perhaps from another motorcycle in the manufacturer's range. The second consideration is the legal requirements in force in your area. The local police may be prepared to help with this point. In the UK for example, there are strict regulations governing the position and use of auxiliary riding lamps and fog lamps.

When fitting electrical equipment always disconnect the battery first to prevent the risk of a short-circuit, and be careful to ensure that all connections are properly made and that they are waterproof. Remember that many electrical accessories are designed primarily for use in cars and that they cannot easily withstand the exposure to vibration and to the weather. Delicate components must be rubber-mounted to insulate them from vibration, and sealed carefully to prevent the entry of rainwater and dirt. Be careful to follow exactly the accessory manufacturer's instructions in conjunction with the wiring loom diagram at the back of this manual.

Accessories – general

Accessories fitted to your motorcycle will rapidly deteriorate if not cared for. Regular washing and polishing will maintain the finish and will provide an opportunity to check that all mounting bolts and nuts are securely fastened. Any sign of chaffing or wear should be watched for, and the cause cured as soon as possible before serious damage occurs.

As a general rule, do not expect the re-sale value of your motorcycle to increase by an amount proportional to the amount of money and effort put into fitting accessories. It is usually the case that an absolutely standard motorcycle will sell more easily at a better price than one that has been modified. If you are in the habit of exchanging your machine for another at frequent intervals, this factor should be borne in mind to avoid loss of money.

Fault diagnosis

Contents

1 Introduction

This Section provides an easy reference-guide to the more common ailments likely to afflict your machine. Obviously, the opportunities are almost limitless for faults to occur as a result of obscure failures, and to try and cover all eventualities would require a book. Indeed, a number have been written on the subject.

Successful fault diagnosis is not a mysterious 'black art' but the application of a little knowledge combined with a systematic and logical approach to the problem. Approach any fault diagnosis by first accurately identifying the symptom and then checking through the list of possible causes, starting with the simplest or most obvious and progressing in stages to the most complex. Take nothing for granted, but above all apply liberal quantities of common sense.

The main symptom of a fault is given in the text as a major heading below which are listed, as Section headings, the various systems or areas which may contain the fault. Details of each possible cause for a fault and the remedial action to be taken are given, in brief, in the paragraphs below each Section heading. Further information should be sought in the relevant Chapter.

Starter motor problems

2 Starter motor not rotating

● Engine stop switch off.
● Fuse blown. Check the main fuse located behind the left-hand side panel.
● Battery voltage low. Switching on the headlamp and operating the horn will give a good indication of the charge level. If necessary recharge the battery from an external source.
● Faulty clutch interlock switch. Check the switch wiring and switch for correct operation.
● Ignition switch defective. Check switch for continuity and connections for security.
● Engine stop switch defective. Check switch for continuity in 'Run' position. Fault will be caused by broken, wet or corroded switch contacts. Clean or renew as necessary.
● Starter button switch faulty. Check continuity of switch. Faults as for engine stop switch.
● Starter relay (solenoid) faulty. If the switch is functioning correctly a pronounced click should be heard when the starter button is depressed. This presupposes that current is flowing to the solenoid when the button is depressed.
● Wiring open or shorted. Check first that the battery terminal connections are tight and corrosion free. Follow this by checking that all wiring connections are dry, tight and corrosion free. Check also for frayed or broken wiring. Occasionally a wire may become trapped between two moving components, particularly in the vicinity of the steering head, leading to breakage of the internal core but leaving the softer but more resilient outer cover intact. This can cause mysterious intermittent or total power loss.
● Starter motor defective. A badly worn starter motor may cause high current drain from a battery without the motor rotating. If current is found to be reaching the motor, after checking the starter button and starter relay, suspect a damaged motor. The motor should be removed for inspection.

3 Starter motor rotates but engine does not turn over

● Starter motor clutch defective. Suspect jammed or worn engagement rollers, plungers and springs.
● Damaged starter motor drive train. Inspect and renew component where necessary. Failure in this area is unlikely.

4 Starter motor and clutch function but engine will not turn over

● Engine seized. Seizure of the engine is always a result of damage to internal components due to lubrication failure, or component breakage resulting from abuse, neglect or old age. A seizing or partially seized component may go un-noticed until the engine has cooled down and an attempt is made to restart the engine. Suspect first seizure of the valves, valve gear and the piston. Instantaneous seizure whilst the engine is running indicates component breakage. In either case major dismantling and inspection will be required.

Engine does not start when turned over

5 No fuel flow to carburettor

● No fuel or insufficient fuel in tank.
● Fuel tap lever position incorrectly selected.
● Tank filler cap air vent obstructed. Usually caused by dirt or water. Clean the vent orifice.
● Fuel tap or filter blocked. Blockage may be due to accumulation of rust or paint flakes from the tank's inner surface or of foreign matter from contaminated fuel. Remove the tap and clean it and the filter. Look also for water droplets in the fuel.
● Fuel line blocked. Blockage of the fuel line is more likely to result from a kink in the line rather than the accumulation of debris.

6 Fuel not reaching cylinder

● Float chamber not filling. Caused by float needle or floats sticking in up position. This may occur after the machine has been left standing for an extended length of time allowing the fuel to evaporate. When this occurs a gummy residue is often left which hardens to a varnish-like substance. This condition may be worsened by corrosion and crystaline deposits produced prior to the total evaporation of contaminated fuel. Sticking of the float needle may also be caused by wear. Removal of the float chamber will be necessary for inspection and cleaning.
● Blockage in the starting circuit, slow running circuit or jets. Blockage of these items may be attributable to debris from the fuel tank by-passing the filter system or to gumming up as described in paragraph 1. Water droplets in the fuel will also block jets and passages. The carburettor should be dismantled for cleaning.
● Fuel level too low. The fuel level in the float chamber is controlled by float height. The float height may increase with wear or damage but will never reduce, thus a low float height is an inherent rather than developing condition. Check the float height and make any necessary adjustment.

7 Engine flooding

● Float valve needle worn or stuck open. A piece of rust or other debris can prevent correct seating of the needle against the valve seat thereby permitting an uncontrolled flow of fuel. Similarly, a worn needle or needle seat will prevent valve closure. Dismantle the carburettor float bowl for cleaning and, if necessary, renewal of the worn components.
● Fuel level too high. The fuel level is controlled by the float height which may increase due to wear of the float needle, pivot pin or operating tang. Check the float height, and make any necessary adjustment. A leaking float will cause an increase in fuel level, and thus should be renewed.
● Cold starting mechanism. Check the choke (starter mechanism) for correct operation. If the mechanism jams in the 'On' position subsequent starting of a hot engine will be difficult.
● Blocked air filter. A badly restricted air filter will cause flooding. Check the filter and clean or renew as required. A collapsed inlet hose will have a similar effect.

8 No spark at plug

● Ignition switch not on.
● Engine stop switch off.
● Fuse blown. Check fuse.
● Battery voltage low. The current draw required by a starter motor is sufficiently high that an under-charged battery may not have enough spare capacity to provide power for the ignition circuit during starting. Bump starting is recommended until the battery has been recharged either by the machine's generator or from an external charger.

● Starter motor inefficient. A starter motor with worn brushes and a worn or dirty commutator will draw excessive amounts of current causing power starvation in the ignition system. See the preceding paragraph. Starter motor overhaul will be required.

● Spark plug failure. Clean the spark plug thoroughly and reset the electrode gap. Refer to the spark plug section and the　condition guide in Routine Maintenance. If the spark plug shorts internally or has sustained visible damage to the electrodes, core or ceramic insulator it should be renewed. On rare occasions a plug that appears to spark vigorously will fail to do so when refitted to the engine and subjected to the compression pressure in the cylinder.

● Spark plug cap or high tension (HT) lead faulty. Check condition and security. Replace if deterioration is evident.

● Spark plug cap loose. Check that the spark plug cap fits securely over the plug and, where fitted, the screwed terminal on the plug end is secure.

● Shorting due to moisture. Certain parts of the ignition system are susceptible to shorting when the machine is ridden or parked in wet weather. Check particularly the area from the spark plug cap back to the ignition coil. A water dispersant spray may be used to dry out waterlogged components. Recurrence of the problem can be prevented by using an ignition sealant spray after drying out and cleaning.

● Ignition or stop switch shorted. May be caused by water, corrosion or wear. Water dispersant and contact cleaning sprays may be used. If this fails to overcome the problem dismantling and visual inspection of the switches will be required.

● Shorting or open circuit in wiring. Failure in any wire connecting any of the ignition components will cause ignition malfunction. Check also that all connections are clean, dry and tight.

● Ignition coil failure. Check the coil, referring to Chapter 3.

● Electronic ignition component failure, see Chapter 3.

9 Weak spark at plug

● Feeble sparking at the plug may be caused by any of the faults mentioned in the preceding Section other than those items in paragraphs 1 and 2. Check first the spark plug cap and the spark plug, these being the most likely culprits.

10 Compression low

● Spark plug loose. This will be self-evident on inspection, and may be accompanied by a hissing noise when the engine is turned over. Remove the plug and check that the threads in the cylinder head are not damaged. Check also that the plug sealing washer is in good condition.

● Cylinder head gasket leaking. This condition is often accompanied by a high pitched squeak from around the cylinder head and oil loss, and may be caused by insufficiently tightened cylinder head fasteners, a warped cylinder head or mechanical failure of the gasket material. Re-torqueing the fasteners to the correct specification may seal the leak in some instances but if damage has occurred this course of action will provide, at best, only a temporary cure.

● Valve not seating correctly. The failure of a valve to seat may be caused by insufficient valve clearance, pitting of the valve seat or face, carbon deposits on the valve seat or seizure of the valve stem or valve gear components. Valve spring breakage will also prevent correct valve closure. The valve clearances should be checked first and then, if these are found to be in order, further dismantling will be required to inspect the relevant components for failure.

● Cylinder, piston and ring wear. Compression pressure will be lost if any of these components are badly worn. Wear in one component is invariably accompanied by wear in another. A top end overhaul will be required.

● Piston rings sticking or broken. Sticking of the piston rings may be caused by seizure due to lack of lubrication or heating as a result of poor carburation or incorrect fuel type. Gumming of the rings may result from lack of use, or carbon deposits in the ring grooves. Broken rings result from over-revving, overheating or general wear. In either case a top-end overhaul will be required.

Engine stalls after starting

11 General causes

● Improper cold start mechanism operation. Check that the operating controls function smoothly and, where applicable, are correctly adjusted. A cold engine may not require application of an enriched mixture to start initially but may baulk without use of the choke once it has fired. Likewise a hot engine may start with an enriched mixture but will stop almost immediately if the choke is inadvertently in operation.

● Ignition malfunction. See Section 9, 'Weak spark at plug'.

● Carburettor incorrectly adjusted. Maladjustment of the mixture strength or idle speed may cause the engine to stop immediately after starting. See Chapter 2.

● Fuel contamination. Check for filter blockage by debris or water which reduces, but does not completely stop, fuel flow or blockage of the slow speed circuit in the carburettor by the same agents. If water is present it can often be seen as droplets in the bottom of the float bowl. Clean the filter and, where water is in evidence, drain and flush the fuel tank and float bowl.

● Intake air leak. Check for security of the carburettor mounting and hose connections, and for cracks or splits in the hoses. Check also that the carburettor top is secure and that the vacuum gauge adaptor plug is tight.

● Air filter blocked or omitted. A blocked filter will cause an over-rich mixture; the omission of a filter will cause an excessively weak mixture. Both conditions will have a detrimental affect on carburation. Clean or refit the filter as necessary.

● Fuel filler cap air vent blocked. Usually caused by dirt or water. Clean the vent orifice.

Poor running at idle and low speed

12 Weak spark at plug or erratic firing

● Battery voltage low. In certain conditions low battery charge, especially when coupled with a badly sulphated battery, may result in misfiring. If the battery is in good general condition it should be recharged; an old battery suffering from sulphated plates should be renewed.

● Spark plug fouled, faulty or incorrectly adjusted. See Section 8 or refer to Chapter 3.

● Spark plug cap or high tension lead shorting. Check the condition of both these items ensuring that they are in good condition and dry and that the cap is fitted correctly.

● Spark plug type incorrect. Fit plug of correct type and heat range as given in Specifications. In certain conditions a plug of hotter or colder type may be required for normal running.

● Igniting timing incorrect. Check the ignition timing statically and dynamically, ensuring that the advance is functioning correctly.

● Faulty ignition coil. Partial failure of the coil internal insulation will diminish the performance of the coil. No repair is possible, a new component must be fitted.

● Ignition system failure, see Chapter 3.

13 Fuel/air mixture incorrect

● Intake air leak. See Section 11.

● Mixture strength incorrect. Adjust slow running mixture strength using pilot adjustment screw.

● Pilot jet or slow running circuit blocked. The carburettor should be removed and dismantled for thorough cleaning. Blow through all jets and air passages with compressed air to clear obstructions.

● Air cleaner clogged or omitted. Clean or fit air cleaner element as necessary. Check also that the element and air filter cover are correctly seated.

● Cold start mechanism in operation. Check that the choke has not been left on inadvertently and the operation is correct.

● Fuel level too high or too low. Check the float height and adjust as necessary. See Section 7.

● Fuel tank air vent obstructed. Obstruction usually caused by dirt or water. Clean vent orifice.
● Valve clearance incorrect. Check, and if necessary, adjust, the clearances.

14 Compression low

● See Section 10.

Acceleration poor

15 General causes

● All items as for previous Section.
● Timing not advancing.
● Brakes binding. Usually caused by maladjustment or partial seizure of the operating mechanism due to poor maintenance. Check brake adjustment (where applicable). A bent wheel spindle or warped brake drum can produce similar symptoms.

Poor running or lack of power at high speeds

16 Weak spark at plug or erratic firing

● All items as for Section 12.
● HT lead insulation failure. Insulation failure of the HT lead and spark plug cap due to old age or damage can cause shorting when the engine is driven hard. This condition may be less noticeable, or not noticeable at all at lower engine speeds.

17 Fuel/air mixture incorrect

● All items as for Section 13, with the exception of items 2 and 3.
● Main jet blocked. Debris from contaminated fuel, or from the fuel tank, and water in the fuel can block the main jet. Clean the fuel filter, the float bowl area, and if water is present, flush and refill the fuel tank.
● Main jet is the wrong size. The standard carburettor jetting is for sea level atmospheric pressure. For high altitudes, usually above 5000 ft, a smaller main jet will be required.
● Jet needle and needle jet worn. These can be renewed individually but should be renewed as a pair. Renewal of both items requires partial dismantling of the carburettor.
● Air bleed holes blocked. Dismantle carburettor and use compressed air to blow out all air passages.
● Reduced fuel flow. A reduction in the maximum fuel flow from the fuel tank to the carburettor will cause fuel starvation, proportionate to the engine speed. Check for blockages through debris or a kinked fuel line.

18 Compression low

● See Section 10.

Knocking or pinking

19 General causes

● Carbon build-up in combustion chamber. After high mileages have been covered large accumulation of carbon may occur. This may glow red hot and cause premature ignition of the fuel/air mixture, in advance of normal firing by the spark plug. Cylinder head removal will be required to allow inspection and cleaning.
● Fuel incorrect. A low grade fuel, or one of poor quality may result in compression induced detonation of the fuel resulting in knocking and pinking noises. Old fuel can cause similar problems. A too highly leaded fuel will reduce detonation but will accelerate deposit formation in the combustion chamber and may lead to early pre-ignition as described in item 1.

● Spark plug heat range incorrect. Uncontrolled pre-ignition can result from the use of a spark plug the heat range of which is too hot.
● Weak mixture. Overheating of the engine due to a weak mixture can result in pre-ignition occurring where it would not occur when engine temperature was within normal limits. Maladjustment, blocked jets or passages and air leaks can cause this condition.

Overheating

20 Firing incorrect

● Spark plug fouled, defective or maladjusted. See Section 6.
● Spark plug type incorrect. Refer to the Specifications and ensure that the correct plug type is fitted.
● Incorrect ignition timing. Timing that is far too much advanced or far too much retarded will cause overheating. Check the ignition timing is correct and that the advance is functioning.

21 Fuel/air mixture incorrect

● Slow speed mixture strength incorrect. Adjust pilot air screw.
● Main jet wrong size. The carburettor is jetted for sea level atmospheric conditions. For high altitudes, usually above 5000 ft, a smaller main jet will be required.
● Air filter badly fitted or omitted. Check that the filter element is in place and that it and the air filter box cover are sealing correctly. Any leaks will cause a weak mixture.
● Induction air leaks. Check the security of the carburettor mountings and hose connections, and for cracks and splits in the hoses. Check also that the carburettor top is secure and that the vacuum gauge adaptor plug is tight.
● Fuel level too low. See Section 6.
● Fuel tank filler cap air vent obstructed. Clear blockage.

22 Lubrication inadequate

● Engine oil too low. Not only does the oil serve as a lubricant by preventing friction between moving components, but it also acts as a coolant. Check the oil level and replenish.
● Engine oil overworked. The lubricating properties of oil are lost slowly during use as a result of changes resulting from heat and also contamination. Always change the oil at the recommended interval.
● Engine oil of incorrect viscosity or poor quality. Always use the recommended viscosity and type of oil.
● Oil filter and filter by-pass valve blocked. Clean filter and by-pass valve.

23 Miscellaneous causes

● Engine fins clogged. A build-up of mud in the cylinder head and cylinder barrel cooling fins will decrease the cooling capabilities of the fins. Clean the fins as required.

Clutch operating problems

24 Clutch slip

● No clutch lever play. Adjust clutch lever end play according to the procedure in Routine Maintenance.
● Friction plates worn or warped. Overhaul clutch assembly, replacing plates out of specification (Chapter 1).
● Steel plates worn or warped. Overhaul clutch assembly, replacing plates out of specification (Chapter 1).
● Clutch springs broken or worn. Old or heat-damaged (from slipping clutch) springs should be replaced with new ones (Chapter 1).
● Clutch release not adjusted properly. See the adjustments section of Chapter 1.
● Clutch inner cable snagging. Caused by a frayed cable or kinked outer cable. Replace the cable with a new one. Repair of a frayed cable is not advised.

● Clutch release mechanism defective. Worn or damaged parts in the clutch release mechanism could include the shaft, cam, actuating arm or pilot. Replace parts as necessary (Chapter 1).
● Clutch centre and outer drum worn. Severe indentation by the clutch plate tangs of the channels in the centre and drum will cause snagging of the plates preventing correct engagement. If this damage occurs, renewal of the worn components is required.
● Lubricant incorrect. Use of a transmission lubricant other than that specified may allow the plates to slip.

25 Clutch drag

● Clutch lever play excessive. Adjust lever at bars or at cable end if necessary (See Routine Maintenance).
● Clutch plates warped or damaged. This will cause a drag on the clutch, causing the machine to creep. Overhaul clutch assembly (Chapter 1).
● Clutch spring tension uneven. Usually caused by a sagged or broken spring. Check and replace springs (Chapter 1).
● Engine oil deteriorated. Badly contaminated engine oil and a heavy deposit of oil sludge and carbon on the plates will cause plate sticking. The oil recommended for this machine is of the detergent type, therefore it is unlikely that this problem will arise unless regular oil changes are neglected.
● Engine oil viscosity too high. Drag in the plates will result from the use of an oil with too high a viscosity. In very cold weather clutch drag may occur until the engine has reached operating temperature.
● Clutch centre and outer drum worn. Indentation by the clutch plate tangs of the channels in the centre and drum will prevent easy plate disengagement. If the damage is light the affected areas may be dressed with a fine file. More pronounced damage will necessitate renewal of the components.
● Clutch housing seized to shaft. Lack of lubrication, severe wear or damage can cause the housing to seize to the shaft. Overhaul of the clutch, and perhaps the transmission, may be necessary to repair damage (Chapter 1).
　Clutch release mechanism defective. Worn or damaged release mechanism parts can stick and fail to provide leverage. Overhaul clutch release components (Chapter 1).
● Loose clutch centre nut. Causes drum and centre misalignment, putting a drag on the engine. Engagement adjustment continually varies. Overhaul clutch assembly (Chapter 1).

Gear selection problems

26 Gear lever does not return

● Weak or broken centraliser spring. Renew the spring.
● Gearchange shaft bent or seized. Distortion of the gearchange shaft often occurs if the machine is dropped heavily on the gear lever. Provided that damage is not severe straightening of the shaft is permissible.

27 Gear selection difficult or impossible

● Clutch not disengaging fully. See Section 25.
● Gearchange shaft bent. This often occurs if the machine is dropped heavily on the gear lever. Straightening of the shaft is permissible if the damage is not too great.
● Gearchange arms, pawls or pins worn or damaged. Wear or breakage of any of these items may cause difficulty in selecting one or more gears. Overhaul the selector mechanism.
● Gearchange arm spring broken. Renew spring.
● Selector drum detent roller damage. Failure, rather than wear, of these items may jam the drum thereby preventing gearchanging. The damaged items must be renewed.
● Selector forks bent or seized. This can be caused by dropping the machine heavily on the gearchange lever or as a result of lack of lubrication. Though rare, bending of a shaft can result from a missed gearchange or false selection at high speed.
● Selector fork end and pin wear. Pronounced wear of these items

and the grooves in the gearchange drum can lead to imprecise selection and, eventually, no selection. Renewal of the worn components will be required.
● Structural failure. Failure of any one component of the selector rod and change mechanism will result in improper or fouled gear selection.

28 Jumping out of gear

● Detent roller assembly worn or damaged. Wear of the roller and the track with which it locates and breakage of the detent spring can cause imprecise gear selection resulting in jumping out of gear. Renew the damaged components.
● Gear pinion dogs worn or damaged. Rounding off the dog edges and the mating recesses in adjacent pinion can lead to jumping out of gear when under load. The gears should be inspected and renewed. Attempting to reprofile the dogs is not recommended.
● Selector forks, selector drum and pinion grooves worn. Extreme wear of these interconnected items can occur after high mileages especially when lubrication has been neglected. The worn components must be renewed.
● Gear pinions, bushes and shafts worn. Renew the worn components.
● Bent gearchange shaft. Often caused by dropping the machine on the gear lever.
● Gear pinion tooth broken. Chipped teeth are unlikely to cause jumping out of gear once the gear has been selected fully; a tooth which is completely broken off, however, may cause problems in this respect and in any event will cause transmission noise.

29 Overselection

● Pawl spring weak or broken. Renew the spring.
● Detent roller worn or broken. Renew the damaged items.
● Stopper arm spring worn or broken. Renew the spring.
● Gearchange arm stop pads worn. Repairs can be made by welding and reprofiling with a file.

Abnormal engine noise.

30 Knocking or pinking

● See Section 19.

31 Piston slap or rattling from cylinder

● Cylinder bore/piston clearance excessive. Resulting from wear, partial seizure or improper boring during overhaul. This condition can often be heard as a high, rapid tapping noise when the engine is under little or no load, particularly when power is just beginning to be applied. Reboring to the next correct oversize should be carried out and a new oversize piston fitted.
● Connecting rod bent. This can be caused by over-revving, trying to start a very badly flooded engine (resulting in a hydraulic lock in the cylinder) or by earlier mechanical failure such as a dropped valve. Attempts at straightening a bent connecting rod from a high performance engine are not recommended. Careful inspection of the crankshaft should be made before renewing the damaged connecting rod.
● Gudgeon pin, piston boss bore or small-end bearing wear or seizure. Excess clearance or partial seizure between normal moving parts of these items can cause continuous or intermittent tapping noises. Rapid wear or seizure is caused by lubrication starvation resulting from an insufficient engine oil level or oilway blockage.
● Piston rings worn, broken or sticking. Renew the rings after careful inspection of the piston and bore.

32 Valve noise or tapping from the cylinder head

● Valve clearance incorrect. Adjust the clearances with the engine cold.

● Valve spring broken or weak. Renew the spring set.

● Camshaft or cylinder head bearing surfaces worn or damaged. The camshaft lobes are the most highly stressed of all components in the engine and are subject to high wear if lubrication becomes inadequate. The bearing surfaces on the camshaft and cylinder head are also sensitive to a lack of lubrication. Lubrication failure due to blocked oilways can occur, but over-enthusiastic revving before engine warm-up is complete is the usual cause.

● Rocker arm or spindle wear. Rapid wear of a rocker arm, and the resulting need for frequent valve clearance adjustment, indicates breakthrough or failure of the surface hardening on the rocker arm tips. Similar wear in the cam lobes can be expected. Renew the worn components after checking for lubrication failure.

● Worn camshaft drive components. A rustling noise or light tapping which is not improved by correct re-adjustment of the cam chain tension can be caused by a worn cam chain or worn sprockets and chain. If uncorrected, subsequent cam chain breakage may cause extensive damage. The worn components must be renewed before wear becomes too far advanced.

33 Other noises

● Big-end bearing wear. A pronounced knock from within the crankcase which worsens rapidly is indicative of big-end bearing failure as a result of extreme normal wear or lubrication failure. Remedial action in the form of a bottom end overhaul should be taken; continuing to run the engine will lead to further damage including the possibility of connecting rod breakage.

● Main bearing failure. Extreme normal wear or failure of the main bearings is characteristically accompanied by a rumble from the crankcase and vibration felt through the frame and footrests. Renew the worn bearings and carry out a very careful examination of the crankshaft.

● Crankshaft excessively out of true. A bent crank may result from over-revving or damage from an upper cylinder component or gearbox failure. Damage can also result from dropping the machine on either crankshaft end. Straightening of the crankshaft is not possible in normal circumstances; a replacement item should be fitted.

● Engine mounting loose. Tighten all the engine mounting nuts and bolts.

● Cylinder head gasket leaking. The noise most often associated with a leaking head gasket is a high pitched squeaking, although any other noise consistent with gas being forced out under pressure from a small orifice can also be emitted. Gasket leakage is often accompanied by oil seepage from around the mating joint or from the cylinder head holding down bolts and nuts. Leakage into the cam chain tunnel or oil return passages will increase crankcase pressure and may cause oil leakage at joints and oil seals. Also, oil contamination will be accelerated. Leakage results from insufficient or uneven tightening of the cylinder head fasteners, or from random mechanical failure. Retightening to the correct torque figure will, at best, only provide a temporary cure. The gasket should be renewed at the earliest opportunity.

● Exhaust system leakage. Popping or crackling in the exhaust system, particularly when it occurs with the engine on the overrun, indicates a poor joint either at the cylinder port or at the exhaust pipe/silencer connection. Failure of the gasket or looseness of the clamp should be looked for.

Abnormal transmission noise

34 Clutch noise

● Clutch outer drum/friction plate tang clearance excessive.
● Clutch outer drum/spacer clearance excessive.
● Clutch outer drum/thrust washer clearance excessive.
● Primary drive gear teeth worn or damaged.
● Clutch shock absorber assembly worn or damaged.

35 Transmission noise

● Bearing or bushes worn or damaged. Renew the affected components.

● Gear pinions worn or chipped. Renew the gear pinions.

● Metal chips jams in gear teeth.This can occur when pieces of metal from any failed component are picked up by a meshing pinion. The condition will lead to rapid bearing wear or early gear failure.

● Engine/transmission oil level too low. Top up immediately to prevent damage to gearbox and engine.

● Gearchange mechanism worn or damaged. Wear or failure of certain items in the selection and change components can induce mis-selection of gears (see Section 27) where incipient engagement of more than one gear set is promoted. Remedial action, by the overhaul of the gearbox, should be taken without delay.

● Loose gearbox chain sprocket. Remove the sprocket and check for impact damage to the splines of the sprocket and shaft. Excessive slack between the splines will promote loosening of the securing bolts; renewal of the worn components is required. When retightening the bolts ensure that they are tightened fully and that thread locking compound is employed.

● Chain snagging on cases or cycle parts. A badly worn chain or one that is excessively loose may snag or smack against adjacent components.

Exhaust smokes excessively

36 White/blue smoke (caused by oil burning)

● Piston rings worn or broken. Breakage or wear of any ring, but particularly the oil control ring, will allow engine oil past the piston into the combustion chamber. Overhaul the cylinder barrel and piston.

● Cylinder cracked, worn or scored. These conditions may be caused by overheating, lack of lubrication, component failure or advanced normal wear. The cylinder barrel should be renewed or rebored and the next oversize piston fitted.

● Valve oil seal damaged or worn. This can occur as a result of valve guide failure or old age. The emission of smoke is likely to occur when the throttle is closed rapidly after acceleration, for instance, when changing gear. Renew the valve oil seals and, if necessary, the valve guides.

● Valve guides worn. See the preceding paragraph.

● Engine oil level too high. This increases the crankcase pressure and allows oil to be forced pass the piston rings. Often accompanied by seepage of oil at joints and oil seals.

● Cylinder head gasket blown between cam chain tunnel or oil return passage. Renew the cylinder head gasket.

● Abnormal crankcase pressure. This may be caused by blocked breather passages or hoses causing back-pressure at high engine revolutions.

37 Black smoke (caused by over-rich mixture)

● Air filter element clogged. Clean or renew the element.

● Main jet loose or too large. Remove the float chamber to check for tightness of the jet. If the machine is used at high altitudes rejetting will be required to compensate for the lower atmospheric pressure.

● Cold start mechanism jammed on. Check that the mechanism works smoothly and correctly.

● Fuel level too high. The fuel level is controlled by the float height which can increase as a result of wear or damage. Remove the float bowl and check the float height. Check also that floats have not punctured; a punctured float will loose buoyancy and allow an increased fuel level.

● Float valve needle stuck open. Caused by dirt or a worn valve. Clean the float chamber or renew the needle and, if necessary, the valve seat.

Lubrication problems

38 Engine lubrication system failure

● Engine oil defective. Oil pump shaft or locating pin sheared off from ingesting debris or seizing from lack of lubrication (low oil level) (Chapter 1).

● Engine oil screen clogged. Change oil and clean both filter gauzes. See Routine Maintenance.

● Engine oil level too low. Inspect for leak or other problem causing low oil level and add recommended lubricant (Chapter 1 and Routine Maintenance).

● Engine oil viscosity too low. Very old, thin oil, or an improper weight of oil used in engine. Change to correct lubricant. (See Routine Maintenance).

● Camshaft or journals worn. High wear causing drop in oil pressure. Replace cam and/or head. Abnormal wear could be caused by oil starvation at high rpm from low oil level or improper oil weight or type.

● Crankshaft and/or bearings worn. Same problems as paragraph 5. Overhaul lower end (Chapter 1).

Poor handling or roadholding

39   Directional instability

● Steering head bearing adjustment too tight. This will cause rolling or weaving at low speeds. Re-adjust the bearings.

● Steering head bearing worn or damaged. Correct adjustment of the bearing will prove impossible to achieve if wear or damage has occurred. Inconsistent handling will occur including rolling or weaving at low speed and poor directional control at indeterminate higher speeds. The steering head bearing should be dismantled for inspection and renewed if required. Lubrication should also be carried out.

● Bearing races pitted or dented. Impact damage caused, perhaps, by an accident or riding over a pot-hole can cause indentation of the bearing, usually in one position. This should be noted as notchiness when the handlebars are turned. Renew and lubricate the bearings.

● Steering stem bent. This will occur only if the machine is subjected to a high impact such as hitting a curb or a pot-hole. The lower yoke/stem should be renewed; do not attempt to straighten the stem.

● Front or rear tyre pressures too low.

● Front or rear tyre worn. General instability, high speed wobbles and skipping over white lines indicates that tyre renewal may be required. Tyre induced problems, in some machine/tyre combinations, can occur even when the tyre in question is by no means fully worn.

● Swinging arm bearings worn. Difficulties in holding line, particularly when cornering or when changing power settings indicates wear in the swinging arm bearings. The swinging arm should be removed from the machine and the bearings renewed.

● Swinging arm flexing. The symptoms given in the preceding paragraph will also occur if the swinging arm fork flexes badly. This can be caused by structural weakness as a result of corrosion, fatigue or impact damage, or because the rear wheel spindle is slack.

● Wheel bearings worn. Renew the worn bearings.

● Loose wheel spokes. The spokes should be tightened evenly to maintain tension and trueness of the rim.

● Tyres unsuitable for machine. Not all available tyres will suit the characteristics of the frame and suspension, indeed, some tyres or tyre combinations may cause a transformation in the handling characteristics. If handling problems occur immediately after changing to a new tyre type or make, revert to the original tyres to see whether an improvement can be noted. In some instances a change to what are, in fact, suitable tyres may give rise to handling deficiencies. In this case a thorough check should be made of all frame and suspension items which affect stability.

40   Steering bias to left or right

● Rear wheel out of alignment. Caused by uneven adjustment of chain tensioner adjusters allowing the wheel to be askew in the fork ends. A bent rear wheel spindle will also misalign the wheel in the swinging arm.

● Wheels out of alignment. This can be caused by impact damage to the frame, swinging arm, wheel spindles or front forks. Although occasionally a result of material failure or corrosion it is usually as a result of a crash.

● Front forks twisted in the steering yokes. A light impact, for instance with a pot-hole or low curb, can twist the fork legs in the steering yokes without causing structural damage to the fork legs or the yokes themselves. Re-alignment can be made by loosening the yoke pinch bolts, wheel spindle and mudguard bolts. Re-align the wheel with the handlebars and tighten the bolts working upwards from the wheel spindle. This action should be carried out only when there is no chance that structural damage has occurred.

41   Handlebar vibrates or oscillates

● Tyres worn or out of balance. Either condition, particularly in the front tyre, will promote shaking of the fork assembly and thus the handlebars. A sudden onset of shaking can result if a balance weight is displaced during use.

● Tyres badly positioned on the wheel rims. A moulded line on each wall of a tyre is provided to allow visual verification that the tyre is correctly positioned on the rim. A check can be made by rotating the tyre; any misalignment will be immediately obvious.

● Wheel rims warped or damaged. Inspect the wheels for runout as described in Chapter 5.

● Swinging arm bearings worn. Renew the bearings.

● Wheel bearings worn. Renew the bearings.

● Steering head bearings, incorrectly adjusted. Vibration is more likely to result from bearings which are too loose rather than too tight. Re-adjust the bearings.

● Loosen fork component fasteners. Loose nuts and bolts holding the fork legs, wheel spindle, mudguards or steering stem can promote shaking at the handlebars. Fasteners on running gear such as the forks and suspension should be check tightened occasionally to prevent dangerous looseness of components occurring.

● Engine mounting bolts loose. Tighten all fasteners.

42   Poor front fork performance

● Damping fluid level incorrect. If the fluid level is too low poor suspension control will occur resulting in a general impairment of roadholding and early loss of tyre adhesion when cornering and braking. Too much oil is unlikely to change the fork characteristics unless severe overfilling occurs when the fork action will become stiffer and oil seal failure may occur.

● Damping oil viscosity incorrect. The damping action of the fork is directly related to the viscosity of the damping oil. The lighter the oil used, the less will be the damping action imparted. For general use, use the recommended viscosity of oil, changing to a slightly higher or heavier oil only when a change in damping characteristics is required. Overworked oil, or oil contaminated with water which has found its way past the seals, should be renewed to restore the correct damping performance and to prevent bottoming of the forks.

● Damping components worn or corroded. Advanced normal wear of the fork internals is unlikely to occur until a very high mileage has been covered. Continual use of the machine with damaged oil seals which allows the ingress of water, or neglect, will lead to rapid corrosion and wear. Dismantle the forks for inspection and overhaul. See Chapter 4.

● Weak fork springs. Progressive fatigue of the fork springs, resulting in a reduced spring free length, will occur after extensive use. This condition will promote excessive fork dive under braking, and in its advanced form will reduce the at-rest extended length of the forks and thus the fork geometry. Renewal of the springs as a pair is the only satisfactory course of action.

● Bent stanchions or corroded stanchions. Both conditions will prevent correct telescoping of the fork legs, and in an advanced state can cause sticking of the fork in one position. In a mild form corrosion will cause stiction of the fork thereby increasing the time the suspension takes to react to an uneven road surface. Bent fork stanchions should be attended to immediately because they indicate that impact damage has occurred, and there is a danger that the forks will fail with disastrous consequences.

43   Front fork judder when braking (see also Section 51)

● Wear between the fork stanchions and the fork legs. Renewal of the affected components is required.

● Slack steering head bearings. Re-adjust the bearings.

● Warped brake disc (models with front disc brakes). If irregular braking action occurs, fork judder can be induced in what are normally serviceable forks. Renew the damaged brake components.

● Warped brake drum. If irregular braking action occurs fork judder can be induced in what are normally serviceable forks. Renew the damaged brake components.

44   Poor rear suspension performances

● Rear suspension unit damper worn out or leaking. The damaging performance of most rear suspension units falls off with age. This is a gradual process, and thus may not be immediately obvious. Indications of poor damping include hopping of the rear end when cornering or braking, and a general loss of positive stability. See Chapter 4.
● Weak rear springs. If the suspension unit springs fatigue they will promote excessive pitching of the machine and reduce the ground clearance when cornering.
● Swinging arm flexing or bearings worn. See Sections 39 and 40.
● Bent suspension unit damper rod. This is likely to occur only if the machine is dropped or if seizure or the piston occurs. If either happens the suspension units should be renewed as a pair.

Abnormal frame and suspension noise

45   Front end noise

● Oil level low or too thin. This can cause a 'spurting' sound and is usually accompanied by irregular fork action.
● Spring weak or broken. Makes a clicking or scraping sound. Fork oil will have a lot of metal particles in it.
● Steering head bearings loose or damaged. Clicks when braking. Check, adjust or replace.
● Fork clamps loose. Make sure all fork clamp pinch bolts are tight.
● Fork stanchion bent. Good possibility if machine has been dropped. Repair or replace tube.

46   Rear suspension noise

● Fluid level too low. Leakage of a suspension unit, usually evident by oil on the outer surfaces, can cause a spurting noise. The suspension units should be renewed as a pair.
● Defective rear suspension unit with internal damage. Renew the suspension units as a pair.

Brake problems

47   Brakes are spongy or ineffective

Drum brakes
● Brake cable deterioration. Damage to the outer cable by stretching or being trapped will give a spongy feel to the brake lever. The cable should be renewed. A cable which has become corroded due to old age or neglect of lubrication will partially seize making operation very heavy. Lubrication at this stage may overcome the problem but the fitting of a new cable is recommended.
● Worn brake linings. Determine lining wear using the external brake wear indicator on the brake backplate, or by removing the wheel and withdrawing the brake backplate. Renew the shoe/lining units as a pair if the linings are worn below the recommended limit.
● Worn brake camshaft. Wear between the camshaft and the bearing surface will reduce brake feel and reduce operating efficiency. Renewal of one or both items will be required to rectify the fault.
● Worn brake cam and shoe ends. Renew the worn components.
● Linings contaminated with dust or grease. Any accumulations of dust should be cleaned from the brake assembly and drum using a petrol dampened cloth. Do not blow of brush off the dust because it is asbestos based and thus harmful if inhaled. Light contamination from grease can be removed from the surface of the brake linings using a solvent; attempts at removing heavier contamination are less likely to be successful because some of the lubricant will have been absorbed by the lining material which will severely reduce the braking performance.

Front disc brake
● Air in brake circuit. This is only likely to happen in service due to neglect in checking the fluid level or because a leak has developed. The problem should be identified and the brake system bled of air.
● Pads worn. Check the pad wear as described in Chapter 7.
● Contaminated pads. Cleaning pads which have been contaminated with oil, grease or brake fluid is unlikely to prove successful; the pads should be renewed.
● Pads glazed. This is usually caused by overheating. The surface of the pads may be roughened using glass-paper or a fine file.
● Brake fluid deterioration. A brake which on initial operation is firm but rapidly becomes spongy in use may be failing due to water contamination of the fluid. The fluid should be drained and then the system refilled and bled.
● Master cylinder seal failure. Wear or damage of master cylinder internal parts will prevent pressurisation of the brake fluid. Overhaul the master cylinder unit.
● Caliper seal failure. This will almost certainly be obvious by loss of fluid, a lowering of fluid level in the master cylinder reservoir and contamination of the brake pads and caliper. Overhaul the caliper assembly.

48   Brake drag

Drum brakes
● Incorrect adjustment. Re-adjust the brake operating mechanism.
● Drum warped or oval. This can result from overheating, impact or uneven tension of the wheel spokes. The condition is difficult to correct, although if slight ovality only occurs, skimming the surface of the brake drum can provide a cure. This is work for a specialist engineer. Renewal of the complete wheel hub is normally the only satisfactory solution.
● Weak brake shoe return springs. This will prevent the brake lining/shoe units from pulling away from the drum surface once the brake is released. The springs should be renewed.
● Brake camshaft, lever pivot or cable poorly lubricated. Failure to attend to regular lubrication of these areas will increase operating resistance which, when compounded, may cause tardy operation and poor release movement.

Front disc brake
● Disc warped. The disc must be renewed.
● Caliper piston, caliper or pads corroded. The brake caliper assembly is vulnerable to corrosion due to water and dirt, and unless cleaned at regular intervals and lubricated in the recommended manner will become sticky in operation.
● Piston seal deteriorated. The seal is designed to return the piston into the caliper to the retracted position when the brake is released. Wear or old age can affect this function. The caliper should be overhauled if this occurs.
● Brake pad damaged. Pad material separating from the backing plate due to wear or faulty manufacture. Renew the pads. Faulty installation of a pad will also cause dragging.
● Brake lever not returning. Check that the lever works smoothly throughout its operating range and does not snag on any adjacent cycle parts. Lubricate the pivot if necessary.
● Twisted caliper mounting bracket. This is likely to occur only after impact in an accident. No attempt should be made to re-align the caliper; the bracket should be renewed.
● Insufficient brake lever freeplay. Adjust as described in Chapter 7.

49   Brake lever or pedal pulsates in operation

Drum brakes
● Drums warped or oval. This can result from overheating, impact or uneven spoke tension. The condition is difficult to correct, although if slight ovality only occurs, skimming the surface of the brake drum can provide a cure. This is work for a specialist engineer. Renewal of the complete wheel hub is normally the only satisfactory solution.

Front disc brake
● Disc warped or irregularly worn. The disc must be renewed.
● Brake caliper or mounting bracket bolts loose.

50 Brake noise

Drum brakes
● Drum warped or oval. This can cause intermittent rubbing of the brake linings against the drum. See the preceding Section.
● Brake linings glazed. This condition, usually accompanied by heavy lining dust contamination, often induces brake squeal. The surface of the linings may be roughened using glass-paper or a fine file.

Front disc brake
● Brake squeal. This can be caused by the omission or incorrect installation of the anti-squeal shim. Squealing can also be caused by dust on the pads, usually in combination with glazed pads, or other contamination from oil, grease, brake fluid or corrosion. Persistent squealing which cannot be traced to any of the normal causes can often be cured by applying a thin layer of copper-based grease to the rear of the pads. Make absolutely certain that no grease is allowed to contaminate the braking surface of the pads.
● Glazed pads. This is usually caused by high temperatures or contamination. The pad surfaces may be roughened using glass-paper or a fine file. If this approach does not effect a cure the pads should be renewed.
● Disc warped. This can cause a chattering, clicking or intermittent squeal and is usually accompanied by a pulsating brake lever or pedal or uneven braking. The disc must be renewed.

51 Brake induced fork judder

● Worn front fork stanchions and legs, or worn or badly adjusted steering head bearings. These conditions, combined with uneven or pulsating braking as described in Section 49 will induce more or less judder when the brakes are applied, dependent on the degree of wear and poor brake operation. Attention should be given to both areas of malfunction. See the relevant Section.

Electrical problems

52 Battery dead or weak

● Battery faulty. Battery life should not be expected to exceed 3 to 4 years, particularly where a starter motor is used regularly. Gradual sulphation of the plates and sediment deposits will reduce the battery performance. Plate and insulator damage can often occur as a result of vibration. Complete power failure, or intermittent failure, may be due to a broken battery terminal. Lack of electrolyte will prevent the battery maintaining charge.
● Battery leads making poor contact. Remove the battery leads and clean them and the terminals, removing all traces of corrosion and tarnish. Reconnect the leads and apply a coating of petroleum jelly to the terminals.
● Load excessive. If additional items such as spot lamps, are fitted, which increase the total electrical load above the maximum alternator output, the battery will fail to maintain full charge. Reduce the electrical load to suit the electrical capacity.
● Regulator/rectifier failure.
● Alternator generating coils open-circuit or shorted.

● Charging circuit shorting or open circuit. This may be caused by frayed or broken wiring, dirty connectors or a faulty ignition switch. The system should be tested in a logical manner. See Section 55.

53 Battery overcharged

● Rectifier/regulator faulty. Overcharging is indicated if the battery becomes hot or it is noticed that the electrolyte level falls repeatedly between checks. In extreme cases the battery will boil causing corrosive gases and electrolyte to be emitted through the vent pipes.
● Battery wrongly matched to the electrical circuit. Ensure that the specified battery is fitted to the machine.

54 Total electrical failure

● Fuse blown. Check the main fuse. If a fault has occurred, it must be rectified before a new fuse is fitted.
● Battery fault. See Section 52.
● Earth failure. Check that the frame main earth strap from the battery is securely affixed to the frame and is making a good contact.
● Ignition switch or power circuit failure. Check for current flow through the battery positive lead (red) to the ignition switch. Check the ignition switch for continuity.

55 Circuit failure

● Cable failure. Refer to the machine's wiring diagram and check the circuit for continuity. Open circuits are a result of loose or corroded connections, either at terminals or in-line connectors, or because of broken wires. Occasionally, the core of a wire will break without there being any apparent damage to the outer plastic cover.
● Switch failure. All switches may be checked for continuity in each switch position, after referring to the switch position boxes incorporated in the wiring diagram for the machine. Switch failure may be a result of mechanical breakage, corrosion or water.
● Fuse blown. Replace the fuse, if blown, only after the fault has been identified and rectified.

56 Bulbs blowing repeatedly

● Vibration failure. This is often an inherent fault related to the natural vibration characteristics of the engine and frame and is, thus, difficult to resolve. Modifications of the lamp mounting, to change the damping characteristics may help.
● Intermittent earth. Repeated failure of one bulb, particularly where the bulb is fed directly from the generator, indicates that a poor earth exists somewhere in the circuit. Check that a good contact is available at each connecting point in the circuit.
● Reduced voltage. Where a quartz-halogen bulb is fitted the voltage to the bulb should be maintained or early failure of the bulb will occur. Do not overload the system with additional electrical equipment in excess of the system's power capacity and ensure that all circuit connections are maintained clean and tight.

YAMAHA XT & SR125 SINGLES

Check list

Daily

1 Check the engine/transmission oil level through the sight glass
2 Ensure you have enough petrol to complete your journey
3 Check the operation of both brakes
4 Check the tyre pressures
5 Check the final drive chain adjustment
6 Check the operation of the controls and steering
7 Check the operation of the lights, indicators, horn and speedometer

Two weekly, or every 300 miles (500 km)

1 Check the engine/transmission oil level
2 Check the tyre pressures
3 Check, adjust and lubricate the final drive chain
4 Check the security of all fittings and fasteners

Six weekly, or every 1000 miles (1500 km)

1 Change the engine/transmission oil – additional change
2 Check the battery electrolyte level and terminal condition
3 Inspect the wheels and tyres for damage
4 Check and adjust the brakes
5 Clean the air filter element
6 Check and adjust the clutch
7 Check and adjust the steering head bearings and check the suspension

Three monthly, or every 2000 miles (3000 km)

1 Clean the spark plug
2 Check and adjust the valve clearances
3 Adjust the cam chain
4 Check the carburettor, throttle cable and fuel pipe
5 Clean the fuel filter
6 Change the engine/transmission oil
7 Lubricate all pivot points and control cables

Six monthly, or every 4000 miles (6000 km)

1 Check the compression pressure
2 Check the ignition timing
3 Clean the oil filter
4 Change the front fork oil

Annually, or every 8000 miles (12 000 km)

1 Renew the spark plug
2 Grease the wheel bearings and speedometer drive
3 Overhaul the brakes
4 Grease the steering head bearings
5 Grease the rear suspension pivot bearings

Adjustment data

Valve clearances
Inlet   0.05 - 0.09 mm (0.002 - 0.003 in)
Exhaust   0.11 - 0.15 mm (0.004 - 0.006 in)

Spark plug gap   0.6 - 0.7 mm (0.024 - 0.028 in)

Spark plug type   NGK D8EA

Idle speed   1250 - 1350 rpm

Tyre pressures - SR125

	Front	Rear
0-198 lb (90 kg)- low speed	25 psi (1.72 kg/cm²)	28 psi (1.96 kg/cm²)
0-198 lb (90 kg)- high speed, 198-353 lb (90-160 kg)	25 psi (1.72 kg/cm²)	31 psi (2.20 kg/cm²)

Tyre pressures - XT125

	Front	Rear
0-254 lb (115 kg)	18 psi (1.27 kg/cm²)	21 psi (1.47 kg/cm²)
254-408 lb (115-185 kg)	18 psi (1.27 kg/cm²)	26 psi (1.77 kg/cm²)

Note: the weights given are the total permissible weight of the rider, passenger and any accessories or luggage.

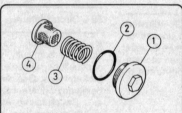

Engine/transmission oil drain plug filter assembly

1 Cap
2 O-ring
3 Spring
4 Filter gauze

Recommended lubricants

Component	Quantity	Type/viscosity
1 Engine/transmission	1.0 litre (1.8 pint)	Good quality SAE 20W40 SE engine oil
2 Front forks:		
SR125	184 cc (6.48 fl oz)	10W30 SE engine oil
XT125	249 cc (8.77 fl oz)	10W30 SE engine oil or SAE 10 fork oil
3 Final drive chain	As required	Aerosol chain lubricant
4 Wheel bearings	As required	High melting point grease
5 Steering head bearings	As required	High melting point grease
6 Rear suspension pivot bearings	As required	High melting point grease
7 Pivot points	As required	High melting point grease
8 Control cables	As required	Light machine oil

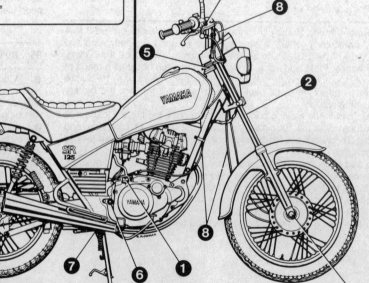

ROUTINE MAINTENANCE GUIDE

Routine maintenance

Refer to Chapter 7 for information relating to the 1991-on SR125 models

Periodic routine maintenance is a continuous process which should commence immediately the machine is used. The object is to maintain all adjustments and to diagnose and rectify minor defects before they develop into more extensive, and often more expensive, problems.

It follows that if the machine is maintained properly, it will both run and perform with optimum efficiency, and be less prone to unexpected breakdowns. Regular inspection of the machine will show up any parts which are wearing, and with a little experience, it is possible to obtain the maximum life from any one component, renewing it when it becomes so worn that it is liable to fail.

Regular cleaning can be considered as important as mechanical maintenance. This will ensure that all the cycle parts are inspected regularly and are kept free from accumulations of road dirt and grime.

Cleaning is especially important during the winter months, despite its appearance of being a thankless task which very soon seems pointless. On the contrary, it is during these months that the paintwork, chromium plating, and the alloy casings suffer the ravages of abrasive grit, rain and road salt. A couple of hours spent weekly on cleaning the machine will maintain its appearance and value, and highlight small points, like chipped paint, before they become a serious problem.

The various maintenance tasks are described under their respective mileage and calendar headings, and are accompanied by diagrams and photographs where pertinent.

It should be noted that the intervals between each maintenance task serve only as a guide. As the machine gets older, or if it is used under particularly arduous conditions, it is advisable to reduce the period between each check.

For ease of reference, most service operations are described in detail under the relevant heading. However, if further general information is required, this can be found under the pertinent Section heading and Chapter in the main text.

Although no special tools are required for routine maintenance, a good selection of general workshop tools is essential. Included in the tools must be a range of metric ring or combination spanners, a selection of crosshead screwdrivers, and two pairs of circlip pliers, one external opening and the other internal opening. Additionally, owing to the extreme tightness of most casing screws on Japanese machines, an impact screwdriver, together with a choice of large or small crosshead screw bits, is absolutely indispensable. This is particularly so if the engine has not been dismantled since leaving the factory. Another tool which is essential for XT125 owners is a stand of some sort. A strong wooden box is normally recommended, but this is not always convenient for routine maintenance tasks, and so the purchase or fabrication of a metal stand, which will support the machine securely upright with enough height for either wheel to be removed, is advised. 'Paddock' type stands are frequently advertised in the national motorcycle press and are, in the author's view, well worth the money spent. XT125 owners should note that where a centre stand is mentioned in the following instructions, they must substitute their own stand.

Daily (pre-riding checks)

Before taking the machine out on the road, there are certain checks which should be completed to ensure that it is in a safe and legal condition to be used.

1 Engine/transmission oil level

With the machine standing upright on its wheels on level ground, check that the oil level visible through the sight glass set in the crankcase right-hand cover is between the lines stamped on the crankcase cover. If topping-up is necessary, add oil slowly via the filler plug orifice in the crankcase cover. Use only a good quality SAE 20W/40 SE engine oil, and refit securely the filler plug. If the engine has just been run, allow one or two minutes for the oil to drain back into the crankcase before checking the level.

Oil level must be between crankcase lines

Use only good quality SAE 20W40SE engine oil when topping up

2   Petrol level

Checking the petrol level may seem obvious, but it is all too easy to forget. Ensure that you have enough petrol to complete your journey, or at least to get you to the nearest petrol station.

3   Brakes

Check that the front and rear brakes work effectively and without binding. Ensure that the rod linkages and the cables, as applicable, are lubricated and properly adjusted.

4   Tyres

Check the tyre pressure with a gauge that is known to be accurate. It is worthwhile purchasing a pocket gauge for this purpose because the gauges on garage forecourt airlines are notoriously inaccurate. The pressures should be checked with the tyres cold. Even a few miles travelled will warm up the tyres to a point where pressures increase and an inaccurate reading will result. Tyre pressures for these models are:

	Front	Rear
SR125		
Up to 198 lb (90 kg) – low speed	25 psi (1.72 kg/cm²)	28 psi (1.96 kg/cm²)
Up to 198 lb (90 kg) – high speed	25 psi (1.72 kg/cm²)	31 psi (2.20 kg/cm²)
198 – 353 lb (90 – 160 kg)		
XT125		
Up to 254 lb (115 kg)	18 psi (1.27 kg/cm²)	21 psi (1.47 kg/cm²)
254 – 408 lb (115 – 185 kg)	18 psi (1.27 kg/cm²)	26 psi (1.77 kg/cm²)

Note: *the weights given are the total permissible weight of rider, passenger and any accessories or luggage.*

At the same time as the tyre pressures are checked, examine the tyres themselves. Check them for damage, especially splitting of the sidewalls. Remove any small stones or other road debris caught between the treads. This is particularly important on the rear tyre, where rapid deflation due to penetration of the inner tube will almost certainly cause total loss of control. When checking the tyres for damage, they should be examined for tread depth in view of both the legal and safety aspects. It is vital to keep the tread depth within the UK legal limits of 1 mm of depth over three-quarters of the tread breadth around the entire circumference with no sign of bald patches. Many riders, however, consider nearer 2 mm to be the limit for secure roadholding, traction, and braking, especially in adverse weather conditions.

5   Final drive chain

Check that the final drive chain is correctly adjusted and well lubricated. Remember that if the machine is used in adverse conditions the chain will require frequent, even daily, lubrication. Refer to the 2 weekly/300 mile service interval.

6   Controls and steering

Check throttle, clutch, gear lever and footrests to ensure that they are securely fastened and working properly. If a bolt is going to work loose, or a cable snap, it is better that it does so with the machine at a standstill than when riding. Check also that the steering and suspension are working correctly.

7   Lights and speedometer

Check that all lights, flashing indicators, horn and speedometer are working correctly to make sure that the machine complies with all legal requirements in this respect.

Two weekly or every 300 miles (500 km)

This is where the proper procedure of routine maintenance begins. The daily checks serve to ensure that the machine is safe and legal to use, but contribute little to maintenance other than to give the owner an accurate picture of what item needs attention. However, if done conscientiously, they will give early warning, as has been stated, of any faults which are about to appear. When performing the following maintenance tasks, therefore, carry out the daily checks first.

1   Check the engine/transmission oil level

Although this has already been included under the daily tasks, it is mentioned again to remind owners that the quality and quantity of oil is vital to the engine's efficiency and reliability. Never allow the engine to run with the oil level outside the level reference marks.

2   Check tyre pressures

This is also repeated to stress the vital part that tyre pressures play in the machine's stability and safety. Ensure that the pressures are correct at all times.

3   Check, adjust and lubricate the final drive chain

The chain consists of a multitude of small bearing surfaces which will wear rapidly, and expensively, if the chain is not regularly lubricated and adjusted. A simple check for wear is as follows. With the chain fully lubricated and correctly adjusted as described below, attempt to pull the chain backwards off the rear sprocket. If the chain can be pulled clear of the sprocket teeth it must be considered worn out and renewed; chains should be renewed always in conjunction with the sprockets since the running together of new and part-worn components will greatly increase the rate of wear of both, necessitating renewal much sooner than would otherwise be the case.

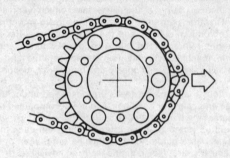

Checking for an excessively worn final drive chain

A more accurate measurement of chain wear can be applied which involves the removal of the chain from the machine and its thorough cleaning. Disconnect the chain at its split connecting link and pull the entire length of the chain clear of the sprockets. Note that refitting the chain is greatly simplified if a worn out length is temporarily connected to it. As the original chain is pulled off the sprockets, the worn-out chain will follow it and remain in place while the task of cleaning and examination is carried out. On reassembly, the process is repeated, pulling the worn-out chain over the sprockets so that the new chain, or the freshly cleaned and lubricated chain, is pulled easily into place.

To clean the chain, immerse it in a bath containing a mixture of petrol and paraffin and use a stiff-bristled brush to scrub away all the traces of road dirt and old lubricant. Take the necessary fire precautions when using this flammable solvent. Swill the chain around to ensure that the solvent penetrates fully into the bushes and rollers and can remove any lubricant which may still be present. When the chain is completely clean, remove it from the bath and hang it up to dry.

To assess accurately the amount of wear present in the chain, it must be cleaned and dried as described above, then laid out on a flat surface. Compress the chain fully and measure its length from end to end. Anchor one end of the chain and pull on the other end, drawing the chain out to its fullest extent. Measure the stretched length. If the stretched measurement exceeds the compressed measurement by more than $\frac{1}{4}$ in per foot, the chain must be considered worn out and be renewed.

Chain lubrication is best carried out by immersing the chain in a molten lubricant such as Chainguard or Linklyfe. Lubrication carried out in this manner must be preceded by removing the chain from the machine, cleaning it, and drying it as described above. Follow the manufacturer's instructions carefully when using Chainguard or Linklyfe, and take great care to swill the chain gently in the molten lubricant to ensure that all bearing surfaces are fully greased.

Refitting a new, or freshly-lubricated, chain is a potentially messy affair which is greatly simplified by the substitution of a worn-out length of chain during removal. The new chain can then be connected to the worn-out length and pulled easily around the sprockets. Refit the connecting link, ensuring that the spring clip is fitted with its closed end facing the normal direction of travel of the chain.

For the purpose of daily or weekly lubrication, one of the many proprietary aerosol-applied chain lubricants is a far better proposition since this can be applied very quickly, while the chain is in place on the machine, and makes very little mess. It should be applied at least once a week, and daily if the machine is used in wet weather conditions. If the roller surfaces look dry, then they need lubrication. Engine oil can be used for this task, but remember that it is flung off the chain far more easily than grease, thus making the rear end of the machine unnecessarily dirty, and requires more frequent application if it is to perform its task adequately. Also remember that surplus oil will eventually find its way on to the tyre, with quite disastrous consequences.

It is necessary to check the chain tension at regular intervals to compensate for wear. Since this wear does not take place evenly along the length of the chain, tight spots will appear which must be compensated for when adjustment is made. Chain tension is checked with the transmission in neutral; on SR125 models place the machine on its centre stand, but on XT125 models the machine must be standing on its wheels. Find the tightest spot in the chain by revolving the rear wheel and pushing upwards on the bottom run of the chain, midway between the front and rear sprockets, testing along the entire length of the chain. When the tightest spot has been found, measure the total amount of up and down movement available. This should be between 45 – 55 mm (1.8 – 2.2 in) on XT125 models; on SR125 models the pin heads in each chain sideplate must not be outside the limits set by the 'Usable Range' marking on the chaincase side, as shown in the accompanying illustration.

If adjustment is necessary, remove the split pin, slacken the rear wheel spindle nut by just enough to permit the spindle to be moved, then draw the spindle back by rotating the snail cams. Use the numbers stamped in each cam to ensure that the spindle is moved back by the same amount on each side, thus preserving accurate wheel alignment. A final check of accurate wheel alignment can be

Ensure spring clip is always refitted with closed end facing direction of chain travel

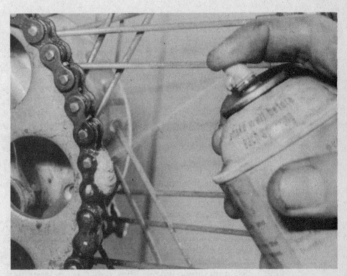

Aerosol spray is the most convenient form of chain lubrication

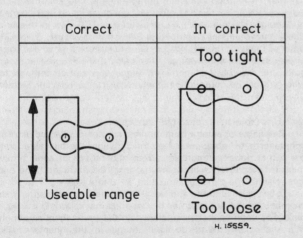

Chain tension limit marks – SR125

Numbers stamped in snail cams help to preserve wheel alignment

made by laying a plank of wood or drawing a length of string parallel to the machine so that it touches both walls of the rear tyre. Wheel alignment is correct when the plank or string is equidistant from both walls of the front tyre when tested on both sides of the machine. Note that if the front tyre is of smaller section than the rear, the plank or string will not touch the walls of the front tyre, as shown in the accompanying illustration. The task of preserving correct rear wheel alignment is made easier if care is taken to draw the spindle back in small stages, turning each cam by exactly the same amount.

When the chain is correctly tensioned, apply the rear brake to centralise the shoes on the drum, and tighten the spindle retaining nut to a torque setting of 8.5 kgf m (61.5 lbf ft) on XT125 models and 6.5 kgf m (47 lbf ft) on SR125 models. Remember that if the chain tension has been altered significantly, the rear brake and stop lamp rear switch adjustment will also require resetting. These should be checked as a matter of course before taking the machine out on the road.

Note that replacement chains are now available in standard metric sizes from Renold Limited, the British chain manufacturer. When ordering a new chain, always quote the size, the number of chain links and the type of machine to which the chain is to be fitted. Both machines featured in this Manual use a 428 ($\frac{1}{2}$ x $\frac{5}{16}$ in) size chain, the number of links varying between 118 – 120 depending on for which model the chain is being ordered, and what size of sprocket is fitted.

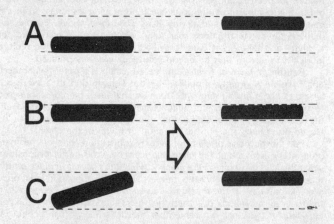

Checking the wheel alignment

A & C – Incorrect   B – Correct

4 Check all fittings, fasteners, lights and signals

Check around the machine, looking for loose nuts, bolts or screws, retightening them as necessary. Check the stand and lever pivots for security and lubricate them with light machine oil or engine oil. Make sure that the stand springs are in good condition.

It is advisable to lubricate the handlebar switches and stop lamp switches with WD40 or a similar water dispersant lubricant. This will keep the switches working properly and prolong their life, especially if the machine is used in adverse weather conditions. Apply a few drops of engine oil to the exposed inner portion of each control cable. This will prevent the cables drying up between the more thorough lubrications that should be carried out at each 3-monthly/2000 mile service. Check that all lights, turn signals, the horn and speedometer are working properly and that their mountings and connections are securely fastened.

Six weekly, or every 1000 miles (1500 km)

Complete the operations under the previous mileage/time heading, then carry out the following:

1 Additional engine/transmission oil change

The manufacturer's scheduled oil change interval is every 2000 miles (3000 km), but since the engine relies so heavily on the quantity and quality of its oil, and since the oil in any motorcycle engine is worked far harder than in other vehicles, it is recommended that the engine oil is changed at more frequent intervals if the machine is used at very high speeds for long periods of time or if it is used only at very slow speed or for very short journeys.

If the additional oil change is to be carried out, follow the instructions given under the 3-monthly/2000 mile service heading.

2 Check the battery

It is essential that the battery is maintained in excellent condition to prolong its life. In addition to the check of the electrolyte level, the condition of the terminals should be examined. The exposed terminals employed on the battery fitted to the SR125 models are prone to corroding, producing a variety of faults in the electrical system if allowed to go unchecked. Clean away all traces of dirt and corrosion, scraping the terminals and connections with a knife and using emery cloth to finish off. Remake the connections while the joint is still clean and then smear the assembly with petroleum jelly (not grease) to prevent recurrence of the corrosion. Finish off by checking that the battery is securely clamped in its mountings and that the vent tube is quite clean and free from kinks or blockages.

The electrolyte level must be maintained between the level marks on the casing. Top up, if necessary, using only distilled water.

Electrolyte level must be maintained between level lines on battery casing

3 Check the wheels and tyres

Make a thorough check of the tyre treads, checking the degree of wear, removing stones and other foreign bodies, and looking for signs of damage. The tyre must be renewed if seriously worn or damaged. Check the wheels as described in Section 2 of Chapter 5, looking for signs of loose or broken spokes, bent or distorted rims, and for signs of play in the wheel bearings. Check also that the sprocket mounting bolts are securely fastened. Any signs of wear or damage to the wheels must be cured immediately; refer to the relevant Sections of Chapter 5.

4 Check and adjust the brakes

The cable-operated front brakes require regular adjustment to compensate for shoe wear and for variations in the cable itself. To check that the adjustment is correct, apply the front brake firmly and measure the distance between the handlebar lever butt end and the lever clamp. The distance should be 5 – 8 mm (0.2 – 0.3 in) when the handlebar lever is firmly applied. If adjustment is necessary, it should be made at the adjuster set in the brake backplate. Once the front brake has been correctly adjusted, spin the front wheel and apply the front brake hard to settle the cable and brake components. Check that the adjustment has not been altered, re-setting it if necessary, and ensure that the adjuster locknuts are securely tightened and that all the rubber cable protecting sleeves are correctly replaced. Check that the front wheel is free to rotate easily. The adjuster at the handlebar

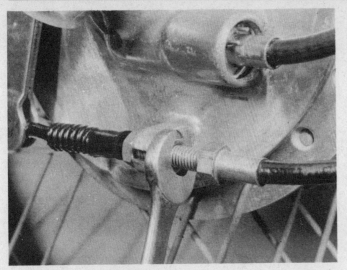

Front brake is adjusted as shown ...

... rear brake is adjusted at rear end of operating rod

lever clamp should be reserved for quick roadside adjustments; be sure that it is screwed fully in before using the lower adjuster.

The rear brake is adjusted by means of a single nut at the rear end of the brake operating rod. Turn the nut clockwise to reduce free play, if necessary, to measure 20 – 30 mm (0.8 – 1.2 in) at the brake pedal tip. Check that the rear wheel rotates freely and that the stop lamp is functioning properly. Remember that the stop lamp switch height must be adjusted every time the rear brake adjustment is altered. To adjust the switch height, turn its plastic sleeve nut as required until the stop lamp bulb lights when the brake pedal free play has been taken up and the rear brake shoes are just beginning to engage the brake drum.

Complete brake maintenance by oiling all lever pivot points, all exposed lengths of cable, cable nipples and the rear brake linkage with a few drops of oil from a can. Remember not to allow excessive oil onto the operating linkage, in case any surplus should find its way into the brake drum or onto the tyre.

Regular checks must be made to ensure that the friction material of the brake shoes is not worn down to a dangerous level, and to ensure that worn items are renewed in good time to maintain peak brake efficiency.

All brakes have external wear indicators which function as follows. A pointer fitted to the brake camshaft aligns with a line cast in the brake backplate, as shown in the accompanying photograph. If, when the brake is correctly adjusted and applied hard, the camshaft is seen to be outside the arc of the backplate line, the friction material is worn to beyond permissible limits and the shoes must be renewed.

Overhauling the brakes must be preceded by the removal of the wheel concerned, as described in the relevant Sections of Chapter 5. The brake components can then be dismantled, cleaned, checked for wear, and reassembled following the instructions given in the same Chapter. It is important that moving parts such as the brake camshaft are lubricated with a smear of high melting-point grease on reassembly.

5 Clean the air filter element

It is vitally important that the air filter element is kept clean and in good condition if the engine is to function properly. If the element becomes choked with dust it follows that the airflow to the engine will be impaired, leading to poor performance and high fuel consumption. Conversely, a damaged air filter will allow excessive amounts of unfiltered air to enter the engine, which can result in an increased rate of wear and possible damage due to the weak nature of the mixture. The interval specified above indicates the maximum time limit between each cleaning operation. Where the machine is used in particularly adverse conditions it is advised that cleaning takes place on a much more frequent basis.

On SR125 models, detach the right-hand side panel and remove the two screws securing the element cover. Withdraw the cover, followed by the plastic supporting frame and the foam element itself.

If the pointer moves outside the arc with the brake applied, brake shoes must be renewed

Remove screws securing filter cover ...

... to gain access to element and supporting frame

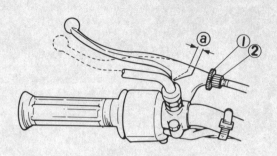

Clutch adjustment

1   Locknut   a   Free play
2   Adjuster

If it is dirty, the steel mesh frame behind the element can be detached for washing in petrol or similar, by removing its two retaining screws. On XT125 models, detach the left-hand side panel and remove the four screws securing the element cover. Withdraw the cover and pull out the element support, which is spring-loaded. The element assembly can then be displaced and the foam element peeled off its supporting steel frame.

Examine the element carefully. It must be renewed if there are any splits or tears, or if the foam appears to be hardened through age. To clean the element, immerse it in a bath of a non-flammable solvent such as white spirit. Petrol may be used, but be careful to take suitable precautions against the risk of fire. When the foam is clean, gently squeeze out the surplus solvent and allow the remainder to evaporate. Do not wring the element out, as this will damage the foam. Soak the cleaned, dry, element in engine oil and gently squeeze out the surplus to leave the element slightly oily to the touch. Filter reassembly is a straightforward reversal of the dismantling procedure, being careful to ensure that both the element and the filter cover are correctly seated so that no unfiltered air can bypass the element and enter the carburettor. A light application of grease to the sealing surfaces of the filter cover will help to achieve good sealing but note that the element cover is fitted with an O-ring seal set in its mating flange; this O-ring must be renewed if split or otherwise damaged.

On no account should the air filter element be omitted while the engine is running in view of the increased noise level and of the high risk of severe damage to the engine due to overheating caused by the resultant weak mixture.

6   Check and adjust the clutch

While the clutch can be adjusted at two points, at the operating mechanism and at the cable itself, it will suffice for the purposes of Routine Maintenance to regard the operating mechanism as set and to make all normal adjustments using the cable length adjusters. The clutch is adjusted correctly when there is 2 – 3 mm (0.08 – 0.12 in) of free play in the cable, the free play being measured between the butt end of the clutch handlebar lever and its handlebar clamp.

Reset the cable free play, if necessary, using the adjusters provided. Use first the lower cable adjuster, reserving the handlebar adjuster for minor alterations.

In the event that adjustment is no longer possible with the cable adjusters, the crankcase right-hand cover must be removed as described in Section 8 of Chapter 1 and the operating mechanism reset as described in Section 38 of the same Chapter. Screw in fully the cable adjusters to achieve the maximum free play in the cable before the mechanism setting is altered.

Complete clutch maintenance by applying a few drops of oil to the lever pivots, to the adjuster threads, and to all exposed lengths of inner cable.

7   Check and adjust the steering head bearings and check the suspension

Place the machine on the centre stand so that the front wheel is clear of the ground. If necessary, place blocks below the crankcase to prevent the motorcycle from tipping forwards.

Grasp the front fork legs near the wheel spindle and push and pull firmly in a fore and aft direction. If play is evident between the top and bottom fork yokes and the head lug casting, the steering head bearings are in need of adjustment. Imprecise handling or a tendency for the front forks to judder may be caused by this fault.

Bearing adjustment is correct when the adjuster ring is tightened, until resistance to movement is felt and then loosened $\frac{1}{8}$ to $\frac{1}{4}$ of a turn. The adjuster ring should be rotated by means of a C-spanner after slackening the steering stem top bolt

Take great care not to overtighten the adjuster ring. It is possible to place a pressure of several tons on the head bearings by over-tightening even though the handlebars may seem to turn quite freely. Overtight bearings will cause the machine to roll at low speeds and give imprecise steering. Adjustment is correct if there is no play in the bearings and the handlebars swing to full lock either side when the machine is on the centre stand with the front wheel clear of the ground. Only a light tap on each end should cause the handlebars to swing. Secure the adjuster ring by tightening the steering stem top bolt to a torque setting of 4.5 kgf m (32.5 lbf ft) on SR125 models, or 5.5 kgf m (40 lbf ft) on XT125 models, then check that the setting has not altered.

Use C-spanner to adjust steering head bearings

At the same time as the steering head bearings are checked, take the opportunity closely to examine the front and rear suspension. Ensure that the front forks work smoothly and progressively by pumping them up and down whilst the front brake is held on. Any faults revealed by this check should be investigated further, as any deterioration in the stability of the machine can have serious consequences. Check carefully for signs of leaks around the front fork oil seals. If any damage is found, it must be repaired immediately as described in the relevant Sections of Chapter 4. Examine the rear suspension in the same way and check for wear in the swinging-arm pivot by pushing and pulling horizontally at its rear end. There should be no discernible play at the pivot.

Three monthly, or every 2000 miles (3000 km)

Complete the operations listed under the previous mileage/time headings, then carry out the following:

1 Clean the spark plug

Detach the spark plug cap, and using the correct spanner remove the spark plug. Clean the electrodes using a wire brush followed by a strip of fine emery cloth or paper. Check the plug gap with a feeler gauge, adjusting it if necessary to within the range of 0.6 – 0.7 mm (0.024 – 0.028 in). Make adjustments by bending the outer electrode, never the inner (central) electrode. Before fitting the spark plug smear the threads with a graphited grease, this will aid subsequent removal. Refit the spark plug by hand only, screwing it down until the sealing washer is firmly seated, then tighten it by a further $\frac{1}{4}$ of a turn with the plug spanner. If a torque wrench is available, tighten the plug to a torque setting of 2.0 kgf m (14.5 lbf ft).

Note that the series of   photographs accompanying the text will assist in giving a good impression of the engine's condition, relying on the colour of the electrodes as a comparison.

2 Check and adjust the valve clearances

The valve clearances must be checked with the engine cold. Remove the sidepanels, the seat, the fuel tank, the spark plug, the inspection caps from the cylinder head and the circular caps from the side of the crankcase left-hand cover. Apply a spanner to the generator rotor retaining nut via the aperture in the side of the crankcase cover and rotate the crankshaft anti-clockwise until the piston is at top dead centre (TDC) on the compression stroke. This is achieved when the timing index mark (a straight line with the letter 'T' adjacent) stamped on the rotor rim and visible via the aperture in the top of the crankcase cover is aligned exactly with the cast arrow on the crankcase, and there is free play at the adjuster ends of both valve rockers.

The valve clearance is measured by sliding feeler gauges between the top of the valve stem and the tip of the adjuster. If the clearance is correct, a feeler gauge of the correct thickness will be a tight sliding fit between the two. The correct clearances are:

Inlet 0.05 – 0.09 mm (0.002 – 0.003 in)
Exhaust 0.11 – 0.15 mm (0.004 – 0.006 in)

To adjust the clearances, slacken the adjuster locknut and use a pair of pliers or small spanner to rotate the adjuster screw. Tighten securely the locknut, but do not overtighten it since this will distort the threads and make future adjustment very difficult; the torque setting specified is 1.4 kgf m (10 lbf ft). Recheck the clearance and repeat the operation on the other valve.

Unless the cam chain tension is about to be adjusted, refit all inspection caps, checking that their sealing O-rings are in good condition, the spark plug and the fuel tank, seat and sidepanels.

3 Adjust the cam chain

Working as described above, set the engine so that the piston is at TDC on the compression stroke, being careful to rotate the crankshaft anti-clockwise only so that all free play is on the chain rear run. Remove the cap from the adjuster assembly set in the rear of the cylinder barrel, slacken the adjuster locknut and rotate the adjuster body in or out until its rear end is flush with that of the pushrod inside the body. Refit the inspection covers to the crankcase left-hand cover and the cylinder head, then refit the spark plug, the fuel tank, the seat

and the sidepanels. Start the engine and watch closely the movement of the pushrod at idle speed. **Do not** increase engine speed above tickover. The pushrod should move very slightly in and out. If there is no movement, the setting is too tight and the adjuster body must be screwed out slightly, if there is excessive movement the setting is too slack and the adjuster body must be screwed in slightly. Tighten the adjuster locknut to a torque setting of 3.0 kgf m (22 lbf ft) and refit the cap, tightening it to a torque setting of 0.5 kgf m (3.5 lbf ft).

Use small spanner to rotate or hold adjuster screw

Adjuster body must be flush with pushrod end, as shown

4 Check the carburettor, throttle cable and fuel pipe

If rough running of the engine has developed, some adjustment of the carburettor pilot setting and tick-over speed may be required. If this is the case refer to Chapter 2, Section 8 for details. Do not make these adjustments unless they are obviously required, there is little to be gained by unwarranted attention to the carburettor. Complete carburettor maintenance by removing the drain plug on the float chamber, turning the petrol on, and allowing a small amount of fuel to drain through, thus flushing any water or dirt from the carburettor. Refit the drain plug securely and switch the petrol off.

Once the carburettor has been checked and reset if necessary, the throttle cable free play can be checked. Open and close the throttle several times, allowing it to snap shut under its own pressure. Ensure that it is able to shut off quickly and fully at all handlebar positions.

Check that there is 2 – 5 mm (0.08 – 0.20 in) free play measured
around the circumference of the inner flange of the rubber twistgrip. If
not, use the adjuster at the twistgrip to achieve the correct setting,
completing the operation, if necessary, with the adjuster on the
carburettor top. Open and close the throttle again to settle the cable
and to check that adjustment is not disturbed.

Give the pipe which connects the fuel tap and carburettor a close
visual examination, checking for cracks or any signs of leakage. In
time, the synthetic rubber pipe will tend to deteriorate, and will
eventually leak. Apart from the obvious fire risk, the leaking fuel will
affect fuel economy. If the pipe is to be renewed, always use the
correct replacement type to ensure as good leak-proof fit. Never use
natural tubing because this will tend to break up when in contact with
petrol and will obstruct the carburettor jets.

5   Clean the fuel filter

Although it is recommended that the fuel filter gauze set in the fuel
tap be cleaned at this interval, this is to a large extent the counsel of
perfection and can be postponed unless symptoms of petrol starvation
have been experienced or signs of dirt or debris have been found on
draining the carburettor float bowl. If the filter is severely blocked it
will be necessary to remove the fuel tank for a thorough swilling out.
Refer to the relevant Sections of Chapter 2.

6   Change the engine/transmission oil

Oil changing is much easier and more efficient if the engine is fully
warmed up so that the oil is thin and flows freely. Place the machine
on its stand so that it is upright on level ground. A maximum of 1300
cc (2.3 pint) of oil is contained in the engine; place a suitable container
under the drain plug, then remove both drain and filler plugs and allow
the oil to drain. Note that the removal of the drain plug will release a
coil spring and a coarse mesh filter gauze. Remove also the Allen
screw from the bottom edge of the filter chamber cap fitted to the
crankcase right-hand cover; this serves as a drain plug for the filter
chamber and will release a certain amount of oil. Carefully wash both
drain plugs, the spring and the filter gauze in clean petrol, taking due
precautions against the risk of fire. Any component that is worn or
damaged, particularly the O-ring set in the larger drain plug, must be
renewed. When the oil has finished draining, wipe away all surplus oil
and refit the filter gauze, the spring and the large drain plug to the
crankcase and the Allen screw to the crankcase right-hand cover. The
large drain plug is tightened to a torque setting of 4.3 kgf m (31 lbf ft)
and the Allen screw to a setting of 1.0 kgf m (7 lbf ft).

Refill the crankcase with 1.0 litre (1.8 pint) of good quality SAE
20W/40 SE engine oil and refit the filler plug. Slacken by one or two
full turns the oil delivery check bolt set in the cylinder head rear right-
hand side, near to the spark plug. Start the engine and allow it to idle.
Oil should trickle past the threads of the check bolt after no more than
a minute, indicating that oil is circulating correctly; if not, stop the

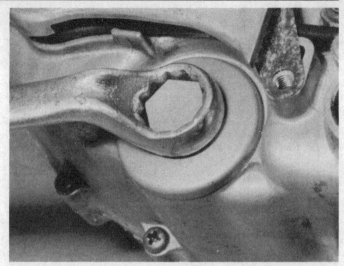

Engine oil is drained by removing large drain plug from crankcase left-
hand side

Coil spring and coarse filter gauze are retained by drain plug – do not
omit

Remove Allen screw to drain filter chamber

Check condition of O-ring before refitting drain plug

Slacken oil delivery check bolt to check oil circulation after every oil change

engine before damage is done and find out what is causing the problem. If all is well, tighten the check bolt to a torque setting of 0.7 kgf m (5 lbf ft) and wipe away any surplus oil. Allow the engine to idle until it is fully warmed up, then stop the engine, allow one or two minutes for the level to settle, and check the oil level.

With the machine standing upright on its wheels on level ground, the oil level should be between the two lines cast next to the inspection window set in the crankcase right-hand cover. If necessary, add (or remove) oil until the level is correct; the engine should never be run with the oil level outside the limits shown by the lines.

Check that the filler plug, drain plugs and check bolt are securely fastened, wipe away all traces of surplus oil and check for any oil leaks which may appear subsequently.

7 General checks and lubrication

Proceed methodically round the machine, checking all nuts, bolts, and screws, tightening securely any that may have worked loose. Be careful not to overtighten any component, and make use of the torque wrench settings given in the Specifications Section of the various Chapters of this Manual to ensure that this does not happen. Pay particular attention to the security of the engine mounting bolts, exhaust system fasteners, cylinder head and barrel retaining nuts, and to the security of any fastener which is known from past experience to slacken off regularly.

Using a spout-type oil can, proceed again around the machine, applying a few drops of oil to all control cables and operating linkages, and to all stand and footrest pivots (where applicable). Ensure that all cable end nipples and any exposed adjuster threads are also lightly lubricated. Similarly, use a water dispersant lubricant such as WD40 to protect and lubricate all exposed electrical components such as the horn and stop lamp switches. Use the long plastic nozzle supplied with the aerosol can to lubricate the internal contacts of the handlebar switches, ignition switch and the fuel tank lock. The above checks are an essential part of the routine maintenance procedure, and play an important role in preserving the smooth and safe operation of the handlebar controls and in offsetting the effects of wear and corrosion.

At regular intervals the centre stand and prop stand (whichever is fitted), the rear brake pedal, and the throttle twistgrip, must be dismantled so that all traces of corrosion and dirt can be removed, and the various components greased. This operation must be carried out to prevent excessive wear and to ensure that the various components can be operated smoothly and easily, in the interests of safety. The opportunity should be taken to examine closely each component, renewing any that show signs of excessive wear or of any damage.

The twistgrip is removed by unscrewing the screws which fasten both halves of the handlebar right-hand switch assembly. The throttle cable upper end nipple can be detached from the twistgrip with a suitable pair of pliers and the twistgrip slid off in the handlebar end. Carefully clean and examine the handlebar end, the internal surface of

the twistgrip, and the two halves of the switch cluster. Remove any rough burrs with a fine file, and apply a coating of grease to all the bearing surfaces. Slide the twistgrip back over the handlebar end, insert the throttle cable end nipple into the twistgrip flange, and reassemble the switch cluster. Check that the twistgrip rotates easily and that the throttle snaps shut as soon as it is released. Tighten the switch retaining screws securely, but do not overtighten them.

Although the regular daily checks will ensure that the control cables are lubricated and maintained in good order, it is recommended that a positive check is made on each cable at this mileage/time interval to ensure that any faults will not develop unnoticed to the point where smooth and safe control operation is impaired. If any doubt exists about the condition of any of the cables, the component in question should be removed from the machine for close examination. Check the outer cables for signs of damage, then examine the exposed portions of the inner cables. Any signs of kinking or fraying will indicate that renewal is required. To obtain maximum life and reliability from the cables they should be thoroughly lubricated. To do the job properly and quickly use one of the hydraulic cable oilers available from most motorcycle shops. Free one end of the cable and assemble the cable oiler as described by the manufacturer's instructions. Operate the oiler until oil emerges from the lower end, indicating that the cable is lubricated throughout its length. This process will expel any dirt or moisture and will prevent its subsequent ingress.

If a cable oiler is not available, an alternative is to remove the cable from the machine. Hang the cable upright and make up a small funnel arrangement using plasticine or by taping a plastic bag around the upper end. Fill the funnel with oil and leave it overnight to drain through. Note that where nylon-lined cables are fitted, they should be used dry or lubricated with a silicone-based lubricant suitable for this application. On no account use ordinary engine oil because this will cause the liner to swell, pinching the cable.

Check all pivots and control levers, cleaning and lubricating them to prevent wear or corrosion. Where necessary, dismantle and clean any moving part which may have become stiff in operation.

When refitting the cables onto the machine, ensure that they are routed in easy curves and that full use is made of any guide or clamps that have been provided to secure the cable out of harm's way. Adjustment of the individual cables is described under previous Routine Maintenance tasks.

Be very careful to ensure that all controls are properly adjusted and are functioning correctly before taking the machine out on the road.

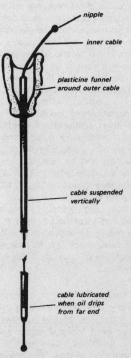

nipple

inner cable

plasticine funnel around outer cable

cable suspended vertically

cable lubricated when oil drips from far end

Oiling a control cable

Six monthly, or every 4000 miles (6000 km)

Complete the tasks listed under the previous mileage/time headings, then carry out the following:

1   Check the compression pressure

The manufacturer recommends that the engine compression pressure be checked at this interval to give some idea of the degree of wear that has taken place in the upper cylinder components. However, since this task requires expensive special tools, it is recommended that it is carried out only when the need arises.

Engine compression pressure is tested using a compression gauge with an adaptor suitable for a 12 mm spark plug thread (Yamaha service tool Part Number 90890-03081). The engine must be fully warmed up, with the valve clearances accurately set and all cylinder head retaining bolts tightened to the correct torque settings. Open fully the throttle twistgrip and turn the engine over several times with the starter motor or kickstart, noting the values recorded by the gauge. If the highest gauge reading is 8 kg/cm² (114 psi) or less, the engine is excessively worn and must be stripped for repair. The areas of wear are the piston/cylinder group, the head gasket, or the valves. The piston/cylinder group can be checked by removing the gauge, pouring a small amount of oil into the cylinder bore, then repeating the test. If the pressure recorded is significantly increased, the piston, piston rings or cylinder barrel are at fault; if the pressure remains unchanged, the head gasket or valves are faulty.

2   Check the ignition timing

It is recommended by the manufacturer that the ignition timing is checked at intervals of 4000 miles (6000 km). While this is commendable as a safety measure, it is not necessary unless a loss of power or other symptoms developed by the engine indicates that a check of the ignition timing would be warranted. Should this be the case, the ignition timing checking procedure is given in Section 9 of Chapter 3.

3   Clean the oil filter

The engine lubrication system employs two filters; one is a coarse mesh gauze located behind the drain plug, and is therefore cleaned whenever the engine oil is changed, the second is a fine mesh filter 'element' that is located in a filter chamber set in the crankcase right-hand cover and must be cleaned at this interval.

First drain the oil as described under the 3-monthly/2000 mile service interval. While the oil is draining, remove the two remaining cross-head screws which secure the chamber cap to the crankcase cover, withdraw the cap and pull out the element. Check it carefully for tears, splits or other damage, and check also the condition of the two O-rings set in the cap. The filter should be renewed if damaged in any way; ideally the O-rings should be renewed whenever the cap is disturbed, but they can be re-used if they are not worn or damaged. Carefully wash the filter in petrol, taking due precautions against the risk of fire, and using a soft-bristled brush to remove any embedded particles of dirt or metal. Allow the filter to dry. Wipe out the filter chamber and refit the filter, noting that the word 'Outside' stamped on one end shows clearly which way round it should be fitted. Refit the O-rings to the chamber cap, using a smear of grease to stick them in place, then refit the cap and its retaining screws. Tighten the two cross-head screws to a torque setting of 0.7 kgf m (5 lbf ft) and the Allen screw drain plug to a torque setting of 1.0 kgf m (7 lbf ft). Wipe away any surplus grease or oil.

Refit the large drain plug, tightening it to a torque setting of 4.3 kgf m (31 lbf ft) and not forgetting to refit the filter gauze and coil spring, then refill the crankcase with oil as previously described. Do not forget to use the oil feed check bolt to ensure that oil is circulating correctly, or to recheck the oil level after the engine has been started and run for a few minutes.

4   Change the fork oil

This is an important task which must be carried out to ensure the continuing stability and safety of the machine on the road. Fork oil gradually degenerates as it loses viscosity and is contaminated by water and dirt, which produces a very gradual loss of damping. This can occur over a long period of time, thus being completely unnoticed by the rider until the machine is in a dangerous condition. Regular changes of the fork oil will eliminate this possibility. Refer to Chapter

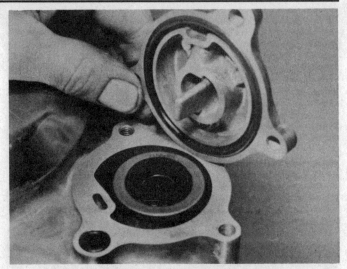

Do not forget to clean second oil filter in crankcase cover

'Outside' marking shows which way round filter must be refitted

4, Sections 2, 3 and 4 for details of removal and refitting. Note that as SR125 models are not fitted with front fork drain plugs, each fork leg must be removed from the machine and inverted to drain the oil. This does, however, offer an excellent opportunity to examine the forks for wear or damage and fits in well with the other maintenance operations that are necessary at this interval.

On XT125 models, drain plugs are provided. To use these, place a suitable container at the side of the front wheel, some distance from the drain plug to be removed and lay a sheet of cardboard or newspaper against the wheel to prevent oil getting on to the brake or tyre. Remove the drain plug and pump gently on the forks to eject the oil by applying the front brake and leaning on the handlebars. When all the oil has been pumped out, repeat the process on the other leg. Leave the machine for a while to allow as much oil as possible to drain to the bottom of the fork legs, then repeat the pumping action to expel the remainder. Refit the drain plugs, tightening them carefully, then remove the fork top bolts and the fork springs and spacers as described in Section 3 of Chapter 4. Take care to support the machine so that it cannot topple over when the springs are removed. Have the full amount of fork oil ready for each leg but remember that as there will be some oil left in the fork leg, a certain amount will be surplus to requirements and that it is more important to have the oil level correct.

Electrode gap check - use a wire type gauge for best results

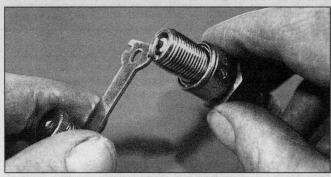

Electrode gap adjustment - bend the side electrode using the correct tool

Normal condition - A brown, tan or grey firing end indicates that the engine is in good condition and that the plug type is correct

Ash deposits - Light brown deposits encrusted on the electrodes and insulator, leading to misfire and hesitation. Caused by excessive amounts of oil in the combustion chamber or poor quality fuel/oil

Carbon fouling - Dry, black sooty deposits leading to misfire and weak spark. Caused by an over-rich fuel/air mixture, faulty choke operation or blocked air filter

Oil fouling - Wet oily deposits leading to misfire and weak spark. Caused by oil leakage past piston rings or valve guides (4-stroke engine), or excess lubricant (2-stroke engine)

Overheating - A blistered white insulator and glazed electrodes. Caused by ignition system fault, incorrect fuel, or cooling system fault

Worn plug - Worn electrodes will cause poor starting in damp or cold weather and will also waste fuel

Using the dipstick described in Section 3 of Chapter 4, add oil until it is 174 mm (6.85 in) from the top of the stanchion when the stanchion is fully compressed and the fork spring and spacers are removed. Gently pump the forks up and down to distribute the oil around each fork leg, then recheck the oil level, adding oil if necessary. When the level is correct, raise the front of the machine to extend fully the forks, then refit the springs, spacers and top bolts as described.

Annually, or every 8000 miles (12 000 km)

Complete all the tasks listed under the previous mileage/time service headings, then carry out the following:

1 Renew the spark plug

It is recommended that the spark plug is renewed at this interval, regardless of its condition. This will assist in maintaining the ignition system at peak efficiency and will minimise the risk of spark plug failure through extended use. It will also prevent the unnecessary waste of fuel. Refer to Section 10 of Chapter 3; always fit the recommended make and type of spark plug, and check that it is correctly gapped before fitting.

2 Grease the wheel bearings and speedometer drive, and overhaul the brakes

Following the instructions given in the relevant Sections of Chapters 4 and 5, remove both front and rear wheels from the machine so that the spindles can be cleaned and greased, the bearings can be checked and renewed or repacked with fresh grease, and so that the speedometer drive can be lubricated.

The speedometer drive cable is retained by a circlip at its lower end and by a large, knurled ring at its upper end. Release the circlip and carefully pull the cable out of its housing in the brake backplate, then unscrew the knurled ring and remove the cable. Remove the inner cable by pulling it out from the bottom of the outer. Carefully examine the inner cable for signs of fraying, kinking, or for any shiny areas which will indicate tight spots, and the outer cable for signs of cracking, kinking or any other damage. Renew the complete cable if necessary. To lubricate the cable, smear a small quantity of grease onto the lower length only of the inner. Do not allow any grease on the top six inches of the cable as the grease will work its way rapidly up the length of the cable as it rotates and get into the instrument itself. This will rapidly ruin the instrument which will then have to be renewed. Insert the inner cable in the outer and refit the cable. Note that the tachometer cable fitted to 1983 and later XT125 models must be lubricated at the same time.

Finally, remember that the opportunity should be taken to check the brake shoes for wear and to grease the brake camshafts, if this has not been done recently during the normal course of Routine Maintenance. Refer to the appropriate Sections of Chapter 5.

3 Grease the steering head bearings

If the steering head bearings have not been dismantled for any other reason, they should be stripped for examination and greasing at this interval. This task would fit in conveniently with the fork oil change, especially on SR125 models, and is described in Chapter 4, Sections 5 and 6.

4 Grease the rear suspension pivot bearings

To offset the effects of wear and corrosion it will be necessary at regular intervals to pack grease into the swinging arm (SR125) or sub-frame (XT125) pivot, and to lubricate similarly the suspension unit mountings (XT125 only). While this can be done without any major dismantling work, as described below, if the regular checks reveal wear of any sort the rear suspension must be dismantled for repair, as described in Chapter 4.

Support the machine securely in an upright position so that the rear wheel is clear of the ground, then wedge a wooden block or similar under the rear tyre so that the weight is taken off the sub-frame pivot. Remove the pivot bolt retaining nut. Using a hammer and a long metal drift, tap out the pivot bolt. If sufficient care is exercised, the sub-frame or swinging arm will not be disturbed.

Thoroughly clean the pivot bolt, removing all traces of dirt and corrosion, then smear it with grease. Pack liberal quantities of grease through the frame apertures and into the pivot bearings, then refit the pivot bolt. It is pushed through from right to left on XT125 models, and from left to right on SR125 models. Place a finger firmly over the frame aperture on the opposite side to the pivot bolt, thus trapping the grease in the pivot bearings as the bolt is pushed through and filling all the tiny cracks where water or road dirt might gather to start the process of corrosion. Refit the pivot bolt retaining nut and its spring or plain washer, then tighten the nut securely to a torque setting of 4.5 kgf m (32.5 lbf ft) on SR125 models, and 8.0 kgf m (58 lbf ft) on XT125 models.

Referring to Section 10 of Chapter 4 where necessary, carry out a similar procedure to grease the mounting bolt and pin of the rear suspension unit. Always use a new split-pin to secure the suspension unit (bottom) mounting pin.

Additional routine maintenance

Cleaning the machine

Keeping the motorcycle clean should be considered as an important part of the routine maintenance, to be carried out whenever the need arises. A machine cleaned regularly will not only succumb less speedily to the inevitable corrosion of external surfaces, and hence maintain its market value, but will be far more approachable when the time comes for maintenance or service work. Furthermore, loose or failing components are more readily spotted when not partially obscured by a mantle of road grime and oil.

Surface dirt should be removed using a sponge and warm, soapy water; the latter being applied copiously to remove the particles of grit which might otherwise cause damage to the paintwork and polished surfaces.

Oil and grease is removed most easily by the application of a cleaning solvent such as 'Gunk' or 'Jizer'. The solvent should be applied when the parts are still dry and worked in with a stiff brush. Large quantities or water should be used when rinsing off, taking care that water does not enter the carburettor, air cleaner or electrics.

If desired, a polish such as Solvol Autosol can be applied to the aluminium alloy parts to restore the original lustre. This does not apply in instances, much favoured by Japanese manufacturers, where the components are lacquered. Application of a wax polish to the cycle parts and a good chrome cleaner to the chrome parts will also give a good finish. Always wipe the machine down if used in the wet, and make sure the chain is well oiled. There is less chance of water getting into control cables if they are regularly lubricated, which will prevent stiffness of action.

Conversion factors

Length (distance)
Inches (in)	X	25.4	= Millimetres (mm)	X 0.0394	= Inches (in)
Feet (ft)	X	0.305	= Metres (m)	X 3.281	= Feet (ft)
Miles	X	1.609	= Kilometres (km)	X 0.621	= Miles

Volume (capacity)
Cubic inches (cu in; in^3)	X	16.387	= Cubic centimetres (cc; cm^3)	X 0.061	= Cubic inches (cu in; in^3)
Imperial pints (Imp pt)	X	0.568	= Litres (l)	X 1.76	= Imperial pints (Imp pt)
Imperial quarts (Imp qt)	X	1.137	= Litres (l)	X 0.88	= Imperial quarts (Imp qt)
Imperial quarts (Imp qt)	X	1.201	= US quarts (US qt)	X 0.833	= Imperial quarts (Imp qt)
US quarts (US qt)	X	0.946	= Litres (l)	X 1.057	= US quarts (US qt)
Imperial gallons (Imp gal)	X	4.546	= Litres (l)	X 0.22	= Imperial gallons (Imp gal)
Imperial gallons (Imp gal)	X	1.201	= US gallons (US gal)	X 0.833	= Imperial gallons (Imp gal)
US gallons (US gal)	X	3.785	= Litres (l)	X 0.264	= US gallons (US gal)

Mass (weight)
Ounces (oz)	X	28.35	= Grams (g)	X 0.035	= Ounces (oz)
Pounds (lb)	X	0.454	= Kilograms (kg)	X 2.205	= Pounds (lb)

Force
Ounces-force (ozf; oz)	X	0.278	= Newtons (N)	X 3.6	= Ounces-force (ozf; oz)
Pounds-force (lbf; lb)	X	4.448	= Newtons (N)	X 0.225	= Pounds-force (lbf; lb)
Newtons (N)	X	0.1	= Kilograms-force (kgf; kg)	X 9.81	= Newtons (N)

Pressure
Pounds-force per square inch (psi; lbf/in^2; lb/in^2)	X	0.070	= Kilograms-force per square centimetre (kgf/cm^2; kg/cm^2)	X 14.223	= Pounds-force per square inch (psi; lbf/in^2; lb/in^2)
Pounds-force per square inch (psi; lbf/in^2; lb/in^2)	X	0.068	= Atmospheres (atm)	X 14.696	= Pounds-force per square inch (psi; lbf/in^2; lb/in^2)
Pounds-force per square inch (psi; lbf/in^2; lb/in^2)	X	0.069	= Bars	X 14.5	= Pounds-force per square inch (psi; lbf/in^2; lb/in^2)
Pounds-force per square inch (psi; lbf/in^2; lb/in^2)	X	6.895	= Kilopascals (kPa)	X 0.145	= Pounds-force per square inch (psi; lbf/in^2; lb/in^2)
Kilopascals (kPa)	X	0.01	= Kilograms-force per square centimetre (kgf/cm^2; kg/cm^2)	X 98.1	= Kilopascals (kPa)

Torque (moment of force)
Pounds-force inches (lbf in; lb in)	X	1.152	= Kilograms-force centimetre (kgf cm; kg cm)	X 0.868	= Pounds-force inches (lbf in; lb in)
Pounds-force inches (lbf in; lb in)	X	0.113	= Newton metres (Nm)	X 8.85	= Pounds-force inches (lbf in; lb in)
Pounds-force inches (lbf in; lb in)	X	0.083	= Pounds-force feet (lbf ft; lb ft)	X 12	= Pounds-force inches (lbf in; lb in)
Pounds-force feet (lbf ft; lb ft)	X	0.138	= Kilograms-force metres (kgf m; kg m)	X 7.233	= Pounds-force feet (lbf ft; lb ft)
Pounds-force feet (lbf ft; lb ft)	X	1.356	= Newton metres (Nm)	X 0.738	= Pounds-force feet (lbf ft; lb ft)
Newton metres (Nm)	X	0.102	= Kilograms-force metres (kgf m; kg m)	X 9.804	= Newton metres (Nm)

Power
Horsepower (hp)	X	745.7	= Watts (W)	X 0.0013	= Horsepower (hp)

Velocity (speed)
Miles per hour (miles/hr; mph)	X	1.609	= Kilometres per hour (km/hr; kph)	X 0.621	= Miles per hour (miles/hr; mph)

Fuel consumption*
Miles per gallon, Imperial (mpg)	X	0.354	= Kilometres per litre (km/l)	X 2.825	= Miles per gallon, Imperial (mpg)
Miles per gallon, US (mpg)	X	0.425	= Kilometres per litre (km/l)	X 2.352	= Miles per gallon, US (mpg)

Temperature
Degrees Fahrenheit = (°C x 1.8) + 32

Degrees Celsius (Degrees Centigrade; °C) = (°F - 32) x 0.56

*It is common practice to convert from miles per gallon (mpg) to litres/100 kilometres (l/100km), where mpg (Imperial) x l/100 km = 282 and mpg (US) x l/100 km = 235

Chapter 1   Engine, clutch and gearbox

Specifications

Note: specifications for XT125 model are given only where they differ from those of the SR125 model

Engine

Type	Air-cooled, single cylinder, overhead camshaft
Bore	57.0 mm (2.24 in)
Stroke	48.8 mm (1.92 in)
Capacity	124 cc (7.56 cu in)
Compression ratio	10 : 1
Compression pressure – engine warm:	
Minimum	114 psi (8 kg/cm^2)
Standard	128 psi (9 kg/cm^2)
Maximum	149 psi (10.5 kg/cm^2)
Vacuum pressure – at idling speed	at least 180 – 200 mm Hg (7.1 – 7.9 in Hg)

Valve clearances – engine cold

Inlet	0.05 – 0.09 mm (0.002 – 0.003 in)
Exhaust	0.11 – 0.15 mm (0.004 – 0.006 in)

Cylinder head
Gasket face maximum distortion .... 0.03 mm (0.0012 in)
Camshaft bearing surface ID .... 20.000 – 20.021 mm (0.7874 – 0.7883 in)

Camshaft, chain and rocker gear
Camshaft lobe height-overall:
    Inlet .... 36.54 – 36.64 mm (1.4386 – 1.4425 in)
    Service limit .... 36.50 mm (1.4370 in)
    Exhaust .... 36.58 – 36.68 mm (1.4402 – 1.4440 in)
    Service limit .... 36.50 mm (1.4370 in)
Camshaft base circle diameter:
    Inlet .... 30.13 – 30.23 mm (1.1862 – 1.1902 in)
    Exhaust .... 30.21 – 30.31 mm (1.1894 – 1.1933 in)
Cam lift:
    Inlet .... 6.31 – 6.51 mm (0.2484 – 0.2563 in)
    Exhaust .... 6.27 – 6.47 mm (0.2469 – 0.2547 in)
Camshaft bearing journal OD:
    Right-hand bearing .... 19.960 – 19.980 mm (0.7858 – 0.7866 in)
    Left-hand bearing .... 24.960 – 24.979 mm (0.9827 – 0.9834 in)
Camshaft bush ID .... 25.000 – 25.021 mm (0.9843 – 0.9851 in)
Camshaft bearing journal/bearing surface clearance .... 0.020 – 0.061 mm (0.0008 – 0.0025 in)
Camshaft maximum runout .... 0.03 mm (0.0012 in)
Camshaft drive chain:
    Type DID25SH
    Number of links 104
Rocker arm ID .... 12.000 – 12.018 mm (0.4724 – 0.4732 in)
Service limit .... 12.046 mm (0.4743 in)
Rocker shaft OD .... 11.985 – 11.991 mm (0.4719 – 0.4721 in)
Service limit .... 11.963 mm (0.4710 in)
Rocker arm/shaft clearance .... 0.009 – 0.033 mm (0.0003 – 0.0013 in)
Service limit .... 0.08 mm (0.0032 in)

Valves, springs and guides
Valve dimensions (refer to Fig. 1 11 for details):-
'A' valve head overall diameter:
    Inlet .... 28.9 – 29.1 mm (1.1378 – 1.1457 in)
    Exhaust .... 23.9 – 24.1 mm (0.9409 – 0.9488 in)
'B' valve face overall width .... 2.4 – 2.8 mm (0.0945 – 0.1102 in)
'C' valve seat width:
    Standard .... 0.9 – 1.1 mm (0.0354 – 0.0433 in)
    Maximum .... 1.6 mm (0.0630 in)
'D' valve head thickness .... 1.2 mm (0.0472 in)
Service limit .... 1.0 mm (0.0394 in)
Valve stem maximum runout .... 0.03 mm (0.0012 in)
Valve stem OD:
    Inlet .... 5.975 – 5.990 mm (0.2352 – 0.2358 in)
    Exhaust .... 5.960 – 5.975 mm (0.2346 – 0.2352 in)
Valve guide ID .... 6.000 – 6.012 mm (0.2362 – 0.2367 in)
Service limit .... 6.100 mm (0.2402 in)
Inlet valve stem/guide clearance .... 0.010 – 0.037 mm (0.0004 – 0.0015 in)
Service limit .... 0.125 mm (0.0049 in)
Exhaust valve stem/guide clearance .... 0.025 – 0.052 mm (0.0009 – 0.0020 in)
Service limit .... 0.140 mm (0.0055 in)
Valve spring free length:
    Inner .... 35.5 mm (1.3976 in)
    Service limit .... 33.5 mm (1.3189 in)
    Outer .... 37.2 mm (1.4646 in)
    Service limit .... 35.2 mm (1.3858 in)
Valve spring installed length – valve closed:
    Inner .... 30.5 mm (1.2008 in)
    Outer .... 32.0 mm (1.2598 in)
Pressure at installed length:
    Inner .... 9.3 kg (20.5 lb)
    Outer .... 18.5 kg (40.8 lb)
Maximum tilt from vertical .... 2.5° or 1.6 mm (0.06 in)

Cylinder barrel
Standard bore size:
    1982 model SR125 only .... 57.000 – 57.020 mm (2.2441 – 2.2449 in)
    All others .... 57.000 – 57.010 mm (2.2441 – 2.2445 in)
    Wear limit .... 57.100 mm (2.2480 in)
Maximum taper:
    1982 model SR125 only .... 0.005 mm (0.0002 in)
    All others .... 0.008 mm (0.0003 in)

Piston and piston rings

Standard OD:
- 1982 models .... 56.960 – 56.975 mm (2.2425 – 2.2431 in)
- 1983 on models .... 56.945 – 56.955 mm (2.2419 – 2.2423 in)

Piston/cylinder clearance:
- 1982 model SR125 .... 0.025 – 0.060 mm (0.0009 – 0.0024 in)
- 1982 model XT125 .... 0.025 – 0.050 mm (0.0009 – 0.0020 in)
- 1983 on models .... 0.045 – 0.065 mm (0.0018 – 0.0026 in)

Top compression ring:
- Type .... Plain
- Thickness .... 1.17 – 1.19 mm (0.0461 – 0.0469 in)
- Width .... 2.30 – 2.50 mm (0.0906 – 0.0984 in)
- End gap – installed .... 0.15 – 0.35 mm (0.0059 – 0.0138 in)
- Service limit – 1982 SR125 only .... 0.60 mm (0.0236 in)
- Service limit – all others .... 0.75 mm (0.0295 in)
- Ring/groove clearance .... 0.03 – 0.07 mm (0.0012 – 0.0028 in)
- Service limit – 1982 SR125 only .... 0.15 mm (0.0059 in)

Second compression ring:
- Type .... Keystone
- Thickness .... 1.17 – 1.19 mm (0.0461 – 0.0469 in)
- Width .... 2.30 – 2.50 mm (0.0906 – 0.0984 in)
- End gap – installed .... 0.15 – 0.35 mm (0.0059 – 0.0138 in)
- Service limit – 1982 SR125 only .... 0.60 mm (0.0236 in)
- Service limit – all others .... 0.75 mm (0.0295 in)
- Ring/groove clearance .... 0.02 – 0.06 mm (0.0008 – 0.0024 in)
- Service limit – 1982 SR125 only .... 0.15 mm (0.0059 in)

Oil scraper ring:
- Type .... Three-piece
- Thickness – 1982 SR125 only .... 2.5 mm (0.0984 in)
- Thickness – all others .... 2.51 – 2.53 mm (0.0988 – 0.0996 in)
- Width – 1982 SR125 only .... 2.8 mm (0.1102 in)
- Width – all others .... 2.64 – 2.96 mm (0.1039 – 0.1165 in)
- Side rail end gap – installed .... 0.3 – 0.9 mm (0.0118 – 0.0354 in)
- Service limit .... N/App
- Ring/groove clearance .... Nil

Crankshaft

- Width across flywheels .... 55.95 – 56.00 mm (2.2028 – 2.2047 in)
- Maximum runout .... 0.03 mm (0.0012 in)
- Big-end side clearance .... 0.35 – 0.65 mm (0.0138 – 0.0256 in)
- Service limit .... 0.70 mm (0.0276 in)
- Big-end bearing deflection – at small-end .... 0.8 – 1.0 mm (0.0315 – 0.0394 in)
- Service limit .... 2.0 mm (0.0787 in)

Primary drive

- Type .... Helical gear
- Reduction ratio .... 3.318 : 1 (73/22T)

Clutch

- Type .... Wet, multi-plate
- Number of friction plates 4
- Number of plain plates 3
- Number of springs 4
- Friction plate thickness .... 2.9 – 3.1 mm (0.1142 – 0.1221 in)
- Service limit .... 2.6 mm (0.1024 in)
- Plain plate thickness .... 1.5 – 1.7 mm (0.0591 – 0.0669 in)
- Plain plate maximum warpage .... 0.05 mm (0.0020 in)
- Spring free length .... 34.9 mm (1.3740 in)
- Service limit .... 33.9 mm (1.3346 in)
- Push rod maximum runout .... 0.2 mm (0.0079 in)

Gearbox

- Type .... 5 speed, constant mesh

Reduction ratios:	SR125	XT125
1st	2.250 : 1 (36/16T)	2.833 : 1 (34/12T)
2nd	1.476 : 1 (31/21T)	1.789 : 1 (34/19T)
3rd	1.125 : 1 (27/24T)	1.318 : 1 (29/22T)
4th	0.926 : 1 (25/27T)	1.040 : 1 (26/25T)
5th	0.793 : 1 (23/29T)	0.821 : 1 (23/28T)

- Input and output shaft maximum runout .... 0.08 mm (0.0032 in)
- Kickstart friction clip resistance – XT125 only .... 0.65 – 1.05 kg (1.43 – 2.32 lb)

Final drive

	SR125	XT125
Type	Chain and sprockets	Chain and sprockets
Reduction ratio	3.500 : 1 (49/14T)	3.571 : 1 (50/14T)
Chain manufacturer	DID	DID
Chain type	428DS ($\frac{1}{2}$ x $\frac{5}{16}$)	428H ($\frac{1}{2}$ x $\frac{5}{16}$)
Number of links	120	118

Torque settings

Component	kgf m	lbf ft
Spark plug	2.0	14.5
Cylinder head:		
8 mm flange bolts	2.2	16.0
8 mm Allen bolts	2.0	14.5
Cylinder barrel retaining Allen bolts	1.0	7.0
Valve inspection cover Allen bolts	1.0	7.0
Cam sprocket cover screws	0.7	5.0
Valve adjuster locknuts	1.4	10.0
Oil feed checking plug	0.7	5.0
Cam bush retainer bolts	0.8	6.0
Cam sprocket retaining bolt	6.0	43.0
Inlet stub Allen bolts	1.2	9.0
Cam chain tensioner locknut	3.0	22.0
Cam chain tensioner cap	0.5	3.5
Stator coil retaining screws	0.7	5.0
Generator rotor mounting bolt	5.0	36.0
Neutral indicator switch	2.0	14.5
Gearbox sprocket retaining bolts	1.0	7.0
Engine oil drain plug	4.3	31.0
Primary drive gear retaining nut	5.0	36.0
Balancer driven gear retaining nut	5.0	36.0
Oil pump mounting screws	0.7	5.0
Clutch centre retaining nut	5.0	36.0
Clutch spring bolts	0.6	4.0
Clutch operating lever retaining screw	1.2	9.0
Clutch operating mechanism adjuster locknut	0.8	6.0
Selector cam Torx screw	1.2	9.0
Tensioner blade bottom mounting bolts	0.8	6.0
Crankcase and crankcase cover retaining screws	0.7	5.0
Oil filter cover retaining screws	0.7	5.0
Oil filter chamber drain plug	1.0	7.0
Engine mounting bolts	3.3	24.0
Sub-frame pivot bolt – XT125	8.0	58.0
Gearchange lever pinch bolt	1.0	7.0
Carburettor hose clamp screws	0.2	1.5
Exhaust pipe/cylinder head Allen bolts	1.2	9.0
Exhaust mounting bolts:		
SR125	2.0	14.5
XT125	2.7	19.5
Exhaust pipe/silencer clamp bolt – XT125	2.0	14.5

1 General description

The Yamaha SR125 and XT125 models share the same basic engine and transmission which is built in one unit, with all major castings in aluminium alloy. The valves of the single cylinder air-cooled engine are opened by a single overhead camshaft which is driven by chain from the crankshaft left-hand end, the vibration produced by any single cylinder engine being largely cancelled out by a single-shaft balancer that is gear-driven from the crankshaft right-hand end. Power is transmitted via primary drive gears to a wet multiplate clutch, from which it passes to a constant mesh, five-speed gearbox.

The engine/gearbox unit is simple and robust in design and construction, requiring a minimum of special tools during dismantling and reassembly.

2 Operations with the engine/gearbox unit in the frame

The following components can be removed for repair or renewal with the engine/gearbox unit in the frame, although if several operations need to be undertaken simultaneously it is worthwhile taking the unit out of the frame to gain better access and more comfortable working conditions.

a) Cylinder head, valves and guides, camshaft and rocker gear
b) Cylinder barrel, piston and rings
c) Cam chain and tensioner components
d) Flywheel generator and ignition components
e) Starter motor and drive components – SR125 only
f) Gearbox sprocket and neutral indicator switch
g) Oil pump and filter screens
h) Clutch assembly and operating mechanism
i) Kickstart mechanism
j) Primary drive gear and balancer shaft driven gear
k) Gear selector mechanism – external components only

3 Operations with the engine/gearbox unit removed from the frame

It will be necessary to remove the engine/gearbox unit from the frame and to separate the crankcase halves to gain access to the following items:

a) Crankshaft and main bearings
b) Balancer shaft
c) Gearbox components
d) Gear selector drum and forks

Engine/gearbox removal is a relatively simple task which can be carried out by one person in no more than one hour.

4 Removing the engine/gearbox unit from the frame

1 When working on an XT125, a stand must be available to hold the machine securely in an upright position. To allow adequate access the stand must bear either on the frame horizontal bracing tube between the footrest mountings or on the footrests themselves. Such a stand can be fabricated or purchased from a supplier advertising in the national motorcycle press.

2 Place the machine on its stand on a convenient working surface noting that work is easier if the machine is raised to a suitable height on an hydraulic ramp or a stout table or a platform constructed from wooden planks supported on blocks. Secure the machine with blocks or ropes to prevent it from falling.

3 Place a suitable container underneath the crankcase, remove the oil filler and drain plugs and allow the oil to drain completely, draining being quicker and more efficient if the engine is warmed up to normal operating temperature. Remove the coil spring and filter gauze from the drain plug orifice, then detach the filter screen cover from the crankcase right-hand cover and withdraw the filter screen, as described in Routine Maintenance.

4 Carefully pull away the sidepanels which are retained by moulded prongs engaging with rubber grommets set in the frame or the base of the fuel tank. Unscrew the two seat mounting bolts and remove the seat.

5 It is good practice to prevent the loss of nuts, bolts and washers by refitting all fasteners in their original positions once any component has been removed.

6 Switch the fuel tap to the 'Off' position, disengage the spring clip securing the fuel pipe upper end, and pull the pipe off the tap spigot. Unscrew the single bolt securing the tank rear mounting, then lift up the tank at the rear and pull it backwards off its front mounting rubbers. Place the tank to one side where it cannot be damaged, and take suitable fire precautions.

7 Disconnect the battery by unscrewing the terminal retaining bolts (SR125) or by removing the fuse (XT125). If the machine is to be out of service for some time the battery should be removed and given regular refresher charges as described in Chapter 6. Store the battery in a safe place to prevent damage.

8 On SR125 models, remove the complete exhaust system, which is retained by two Allen bolts at the exhaust pipe/cylinder head joint and by a single nut at the pillion footrest mounting. Note that it will be necessary to slacken fully the rear brake adjuster so that the pedal can be depressed far enough to release the exhaust pipe. On XT125 models, remove the two Allen bolts at the exhaust pipe/cylinder head joint, slacken fully the exhaust pipe/silencer clamp bolt, and carefully tap the exhaust pipe forwards, using only a soft-faced mallet, to release it. It is not necessary to disturb the silencer assembly.

9 On 1983 on XT125 models only, remove the single screw which secures the tachometer drive cable to the cam sprocket cover and pull the cable carefully out of its housing. Pull the spark plug cap off the spark plug. Trace all electrical leads from the crankcase and disconnect them from the main wiring loom at their respective connectors, then release the leads from any clamps or ties which secure them to the frame. On SR125 models only, disconnect the black heavy-gauge starter motor lead wire from the starter relay and pull the lead clear of the frame.

10 Remove the pinch bolt which secures the gearchange pedal to the gearchange shaft, then pull the pedal off the shaft splines. Remove the two screws which secure the gearbox sprocket cover and withdraw the cover. Unscrew the two sprocket retaining bolts, applying the rear brake firmly to prevent rotation, then withdraw the sprocket retaining plate, rotating it until it can be pulled off the output shaft splines. Pull the sprocket off the shaft splines, disengage it from the chain, and allow the chain to hang over the swinging arm/subframe pivot.

11 Releasing its wire retaining clip, prise the crankcase breather pipe off its stub on the crankcase top. Slacken both upper and lower adjuster locknuts and screw in fully both clutch cable adjusters to gain the maximum cable free play before disengaging the cable lower end from the operating lever and adjuster bracket. Note that there is a small metal tang which must be bent flat to permit the cable end nipple to be released from the operating lever end.

12 Slacken fully both clamps securing the carburettor to the inlet stub and air filter hose, then carefully remove the carburettor and place it on the frame top tube, having removed all surplus fuel by unscrewing the float chamber drain plug.

13 On XT 125 models only, remove the single bolt securing the crankcase bashplate to the frame front downtube and withdraw the bashplate, unhooking it from its rear mounting. Slacken the single bolt retaining the left-hand footrest and swing down the footrest so that the engine lower rear mounting bolt is exposed.

14 On SR125 and XT125 models, remove the four mounting bolts and withdraw the two engine front mounting plates (SR125) or the single plate (XT125). Slacken, but do not remove yet, the retaining nut and bolts of the engine top mounting/cylinder head steady assembly. Make a final check that all components have been removed which will prevent the removal of the engine/gearbox unit, and check that all cables and wiring are secured out of the way.

15 On SR125 models only, remove both the engine upper and lower rear mounting bolts so that the engine/gearbox unit is left hanging by its top mounting. Carefully remove the single retaining nut, support the unit with one hand and withdraw the mounting bolt. Lower the engine/gearbox unit to the ground, manoeuvring it to clear footrests and brake pedal.

16 On XT125 models the engine upper rear mounting is formed by the rear suspension sub-frame pivot bolt, a fact which requires a slight modification of the above procedure. First remove the pivot bolt retaining nut and check that the pivot bolt slides easily through the frame, crankcase, and sub-frame pivot bushes. If it is stuck in place by corrosion, the bolt must be removed using penetrating fluid and a hammer and long metal drift so that it can be cleaned thoroughly, greased and refitted. Obtain a bolt or a length of wooden dowel that is the same diameter as the pivot bolt.

17 Using the bolt or wooden dowel as a drift, tap out the pivot bolt until it is clear of the sub-frame left-hand pivot, then remove the engine lower rear mounting bolt. Pull the pivot bolt out to the right until it clears the crankcase lug and the engine/gearbox unit is felt to drop slightly. **Do not** remove the pivot bolt completely; it is essential that both sides of the sub-frame are correctly supported or it will fall at an awkward angle and jam on the crankcase lug. The engine/gearbox unit will now hang from the engine top mounting/cylinder head steady. Carefully remove the single retaining nut, support the unit with one hand and withdraw the mounting bolt. Lower the engine/gearbox unit to the ground, manoeuvring it to clear the footrests and brake pedal. There are two thick washers set in recesses, one on each side of the crankcase lug; unless firmly fixed in the crankcase, these should be removed for safe storage.

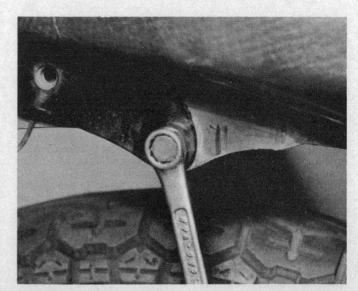

4.4 Seat is retained by two bolts

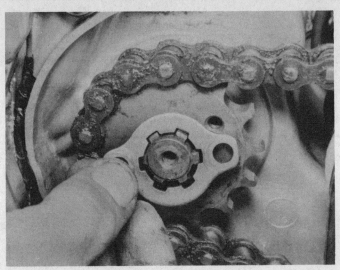

4.10 Gearbox sprocket is secured by retaining plate

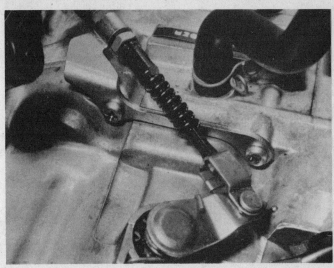

4.11 Flatten metal tang to release cable from clutch operating lever

4.12 Slacken clamp screws to release carburettor

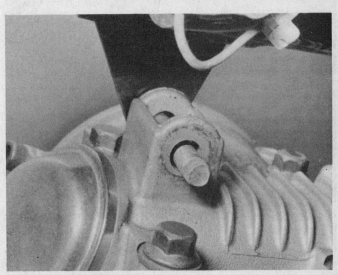

4.15 Allow engine/gearbox unit to hang from top mounting bolt

5 Dismantling the engine/gearbox unit: preliminaries

1   Before any dismantling work is undertaken, the external surfaces of the unit should be thoroughly cleaned and degreased. This will prevent the contamination of the engine internals, and will also make working a lot easier and cleaner. A high flash point solvent, such as paraffin (kerosene) can be used, or better still, a proprietary engine degreaser such as Gunk. Use old paintbrushes and toothbrushes to work the solvent into the various recesses of the engine castings. Take care to exclude solvent or water from the electrical components and inlet and exhaust ports. The use of petrol (gasoline) as a cleaning medium should be avoided, because the vapour is explosive and can be toxic if used in a confined space.

2   When clean and dry, arrange the unit on the workbench leaving a suitable clear area for working. Gather a selection of small containers and plastic bags so that parts can be grouped together in an easily identifiable manner. Some paper and a pen should be on hand to permit notes to be made and labels attached where necessary. A supply of clean rag is also required.

3   Before commencing work, read through the appropriate section so that some idea of the necessary procedure can be gained. When removing the various engine components it should be noted that great force is seldom required, unless specified. In many cases, a component's reluctance to be removed is indicative of an incorrect approach or removal method. If in any doubt, re-check with the text.

6 Dismantling the engine/gearbox unit: removing the cylinder head, cylinder barrel and piston

1   The above components can be removed whether the engine/gearbox unit is in the frame or not, but in the former case the sidepanels, the seat, the fuel tank, the carburettor and the exhaust system or exhaust pipe (as applicable) must be first removed and the tachometer cable (1983 on model XT125 only) and spark plug cap must be disconnected. The engine top mounting/cylinder head steady assembly must also be dismantled, all these operations being described in Section 4 of this Chapter.

2   Remove the two valve adjuster inspection caps, the spark plug and the two circular inspection caps screwed into the crankcase left-hand cover. Applying a spanner to the generator rotor retaining bolt via the larger of the two circular inspection apertures, rotate the engine anti-clockwise until it is at TDC on the compression stroke. This is found by

checking that both rocker arms have free play when the index mark (a straight line with the letter 'T') stamped on the rotor rim aligns exactly with the reference mark (a cast pointer on the smaller inspection aperture rim) set in the crankcase left-hand cover.

3   Remove the cam chain tensioner cap, slacken the tensioner locknut and unscrew the tensioner body. Withdraw the tensioner plunger, the two springs (one spring only on 1982 models) and the rubber damper. Remove the camshaft sprocket cover, which is secured to the cylinder head left-hand side by two screws. Prevent the crankshaft from rotating by applying a spanner to the rotor retaining bolt, then remove the cam sprocket retaining bolt. Pull the sprocket off the camshaft left-hand end, disengage it from the chain and withdraw the sprocket. Prevent the cam chain from dropping into the crankcase by passing a rod through it or by wiring it to a suitable point on the outside of the engine/gearbox unit. Unless it is firmly fixed, remove the sprocket locating pin from the camshaft.

4   The cylinder head and barrel are fastened together and to the crankcase by four long bolts and by four short Allen screws; slacken all eight bolts and screws following the **reverse** of the sequence shown in photograph 41.11. Slacken each fastener in sequence by a turn at

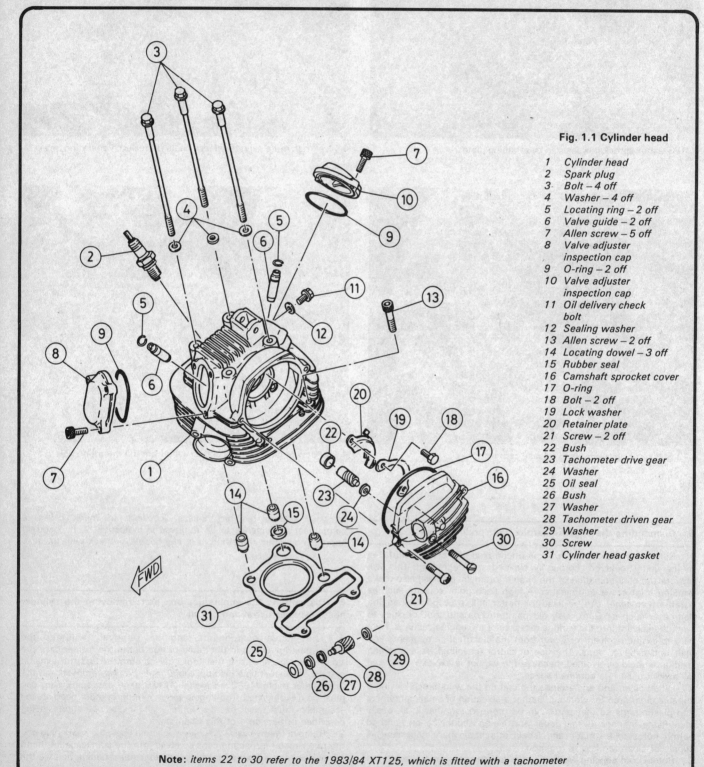

Fig. 1.1 Cylinder head

1   Cylinder head
2   Spark plug
3   Bolt – 4 off
4   Washer – 4 off
5   Locating ring – 2 off
6   Valve guide – 2 off
7   Allen screw – 5 off
8   Valve adjuster
    inspection cap
9   O-ring – 2 off
10 Valve adjuster
    inspection cap
11 Oil delivery check
    bolt
12 Sealing washer
13 Allen screw – 2 off
14 Locating dowel – 3 off
15 Rubber seal
16 Camshaft sprocket cover
17 O-ring
18 Bolt – 2 off
19 Lock washer
20 Retainer plate
21 Screw – 2 off
22 Bush
23 Tachometer drive gear
24 Washer
25 Oil seal
26 Bush
27 Washer
28 Tachometer driven gear
29 Washer
30 Screw
31 Cylinder head gasket

Note: *items 22 to 30 refer to the 1983/84 XT125, which is fitted with a tachometer*

a time until all pressure is released. Remove fully the four long bolts and the two cylinder head/cylinder barrel Allen screws but do not remove yet the two cylinder barrel/crankcase Allen screws.

5   Tap gently around the cylinder head/barrel joint area with a soft-faced mallet to break the seal, then lift away the cylinder head, feeding by hand the cam chain. Remove the cylinder head gasket then secure the cam chain as previously described. If they are loose, the three locating dowels should be removed for safe storage; otherwise they should be refitted in the cylinder barrel top surface. Note the presence of a rubber seal around one of the dowels. Withdraw the cam chain guide blade from the front of the cam chain tunnel.

6   If the cylinder head will not release easily it is probably stuck on the dowels or gasket and must be freed by careful tapping. Use only a soft-faced mallet or a hammer and a wooden drift to tap firmly on the roofs of the inlet and exhaust ports or on any other part of the head where there is no risk of damaging the fins or of distorting the casting. Note that excessive force will not be required and should never be employed. Never attempt to remove the head by levering it away from the barrel.

7   If necessary, rotate the crankshaft to bring the piston to the top of its stroke, then remove the two cylinder barrel retaining Allen bolts. On XT125 models only, if the clutch cable has not been disconnected it should be lifted clear and secured, with the adjuster bracket, well clear of the cylinder barrel. Tap gently around the cylinder base with a soft-faced mallet to break the seal.

8   Lift the cylinder barrel until the base of the piston skirt is exposed then pack the crankcase mouth and cam chain tunnel with clean rag to prevent dirt or debris from falling into the crankcase. Allow the cam chain to drop onto the rag and withdraw the cylinder barrel fully, followed by the base gasket. Unless they are firmly fixed in the crankcase, withdraw the two locating dowels. O-rings are fitted around the base of the cylinder barrel spigot and around the right-hand rear retaining bolt hole; withdraw them both.

9   Use a sharp-pointed instrument to prise out one of the gudgeon pin retaining circlips, press out the gudgeon pin and remove the piston. If the gudgeon pin is a tight fit, soak a rag in boiling water, wring it out, and wrap it around the piston. The heat will expand the piston sufficiently to release its grip on the gudgeon pin. If the pin is still tight, it may be tapped out, using a hammer and a suitable drift, but care must be taken to support the connecting rod firmly while this is being done.

10 The piston rings are removed by holding the piston in both hands and prising the ring ends apart gently with the thumbnails until the rings can be lifted out of their grooves and on to the piston lands, one side at a time. The rings can then be slipped off the piston and put to one side for cleaning and examination. If the rings are stuck in their grooves by excessive carbon deposits use three strips of thin metal sheet to remove them, as shown in the accompanying illustration.

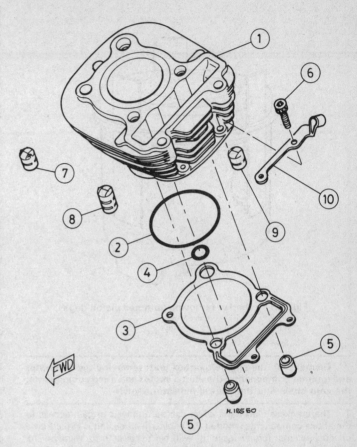

Fig. 1.2 Cylinder barrel

1	Cylinder barrel	7	Damping rubber – 2 off
2	O-ring	8	Damping rubber – 2 off
3	Base gasket	9	Damping rubber
4	O-ring	10	Clutch cable adjuster
5	Locating dowel – 2 off		bracket – XT125
6	Allen bolt – 2 off		

6.7 Clutch cable adjuster bracket is also retained by cylinder barrel Allen screws – XT125 only

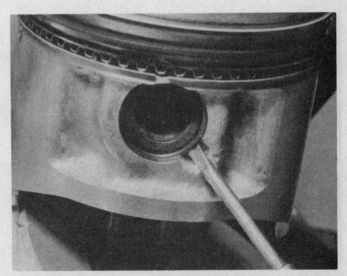

6.9 Use pointed instrument to displace gudgeon pin circlips

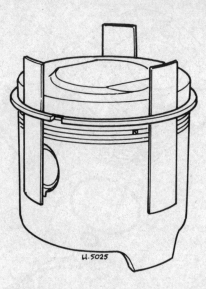

Fig. 1.3 Method of removing gummed piston rings

7 Dismantling the engine/gearbox unit: removing the generator and ignition components, the starter motor and drive components, the cam chain and the neutral indicator switch

1   The crankcase left-hand cover can be removed to gain access to the above components whether the engine/gearbox unit is in the frame or not. In the former case it will be necessary to remove the sidepanels, the seat and the fuel tank to allow the electrical leads to be disconnected, to remove the gearbox sprocket cover and to drain the oil. Note that the cam chain and tensioner blade cannot be removed until the cylinder head has been withdrawn, as described in the previous Section, and that in the case of SR125 models, the starter motor itself cannot be withdrawn until the crankcase right-hand cover has been removed, as described in Section 8.

2   Remove the two circular inspection caps screwed into the crankcase cover and disconnect the neutral indicator switch lead from the switch, then remove the eight screws which retain the cover. Use an impact driver to release the screws, and press each screw into a cardboard template as it is removed to retain it in its correct respective position, as an aid to correct refitting. Lift away the cover and its gasket, noting the presence of the two locating dowels which must be removed for safe storage unless they are firmly fixed in the crankcase.

3   Hold the generator rotor by applying an open-ended spanner to the flats of its centre boss, then remove the rotor retaining bolt and its spring and plain washers. The rotor must be removed using only the correct Yamaha service tool 90890-01080 or a 16mm (thread size) metric bolt; no other method of rotor removal should be attempted.

4   If an ordinary bolt is to be used, damage to the hollow crankshaft end must be prevented, as shown in the accompanying photograph, by inserting first a metal bar approximately 1.5 inches (38 mm) in length and of suitable diameter into the crankshaft end. This will prevent damage by ensuring that the rotor removing bolt bears securely on the crankshaft; the Yamaha service tool has a carefully shaped end and does not need such a spacer. It was found that a 10 mm bolt with the flats of the head ground off is quite suitable.

5   Screw the tool or bolt carefully into the rotor centre boss and tighten it firmly against the crankshaft or spacer, then tap sharply on the tool or bolt head with a hammer; the shock should jar the rotor free. If it does not work at the first attempt, tighten the tool further and tap again. Withdraw the rotor, taking care that on SR125 models only the starter clutch rollers are not displaced.

6   On SR125 models only, displace the rotor locating Woodruff key from the crankshaft keyway, then withdraw the starter clutch driven gear and the thrust washer behind it. Refit the driven gear to the generator rotor to prevent the loss of any of the starter clutch components. Withdraw the starter idler gear and its shaft. On XT125 models the rotor locating Woodruff key should be removed only if necessary.

7   Unscrew the two bolts securing the cam chain tensioner blade bottom mounting and lift the blade assembly upwards through the cam chain tunnel. Drop the cam chain into the crankcase, disengage it from the crankshaft sprocket and withdraw it.

8   Unscrew the neutral indicator switch from the crankcase wall and withdraw it, complete with its sealing washer. The generator and ignition source and pulser coils are retained by screws to the inside of the crankcase left-hand cover, the electrical leads being secured by clamps. Use an impact driver to release the screws and withdraw the coils, noting carefully where each is fitted and the way in which the leads are routed.

9   On SR125 models only, the starter motor can be removed only after the crankcase right-hand cover has been withdrawn, as described in the next Section of this Chapter. If necessary, disconnect the starter lead from the terminal underneath the motor right-hand end, the lead being secured by a nut and plain washer. Use an impact driver to release the two screws securing the motor mounting flange and pull the motor to the right, out of the crankcase.

7.3 Hold generator rotor as shown while removing retaining bolt

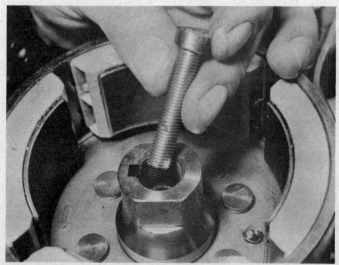

7.4 Rotor removal – spacer must be fabricated if correct service tool is not used

7.5 Ordinary bolt can be used to extract rotor

7.6 SR125 only – Woodruff key must be displaced before driven gear is removed

8 Dismantling the engine/gearbox unit: removing the crankcase right-hand cover

1 The crankcase right-hand cover can be removed with the engine/gearbox unit in the frame or out of it, but in the former case engine oil must be drained and the gauze filter removed, as described in Routine Maintenance. On all XT125 models the kickstart lever must be withdrawn, noting that the pinch bolt must be removed completely before the lever can be pulled off the shaft splines, the stop lamp rear switch spring must be disconnected from the brake pedal, and the two bolts securing the right-hand footrest and brake pedal must be removed so that the footrest/pedal assembly can be displaced and allowed to hang down clear of the engine. On SR125 models, the exhaust system must be removed, as described in Section 4 of this Chapter, and the swinging arm pivot bolt retaining nut unscrewed so that the right-hand footrest can be withdrawn.

2 Use an impact driver to release the nine (SR125) or ten (XT125) screws which secure the cover and remove the screws, pressing each screw through a cardboard template so that all are preserved in their original respective positions. Note that one of the screws securing the oil filter chamber cap also retains the crankcase cover; the chamber cap must be withdrawn before an attempt is made to remove the cover.

3 Tap around the joint with a soft-faced mallet to break the seal, then lift away the cover. Slots are incorporated in the cover at three points to permit the insertion of a suitable lever. If these are used, as shown in the accompanying photograph, do not exert excessive force and be very careful not to mark the machined gasket surface.

4 With the cover removed, peel away the gasket and discard it; a new one should be fitted on reassembly. Unless the two locating dowels are firmly fixed in the crankcase gasket surface, remove them for safe storage. Check that no thrust washers or other components have stuck to the cover or dropped clear as it was removed.

9 Dismantling the engine/gearbox unit: removing the clutch assembly

1 When the crankcase right-hand cover has been removed as described in the previous Section, the clutch assembly can be withdrawn whether the engine/gearbox unit is in the frame or not.

2 Before the clutch is dismantled it should be noted that it may be necessary, in certain circumstances, to have the clutch intact so that the crankshaft can be locked via the transmission while the primary drive gear retaining nut is removed. Refer to Section 10 of this Chapter.

3 Slacken, but do not remove, the locknut of the clutch release mechanism adjuster set in the centre of the clutch pressure plate. Working in a diagonal sequence, progressively slacken, then remove, the clutch spring retaining bolts. Withdraw the clutch springs, the

pressure plate complete with the release mechanism adjuster, and the clutch friction and plain plates. Knock back the raised portion of the clutch centre retaining nut lock washer.

4 The clutch centre must be locked to prevent rotation while the retaining nut is removed. This can be done by applying the Yamaha service tool 90890-01022 to the centre. If the correct tool is not available an alternative tool can be fabricated from two strips of metal, as shown in the accompanying illustration. Alternatively the clutch centre can be locked by selecting top gear and by applying the rear brake hard (if the engine is in the frame) or by refitting the gearbox sprocket and locking it with a length of chain, thus locking the clutch via the transmission. Remove the retaining nut, then withdraw the clutch centre, the thick thrust washer, and the clutch outer drum.

5 Tip the machine or engine unit to the right so that the steel ball and clutch pushrod will slide out of the input shaft centre. If this does not work, use a slim steel rod that has been magnetised by stroking it across the magnets of the generator rotor.

6 Using an impact driver, remove from the crankcase left-hand side the single screw which retains the clutch release shaft, disconnect the clutch cable (if necessary) and pull the shaft upwards out of the crankcase, complete with its return spring. Use circlip pliers to remove the circlip which retains the shaft oil seal; the oil seal can then be levered out and the bush underneath it extracted.

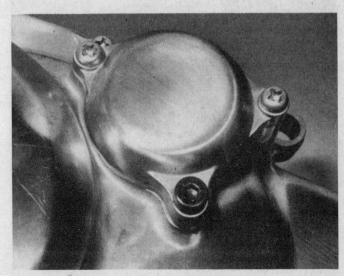

8.1a Remove oil filter chamber cap ...

8.1b ... and withdraw filter before removing crankcase cover

8.1c XT125 only – kickstart and footrest/brake pedal assembly must be removed

8.3 Exercise great care when using leverage to remove cover

9.6 Remove circlip before levering out clutch release shaft oil seal

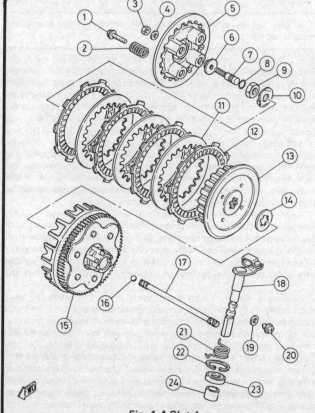

Fig. 1.4 Clutch

1 Bolt – 4 off	13 Clutch centre
2 Spring – 4 off	14 Thick thrust washer
3 Locknut	15 Outer drum
4 Washer	16 Steel ball
5 Pressure plate	17 Pushrod
6 Release mechanism hexagon	18 Release shaft
headed plate	19 Washer
7 Release mechanism adjuster	20 Screw
8 O-ring	21 Return spring
9 Nut	22 Circlip
10 Lock washer	23 Oil seal
11 Plain plate – 3 off	24 Bush
12 Friction plate – 4 off	

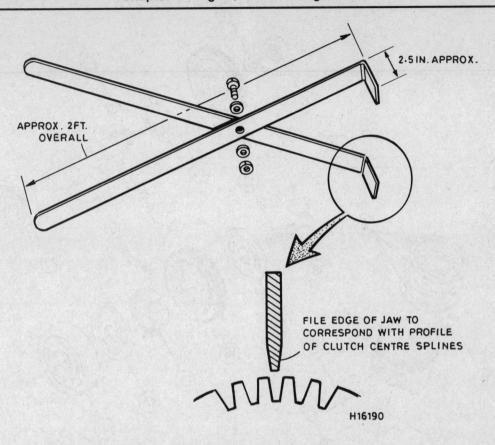

2·5 IN. APPROX.

APPROX. 2FT. OVERALL

FILE EDGE OF JAW TO CORRESPOND WITH PROFILE OF CLUTCH CENTRE SPLINES

H16190

Fig. 1.5 Fabricated clutch holding tool

10 Dismantling the engine/gearbox unit: removing the primary drive and balancer drive gears and the oil pump

1   The above components can be removed, after the crankcase right-hand cover has been removed as described in Section 8, whether the engine/gearbox unit is in the frame or not. Note, however, that only the primary drive gear can be removed easily with the clutch in place; while the oil pump can be manoeuvred out from underneath the clutch, the clutch must be removed before the balancer drive gears can be withdrawn. Refer to Section 9 of this Chapter.

2   Knock back the raised tab of the primary drive gear retaining nut lock washer. Any one of several methods can be employed to lock the crankshaft while the primary drive gear retaining nut is removed. The generator rotor can be held as described in Section 7, or the transmission can be locked as described in Section 9, if the rotor or clutch are still in place. If the engine top half has been dismantled, a close-fitting metal bar can be passed through the connecting rod small-end eye and rested on two wooden blocks placed across the crankcase mouth. Alternatively the clutch outer drum can be refitted temporarily and the primary drive gears spragged, or locked, by wedging between them a wooden or soft alloy bar or a tightly-wadded piece of rag. Unscrew the nut and remove the lock washer and primary drive gear.

3   To remove the oil pump, first prise off the metal cover from around the nylon pump driven gear, then rotate the gear until the apertures cut in it align with the heads of the three countersunk pump retaining screws. Use an impact driver to release the three screws, then remove the pump and its gasket. Note that there is a fourth countersunk screw in approximately the 7 o'clock position from the pump drive shaft (ie to the left of the single lower pump retaining screw); this screw is shorter than the others and should not be disturbed as it secures both halves of the pump body.

4   Knock back the raised tab of the balancer driven gear retaining nut lock washer, then lock the balancer shaft by spragging the drive gears. This involves wedging a wooden or soft alloy bar or a tightly-wadded piece of rag between the two sets of teeth while the retaining nut and

lock washer are removed. Withdraw from the balancer shaft the driven gear and Woodruff key, then withdraw from the crankshaft the first thick washer.

5   The balancer drive gear is in two pieces, joined by six coil springs and three dowel pins; be very careful to remove the gear in one unit, or there is a risk of losing one or more components. Withdraw from the crankshaft the Woodruff key and the remaining thick washer.

6   Apply finger pressure to the oil feed quill set in the crankshaft end while pushing out its retaining pin from the drilling across the crankshaft. Withdraw the feed quill and its spring, then store them carefully with the retaining pin.

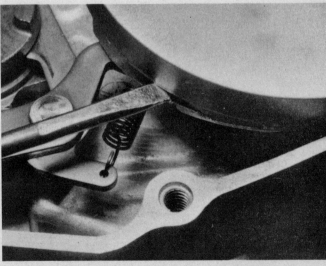

10.3 Oil pump driven gear cover can be levered from position

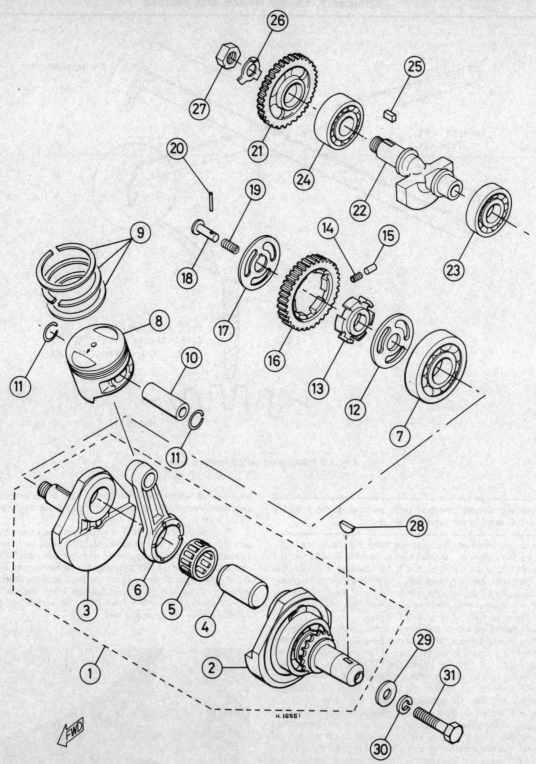

Fig. 1.6 Crankshaft and balancer shaft components

1	Crankshaft assembly	11	Circlip – 2 off
2	Left-hand crankshaft	12	Thick washer
3	Right-hand crankshaft	13	Balancer drive gear
4	Crankpin		inner
5	Big-end bearing	14	Spring – 6 off
6	Connecting rod	15	Dowel pin – 3 off
7	Right-hand main bearing	16	Balancer drive gear
8	Piston		outer
9	Piston rings	17	Thick washer
10	Gudgeon pin		

18	Oil feed quill	25	Woodruff key
19	Spring	26	Lock washer
20	Retaining pin	27	Nut
21	Balancer driven gear	28	Woodruff key
22	Balancer shaft	29	Washer
23	Balancer shaft left-hand	30	Spring washer
	bearing	31	Bolt
24	Balancer shaft right-hand		
	bearing		

11 Dismantling the engine/gearbox unit: removing the kickstart shaft and idler gear – XT125 only

1   The kickstart components can be removed after the crankcase right-hand cover has been withdrawn, as described in Section 8 of this Chapter, and after the clutch has been removed, as described in Section 9.

2   Using a pair of pliers, grasp the kickstart return spring firmly at its outer end, unhook it, and allow it to return slowly to its relaxed position. Care is required as the spring is under tension. Pull the shaft assembly out of the crankcase.

3   Remove from the shaft right-hand end the two thrust washers, displace the circlip and slide off the spring guide. Unhook the spring inner end from the shaft and remove the spring, followed by the plain washer and the kickstart pinion, the latter complete with its friction clip.

4   Remove the first circlip from the output shaft right-hand end, followed by the first thrust washer, the idler gear itself, and the second thrust washer. Displace the second circlip from its shaft groove.

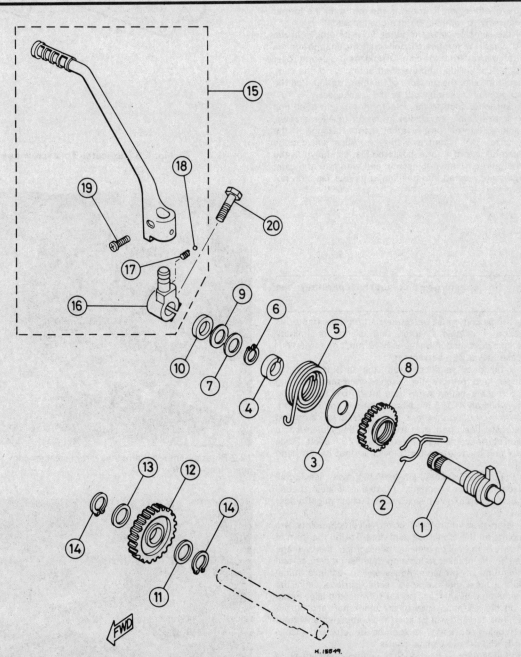

Fig. 1.7 Kickstart assembly – XT125 only

1 Kickstart shaft	6 Circlip	11 Thrust washer	16 Lever knuckle
2 Friction clip	7 Thrust washer	12 Kickstart idler gear	17 Spring
3 Washer	8 Kickstart pinion	13 Thrust washer	18 Steel ball
4 Return spring guide	9 Thrust washer	14 Circlip – 2 off	19 Screw
5 Return spring	10 Oil seal	15 Kickstart lever	20 Pinch bolt

12 Dismantling the engine/gearbox unit: removing the external gear selector components

1   Those components of the selector mechanism that can be removed without separating the crankcase halves are the gearchange shaft and return spring, incorporating the selector claw arm and detent roller arm, and the selector cam. It will be necessary to remove the crankcase right-hand cover, the clutch and the kickstart assembly (XT125 only) to gain access to them, the work being described in Section 8, 9 and 11 of this Chapter. While the task can be carried out whether the engine/gearbox unit is in the frame or not, in the former case it will be necessary to remove the gearchange pedal.

2   Carefully pull the selector claw arm away from its groove in the selector cam, and withdraw the gearchange shaft far enough for the claw arm to be rotated away from the cam. Disengage the detent roller arm from the selector cam, slide it up the shaft until clear of the cam, then slowly release it to relax the pressure of its return spring. Pull the complete gearchange shaft assembly out of the crankcases.

3   The selector cam is retained to the selector drum right-hand end by a single 'Torx' screw. These are similar in design to Allen screws, but have a star shaped internal profile rather than a hexagon. If the correct Torx key (size T30) is not available, an Allen key can be modified by the careful use of a three-cornered file, as shown in the accompanying illustration. Remove the screw and withdraw the cam, noting that four pins are pushed into drillings in its rear face; do not lose any of these pins.

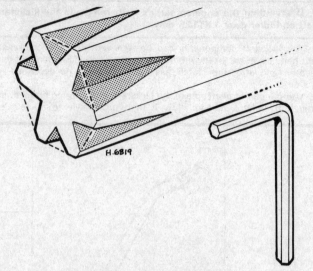

Fig. 1.8 Fabricated Torx screw key

12.2 Press detent roller arm away from selector cam, then remove gearchange shaft

13 Dismantling the engine/gearbox unit: separating the crankcase halves

1   The engine/gearbox unit must be removed from the frame, as described in Section 4 of this Chapter, and all the preliminary dismantling operations described in Sections 5-12 must be carried out before the crankcase halves can be separated.

2   Working in a diagonal sequence from the outside inwards, progressively slacken and remove the twelve crankcase securing screws. On SR125 models eleven screws are fitted from the left and one from the right, while on XT125 models ten screws are fitted from the left and two from the right. Store all screws in a cardboard template as previously described, not forgetting the clutch cable adjuster bracket and starter cable guide fitted on SR125 models. Place the engine/gearbox unit on two wooden blocks so that its left-hand side is uppermost.

3   The object is to pull the crankcase left-hand half away, leaving all components in place in the right-hand half. Make a final check that all screws and other components have been removed which might hinder crankcase separation.

4   As with the crankcase right-hand cover, leverage points are provided at two points on the crankcase joint area. Taking the form of small slots, as shown in the accompanying photograph, the leverage points are adjacent to the crankcase locating dowels; be very careful to apply the minimum of pressure necessary to achieve initial separation and do not mark the machined sealing surface. Once the crankcases have separated evenly, use only a soft-faced mallet to tap gently but firmly on the left-hand ends of the crankshaft and output shaft. The regular, light, tapping will jar apart the components without any excessive force being necessary. As soon as the left-hand case is free, pull it upwards and off the various shafts.

5   Note the presence of a thrust washer on the output shaft left-hand end; check that this is not stuck to the crankcase. Also, the two locating dowels should be removed for safe storage unless they are firmly fixed in the gasket surface of the right-hand crankcase half.

6   If the crankcases are reluctant to separate, never be tempted to tap ever harder in an effort to release them; check again that all fasteners etc. have been removed. It may be that corrosion has formed around the locating dowels, requiring the application of penetrating fluid to release the two castings. If the crankcase halves separate but then stick, ensure that they are square to one another and not tying. If necessary, tap the two halves back together and start again.

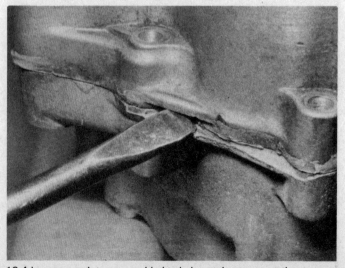

13.4 Leverage points are provided to help crankcase separation

14 Dismantling the engine/gearbox unit: removing the crankshaft, balancer shaft and gearbox components

1 Have ready a spirit-based felt marker. Withdraw first the selector fork shaft to the rear of the selector drum, then withdraw both selector forks. As each fork is withdrawn, mark its left-hand or upper, face with the felt marker so that it can be identified easily on reassembly and refitted the correct way round. Refit both forks to the shaft in their original positions as a further aid to correct reassembly.
2 Withdraw the selector fork shaft from in front of the selector drum, swing the guide pin of the single selector fork away from the selector drum track, and withdraw the drum. Check that the neutral indicator switch contact is firmly fixed in the drum left-hand end. Withdraw the remaining selector fork, mark it as described above, and refit it to its shaft.
3 To prevent the loss of any components, fasten an elastic band around the output shaft left-hand end. Remove as a single unit the two gear clusters, using a soft-faced mallet to tap on the input shaft right-hand end. On SR125 models only, insert a finger as soon as possible to retain the two gear pinions and single thrust washer on the output shaft right-hand end; as soon as the shaft is withdrawn, tighten an elastic band around the shaft end to secure these components.
4 Withdraw the balancer shaft, tapping lightly on its right-hand end with a soft-faced mallet, then remove the crankshaft in the same way.
5 If the crankshaft proves stubborn, support the crankcase right-hand half on two wooden blocks so that the right-hand surface is uppermost. The two blocks must be placed as close around the crankshaft as possible to give the maximum support to the crankcase, and must be of sufficient height to permit the crankshaft to be removed from underneath. Using only a soft-faced mallet, or an ordinary hammer in conjunction with a hard wooden drift, tap the crankshaft downwards out of its main bearing. Hold the crankshaft with the free hand; it must not be allowed to drop clear. Note that excessive force will not be required as a few firm taps should suffice. Be very careful to tap squarely on the crankshaft end, and avoid any risk of damage to the end itself.

15 Dismantling the engine/gearbox unit: removing oil seals and bearings

1 Before removing any oil seal or bearing, check that it is not secured by a retaining plate. If this is the case, use an impact driver or spanner, as appropriate, to release the securing screws or bolts and lift away the retaining plate.
2 Oil seals are easily damaged when disturbed and, thus, should be renewed as a matter of course during overhaul. Prise them out of position using the flat of a screwdriver and taking care not to damage the alloy seal housings.
3 The crankshaft and gearbox bearings are a press fit in their respective crankcase locations. To remove a bearing, the crankcase casting must be heated so that it expands and releases its grip on the bearing, which can then be drifted or pulled out.
4 To prevent casting distortion, it must be heated evenly to a temperature of about 100°C by placing it in an oven; if an oven is not available, place the casting in a suitable container and carefully pour boiling water over it until it is submerged.
5 Taking care to prevent personal injury when handling heated components, lay the casting on a clean surface and tap out the bearing using a hammer and a suitable drift. If the bearing is to be re-used apply the drift only to the bearing outer race, where this is accessible, to avoid damaging the bearing. In some cases it will be necessary to apply pressure to the bearing inner race; in such cases closely inspect the bearing for signs of damage before using it again. When drifting a bearing from its housing it must be kept square to the housing to prevent tying in the housing with the resulting risk of damage. Where possible, use a tubular drift such as a socket spanner which bears only on the bearing outer race; if this is not possible, tap evenly around the outer race to achieve the same result.
6 In some cases, bearings are pressed into blind holes in the castings. These bearings must be removed by heating the casting and tapping it face downwards on to a clean wooden surface to dislodge the bearing under its own weight. If this is not successful the casting should be taken to a motorcycle service engineer who has the correct internally expanding bearing puller. In the case of the bush supporting

the clutch release shaft, a thread can be cut in the bush using a tap of suitable size so that a bolt can be screwed into place. This will provide suitable purchase for the bush to be extracted after heating the crankcase half.

15.2 Oil seals can be levered from their housings as shown

15.5 Heat crankcases as described before removing bearings

16 Examination and renovation: general

1 Before examining the parts of the dismantled engine unit for wear it is essential that they should be cleaned thoroughly. Use a petrol/paraffin mix or a high flash-point solvent to remove all traces of old oil and sludge which may have accumulated within the engine. Where petrol is included in the cleaning agent normal fire precautions should be taken and cleaning should be carried out in a well ventilated place.
2 Examine the crankcase castings for cracks or other signs of damage. If a crack is discovered it will require a specialist repair.
3 Examine carefully each part to determine the extent of wear, checking with the tolerance figures listed in the Specifications section of this Chapter or in the main text. If there is any doubt about the condition of a particular component, play safe and renew.
4 Use a clean lint-free rag for cleaning and drying the various

components. This will obviate the risk of small particles obstructing the internal oilways, and causing the lubrication system to fail.

5   Various instruments for measuring wear are required, including a vernier gauge or external micrometer and a set of standard feeler gauges. Both an internal and external micrometer will also be required to check wear limits. Additionally, although not absolutely necessary, a dial gauge and mounting bracket is invaluable for accurate measurement of end float, and play between components of very low diameter bores – where a micrometer cannot reach.

6   After some experience has been gained the state of wear of many components can be determined visually or by feel and thus a decision on their suitability for continued service can be made without resorting to direct measurement.

17 Examination and renovation: engine cases and covers

1   Small cracks or holes in aluminium castings may be repaired with an epoxy resin adhesive, such as Araldite, as a temporary expedient. Permanent repairs can only be effected by argon-arc welding, and a specialist in this process is in a position to advise on the viability of proposed repair.

2   Damaged threads can be economically reclaimed by using a diamond section wire insert, of the Helicoil type, which is easily fitted after drilling and re-tapping the affected thread. Most motorcycle dealers and small engineering firms offer a service of this kind.

3   Sheared studs or screws can usually be removed with screw extractors, which consist of tapered, left-hand thread screws, of very hard steel. These are inserted by screwing anti-clockwise, into a pre-drilled hole in the stud, and usually succeed in dislodging the most stubborn stud or screw. If a problem arises which seems to be beyond

your scope, it is worth consulting a professional engineering firm before condemning an otherwise sound casing. Many of these firms advertise regularly in the motorcycle papers.

18 Examination and renovation: bearings and oil seals

1   The crankshaft and gearbox bearings can be examined while they are still in place in the crankcase castings. Wash them thoroughly to remove all traces of oil, then feel for free play by attempting to move the inner race up and down, then from side-to-side. Examine the bearing balls or rollers and the bearing tracks for pitting or other signs of wear, then spin hard the bearing. Any roughness caused by defects in the bearing balls or rollers or in the bearing tracks will be felt and heard immediately.

2   If any signs of free play or wear are discovered, or if the bearing is not free and smooth in rotation but runs roughly and slows down jerkily, the bearing must be renewed. Bearing removal is described in Section 15 of this Chapter, and refitting in Section 32.

3   To prevent oil leaks occurring in the future, all oil seals and O-rings should be renewed whenever they are disturbed during the course of an overhaul, regardless of their apparent condition.

19 Examination and renovation: camshaft and rocker gear

1   The camshaft and rocker gear must be very closely inspected, particularly if engine oil changing at the correct interval has been neglected or if the oil level has been allowed to drop too far, even if the engine has been dismantled for some other reason.

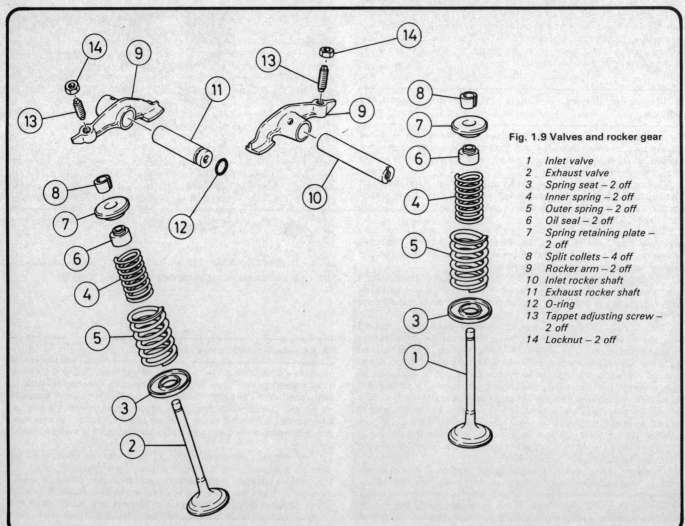

Fig. 1.9 Valves and rocker gear

1   Inlet valve
2   Exhaust valve
3   Spring seat – 2 off
4   Inner spring – 2 off
5   Outer spring – 2 off
6   Oil seal – 2 off
7   Spring retaining plate – 2 off
8   Split collets – 4 off
9   Rocker arm – 2 off
10   Inlet rocker shaft
11   Exhaust rocker shaft
12   O-ring
13   Tappet adjusting screw – 2 off
14   Locknut – 2 off

2   Flatten the raised portions of the lock washer, then remove the two camshaft retainer plate mounting bolts, the lock washer, and the retainer plate. Screw a 6 mm (thread size) metric bolt or screw into the thread tapped on the inside of both rocker shafts, as shown in the accompanying photograph. The bolt or screw head will then provide purchase so that the rocker shaft can be pulled out of the head. Note that the exhaust rocker shaft has an O-ring fitted which will make its removal slightly more difficult; this O-ring should be renewed as a matter of course whenever the shaft is disturbed. If the shafts are a tight fit, the head may be warmed in an oven as described in Section 20 to aid removal; in exceptionally stubborn cases a slide hammer can be attached to the bolt or screw head.

3   Withdraw both rocker shafts and the rocker arms, but be careful to keep separate the inlet and exhaust components; place them in separate, clearly marked, containers to avoid any risk of confusion on reassembly. If excessive wear is to be avoided due to mismatching of part worn components, all parts should be refitted in exactly their original positions.

4   With the rockers removed, the camshaft can be extracted, a task which is carried out in exactly the same way as for the rocker shafts but employing a 10 mm (thread size) metric bolt. If the cam sprocket retaining bolt is employed, take care not to damage it. Note that the camshaft bush will be removed with the camshaft.

5   Examine the camshaft visually for signs of wear. The camshaft lobes should have a smooth surface and be entirely free from scuff marks or indentations. Wear will probably be most evident on the ramps of each cam and where the cam contour changes sharply. It is unlikely that severe wear will be encountered during the normal service life of the machine unless the lubrication system has failed, causing the case hardened surface to wear through. If necessary, check with the Specification given at the beginning of this Chapter and measure the cam lobe height in each case. If either of the cam lobes is below the service limit, the camshaft must be renewed.

6   Examine closely the bearing surfaces of the camshaft, the camshaft bush and the cylinder head; signs of anything other than the slightest scoring or scuffing will mean that the component concerned must be renewed. Reassemble the components and feel for free play which should be immediately evident once the lubricating film of oil has been removed. If excessive free play is encountered, measure the diameter of the camshaft right- and left-hand bearing journals and the inside diameter of the camshaft bush and the cylinder head bearing surface; the clearance can be calculated by subtracting one from the other. If the clearance is beyond the tolerance given in the Specifications Section of this Chapter, any component that is found to be excessively worn must be renewed.

7   Note that if excessive wear is found between the camshaft right-hand end and the cylinder head, there are several light engineering companies advertising in the national motorcycle press who will reclaim such damage by fabricating and fitting separate plain or roller bearings, thus saving the cost of a new cylinder head if it is the cylinder head that is worn.

8   Check the fit of the rocker shafts in the rocker arms and cylinder head; if excessive play is apparent, measure the outside diameter of each rocker shaft and the matching bore of each rocker arm, comparing the measurements obtained with those given in the Specifications Section of this Chapter and renewing any component that is worn. Wear in the rocker gear is revealed by a light tapping noise which should not be confused with the similar noise produced by excessive valve clearances.

9   Check the tip of each rocker arm at the point where the arm makes contact with the cam. If signs of cracking, scuffing or breakthrough in the case hardened surface are evident, fit a new replacement.

10 Check the thread of the tappet adjusting screw, the thread of the rocker arm into which it fits, and the thread of the locknut. The hardened end of the tappet adjuster must also be in good condition.

11 If signs of oil starvation are evident such as dry, badly scored, bearing surfaces, deposits of burnt oil, or excessive heating (or blueing) on any component, the cause must be found and rectified before the engine is reassembled. Examine and clean thoroughly all oilways using compressed air to clean out any that cannot be reached by other means.

12 On reassembly, coat the camshaft and the bearing surfaces of the camshaft bush and cylinder head with a high-quality molybdenum disulphide-based lubricant, or failing this, with a copious supply of clean engine oil. Aligning the camshaft so that its lobes point downwards and to each side, to pass easily through the cutouts in the cylinder head, refit the camshaft, followed by the camshaft bush. Note that the cutout in the bush left-hand surface must face to the rear, or inlet side of the head. Check that the camshaft is free to rotate easily, then turn it to the TDC position, with the sprocket locating pin at 12 o'clock.

13 If the rocker shafts were a tight fit in the cylinder head it may be necessary to warm the head to aid refitting. The inlet rocker shaft is identified by the slot cut across its hollow, threaded, left-hand end, while the exhaust shaft is identified by the groove machined near its left-hand end; note that a new O-ring must be fitted to this groove before the shaft is refitted. Thoroughly lubricate all components then insert the first rocker arm, ensuring that it is fitted in the correct position and the right way round, then push the rocker shaft through the cylinder head and rocker arm bore. Note that the shafts must be refitted with their hollow, threaded ends facing to the left or it will be impossible to remove them in the future. Check that the arm is pressed fully into the head and repeat the process to refit the remaining rocker assembly.

14 Refit the retainer plate, note that its projecting tongues engage with the notch in the camshaft bush and against the inlet rocker shaft end. The lock washer should be renewed if all its locking tabs have previously been used. Fit the lock washer, apply thread locking compound to their threads and refit both retainer plate mounting bolts, tightening them to a torque setting of 0.8 kgf m (6 lbf ft). Secure each bolt by bending up one of the lock washer tabs against one of the flats of its head.

19.2 Using a bolt to extract the exhaust rocker shaft

19.5 Measure camshaft lobe height

19.6a Measuring camshaft bush inside diameter

19.6b Measuring camshaft bearing journal diameter

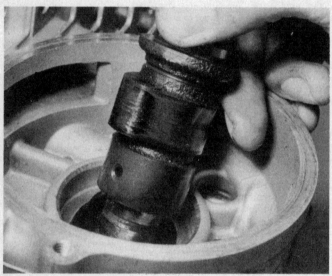

19.12a Thoroughly lubricate camshaft before refitting

19.12b Refit camshaft bush

19.13a Rocker arms must be fitted correct way round

19.13b Note different inlet and exhaust rocker shafts – also that threaded ends are facing outwards

19.14a Note that bush retainer plate also locates inlet rocker shaft

19.14b Secure retainer mounting bolts as shown

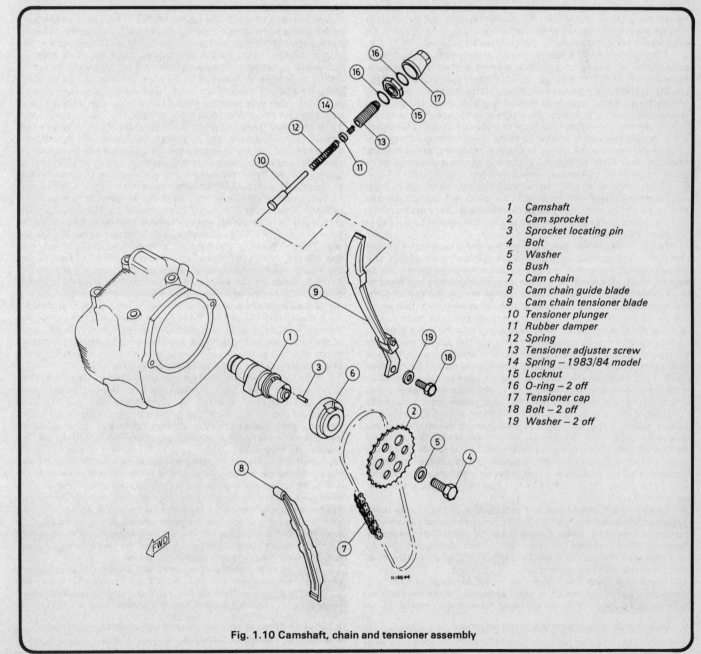

1   Camshaft
2   Cam sprocket
3   Sprocket locating pin
4   Bolt
5   Washer
6   Bush
7   Cam chain
8   Cam chain guide blade
9   Cam chain tensioner blade
10 Tensioner plunger
11 Rubber damper
12 Spring
13 Tensioner adjuster screw
14 Spring – 1983/84 model
15 Locknut
16 O-ring – 2 off
17 Tensioner cap
18 Bolt – 2 off
19 Washer – 2 off

Fig. 1.10 Camshaft, chain and tensioner assembly

20 Examination and renovation: cylinder head, valves, valve seats and guides

1   It is best to remove all carbon deposits from the combustion chamber before the valves are withdrawn for inspection, but do not forget to pay equal attention to cleaning the intake and exhaust ports once the valves have been removed. Use a blunt-ended scraper to avoid damaging the soft alloy, and finish off with a metal polish to achieve a smooth surface.

2   Clean the cylinder head gasket surface and check it for distortion with a straight-edge and a set of feeler gauges. The straight-edge should be laid diagonally across the mating surface from corner to corner and any clearance between its lower edge and the mating surface checked with the gauges. Repeat the procedure with the straight-edge laid between the opposite corners and then at several positions in between the four corners. If the largest clearance found exceeds 0.25 mm (0.01 in), Yamaha recommend that the cylinder head by replaced with a new item. It is worth noting however, that if the amount of distortion found is only slightly greater than the limit given in the Specifications Section of this Chapter, it could well be worth seeking the advice of a competent motorcycle engineer who can advise on whether skimming the mating surface flat is possible without the subsequent risk of the piston coming into contact with the valve heads once the engine is reassembled and started.

3   If the cylinder head is seen to be only slightly warped, the mating surface may be lapped on a surface plate or a sheet of place glass. Place a sheet of 400 or 600 grit abrasive paper on the surface plate. Lay the cylinder head, gasket-face down, on the paper and gently rub it with an oscillating motion to remove any high spots. Lift the head at frequent intervals to inspect the progress of the operation, and take care to remove the minimum amount of material necessary to restore a flat sealing surface. It should be remembered that most cases of cylinder head warpage can be traced to unequal tensioning of the cylinder head nuts and bolts by tightening them in incorrect sequence or by using incorrect or unmeasured torque settings.

4   Finally, make sure that the external cooling fins of the cylinder head are not clogged with oil or road dirt which will prevent the free flow of air and cause the engine to overheat, and check the condition of the spark plug thread; if damaged this can be repaired by the use of a Helicoil thread insert.

5   To remove the valves, first withdraw the rocker assemblies and the camshaft, as described in the previous Section, then obtain two marked containers so that the appropriate valve components can be kept separate once removed. A valve spring compression tool must be used to compress each set of valve springs in turn, thereby allowing the split collets to be freed from the valve stem and the spring retaining plate, the springs, the spring seat and the valve guide oil seal to be removed from the cylinder head along with the valve itself. As each valve is removed, check that it will pass through the guide bore without resistance. Use fine abrasive paper to polish away any burrs or raised edges from the collet groove until the valves can be removed easily. Keep separate the inlet and exhaust valve components; while there is no possibility of confusing the valves, since their heads are of different sizes, the springs, collets, and spring retainers are identical.

6   Using a micrometer, measure the diameter of each valve stem at various points along its length. If any one of the measurements obtained is less than the service limit given in the Specfications Section of this Chapter, the valve should be renewed. Check the amount of valve stem runout by supporting the valve stem on two V-blocks and slowly rotating it whilst measuring the amount of runout with a dial gauge. If the stem is found to be distorted, the valve must be renewed.

7   Examine each valve head and seating face. If the face is burnt, pitted, or damaged, the valve must be renewed; do not attempt to restore a damaged valve seating face by excessive grinding-in. Measure the thickness of the valve head as shown in the accompanying illustration, if the head is worn to 1.0 mm (0.04 in) or less, the valve must be renewed.

8   Check that each valve stem tip is not indented or otherwise damaged; slight wear can be repaired by grinding down the stem but care must be taken that an excessive amount of material is not removed.

9   Check each valve stem/valve guide clearance using a dial gauge and a valve that is either new or known to be within the specified wear limits. Insert the valve into the guide and push it down until it is in the maximum lift position. Clamp the dial gauge to the cylinder head so that its pointer rests against the valve head. Take two measurements, one at 90° to the other, and renew the valve guide if the amount of wear indicated is greater than the service limit given in the Specifications. Alternatively, if the necessary equipment is available, measure the guide internal diameters and calculate the respective clearances by subtracting the valve stem diameter from that of the guide.

10   To renew a valve guide, place the cylinder head in an oven to heat it evenly to about 100°C (212°F). The old guide can now be tapped out from the cylinder side. The correct drift should be shouldered with the small diameter the same size as the valve stem and the larger diameter slightly smaller than the OD of the valve guide. If a suitable drift is not available a plain brass drift may be utilized with great care. Before removing the old guides scrape away any carbon deposits which have accumulated on the guide where it projects into the port. If in doubt, seek the advice of a Yamaha Service Agent. Note that each valve guide is fitted with a metal locating ring which must be discarded along with the guide.

11   Clean out the valve guide holes in the cylider head and lubricate the surface of each hole. Failure to keep the hole lubricated during insertion of the guide may result in damage to the guide or head. Ensure the cylinder head is well supported on a clean flat work surface during insertion of the guides and is heated to the same temperature as for removal. Fit a new locating ring to each new guide and drive each guide into its hole until the locating ring abuts against its recess in the cylinder head. New valve guides, once installed, must be finished to the correct dimensions using a 6 mm (0.24 in) reamer. Be careful to remove all traces of swarf after reaming, and oil the valve guide bore before inserting the valve. Note that if a new valve guide is fitted, the valve seat must be recut to centre the seat with the guide axis, this task being described in paragraphs 14 - 18 of this Section.

12   If the valve faces and seats are in good condition, with only light pitting, they may be restored by grinding-in. Commence by smearing a trace of fine valve grinding compound (carborundum paste) on the valve seat and apply a suction tool to the head of the valve. Oil the first valve stem and insert the valve in the guide so that the two surfaces to be ground in make contact with one another. With a semi-rotary motion, grind in the valve head to the seat, using a backward and forward action. Lift the valve occasionally so that the grinding compound is distributed evenly. Repeat the application until an unbroken ring of light grey matt finish is obtained on both valve and seal. This denotes the grinding operation is now complete. Use only fine grinding compound, never coarse, and be careful to remove only the barest minimum of material necessary to achieve a good seating. Carefully wash off the valve and seat so that all traces of grinding compound are removed, then repeat with the second valve.

13   Measure the width of each valve seating ring, which should be 0.9 - 1.1 mm (0.035 - 0.043 in). If the ring is wider or narrower than this the seat must be recut. Also check that the ring is exactly in the centre of the valve face, as shown in the accompanying illustration; if too high or too low, the seat position must be altered, again by recutting, this task being described in the following paragraphs.

14   If the valve/valve seat contact area cannot be restored correctly by grinding-in, or if new valve guides have been fitted, the valve seats must be recut. This is a task requiring some skill and expensive equipment and should be entrusted, therefore, to a competent Yamaha Service Agent. If it is decided to attempt this task at home, obtain the Yamaha valve seat cutting set, Part Number TLM-90910-43-20, and proceed as follows.

15   Insert the solid pilot into the valve guide with a rotary motion until the pilot shoulder is about 10 mm (0.4 in) from the guide end, fit the 45° cutter attachment to the tool handle and place the cutter over the pilot. Using firm hand pressure, rotate the cutter through one or two full turns to clean the seat, then withdraw the cutter and examine the seat. If the seat is continuous and unmarked by pitting, proceed to the next step, but if pitting is still evident refit the cutter and repeat the procedure until all pitting has been removed. Be very careful to remove only the bare minimum of material necessary.

16   When all pitting has been removed, and a continuous seating ring obtained, remove the cutter and pilot. Coat the valve seat evenly and lightly with Engineers Blue (or fine valve grinding compound), oil the valve stem and attach a suction tool to the valve head. Insert the valve stem into the guide and press the valve on to its seat. Rotate the valve once (or more often if valve grinding compound is being used) and withdraw it. The marks left by the Engineers Blue or valve grinding compound should form a continuous unbroken ring that is of the

correct width on both valve face and seat, and in the centre of the valve face, as described in paragraph 13 above.

17 If the contact area is too narrow, it may be widened by using the 45° cutter. If it is too wide, it may be narrowed by using either the 30° or 60° cutter; note that the latter two cutters will raise or lower the contact area on the valve face. Remove only the minimum of material to prevent the valve from seating too deeply in the head. If this is allowed to happen, performance will be reduced, valve gear wear will be increased, and difficulties will be encountered when adjusting the valve clearances.

18 Once the correct valve seat widths and positions have been achieved, lightly skim the seat surface with the 45° cutter in order to remove any burrs caused by the cutting procedure. The finished seat surfaces should be matt in appearance and have a smooth finish, thus providing the ideal surface for correct bedding in of the valves once the engine is started. It is not necessary to grind the valves in on completion of the recutting procedure. Be careful to wash off all traces of swarf and foreign matter once the seat recutting operation is finished.

19 Examine the condition of the valve collets and the groove on each valve stem in which they seat. If there is any sign of damage, new parts should be fitted. Check that the spring retaining plates are not cracked. If the collets work loose or the plates split whilst the engine is running, a valve could drop into the cylinder and cause extensive damage.

20 Check the free length of each of the valve springs. The springs have reached their serviceable limit when they have compressed to the limit readings given in the Specifications Section of this Chapter.

21 Reassemble the valve and valve springs by reversing the dismantling procedure. Fit new oil seals to each valve guide and oil both the valve stem and the valve guide with a molybdenum disulphide based lubricant prior to reassembly. Take special care to ensure the valve guide oil seals are not damaged when the valves are inserted. As a final check after assembly, give the end of each valve stem a light tap with a hammer, to make sure the split collets have located correctly. Note that each spring must be fitted with its close coil end nearest the cylinder head.

20.5 Valve spring compressor must be used to permit valve removal

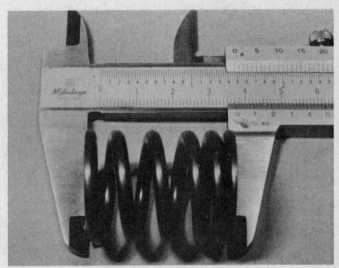

20.20 Measuring valve spring free length

20.21a Fit spring seat over valve guide ...

20.21b ... then fit a new valve guide oil seal

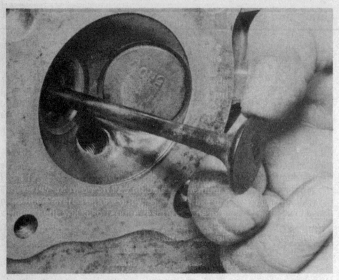

20.21c Oil valve stem before refitting

20.21d Valve spring upper ends identified by dab of paint ...

20.21e ... but note that close-pitched coils are fitted next to cylinder head

20.21f Refit top collar as shown

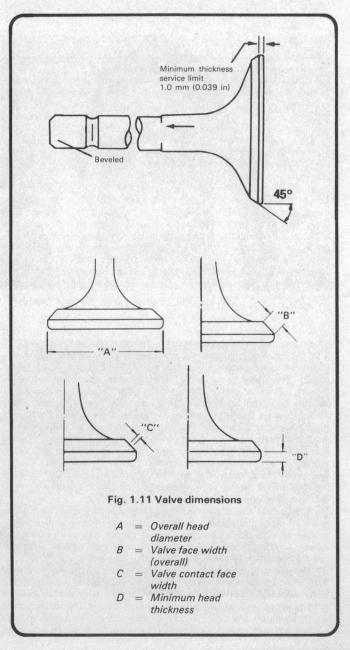

Fig. 1.11 Valve dimensions

A = Overall head diameter
B = Valve face width (overall)
C = Valve contact face width
D = Minimum head thickness

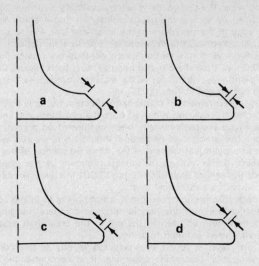

Fig. 1.12 Valve face contact arm

a	Seat too wide	c	Seat too high
b	Correct	d	Seat too low

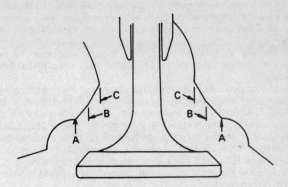

Fig. 1.13 Valve seat re-cutting angles

A 30° cutter
B 45° cutter
C 60° cutter

21 Examination and renovation: cylinder barrel

1   The usual indication of a badly worn cylinder bore and piston is excessive smoking from the exhaust, high crankcase compression which causes oil leaks, and piston slap, a metallic rattle that occurs when there is little or no load on the engine. If the top of the cylinder bore is examined carefully, it will be found that there is a ridge at the front and back, the depth of which will indicate the amount of wear which has taken place. This ridge marks the limit of travel of the top piston ring.

2   Since there is a difference in cylinder wear in different directions, side to side and back to front measurements should be made. Take measurements at three different points down the length of the cylinder bore, starting at a point just below the wear ridge and following this with measurements half way down the bore and at a point just above the lower edge of the bore. If any of these measurements exceed the service limit given in the Specifications Section of this Chapter, the cylinder must be rebored and fitted with an oversize piston. If the barrel has been rebored previously, do not forget to compensate for this by adding the total amount of the rebore to the cylinder standard bore size and service limit.

3   Oversize pistons and piston rings are available in various sizes, according to the year and model. Check with a Yamaha Service Agent before reboring is attempted.

4   If measuring equipment is not available, a reasonable indication of bore wear can be obtained using a set of feeler gauges and a piston that is either new or is known from accurate measurements (See Section 22) to be within the specified wear limits. Insert the piston into the bore from the top, ensuring that the arrow mark cast on the piston crown is facing to the front of the barrel, and push it down until the base of the piston skirt is 20 - 25 mm ($\frac{3}{4}$ - 1 in) below the top surface of the bore. If the gap between the forward side of the piston skirt (ie the thrust face) and the cylinder wall is found to be outside the tolerance for piston/cylinder clearance given in the Specifications Section of this Chapter, the cylinder barrel is excessively worn. Take the piston and barrel to a competent Yamaha Service Agent for accurate checking before reboring is attempted.

5   Check that the surface of the cylinder bore is free from score marks or other damage that may have resulted from an earlier engine seizure or a displaced gudgeon pin. A rebore will be necessary to remove any deep scores, irrespective of the amount of bore wear that has taken place, otherwise a compression leak will occur.

6   When fitting new piston rings to be run in a part-worn cylinder bore, the bore surface must be prepared first by glaze-busting. This is a process which involves the use of a cylinder-bore honing tool, usually in conjunction with an electric drill, to break down the surface glaze which forms on any cylinder bore in normal use. The prepared bore surface will then have a very lightly roughened finish which will assist the new piston rings to bed in rapidly and fully. Furthermore, the lip at the top of the bore, which will have been formed by the bore wearing, must be removed. If this is not done the new top ring will come into contact with the edge and shatter. Most motorcycle dealers have glaze-busting equipment and will be able to carry out the necessary work for a small charge.

7   Clean the cylinder barrel/cylinder head gasket surface and check it for distortion with a straight-edge and a set of feeler gauges. The straight-edge should be laid diagonally across the surface from corner to corner and any clearance between its lower edge and the surface checked with gauges. Repeat the procedure with the straight-edge laid between the opposite corners and then at several positions in between the four corners. If the largest clearance found exceeds 0.05 mm (0.002 in), Yamaha recommend that the cylinder barrel be replaced with a new item. It is worth noting however, that if the amount of distortion found is only slightly greater than the limit given, the advice should be sought of a competent motorcycle engineer who can advise on whether skimming the surface flat is possible without the subsequent risk of the piston coming into contact with the valve heads.

8   Finally, make sure the external cooling fins of the cylinder barrel are not clogged with oil or road dirt which will prevent the free flow of air and cause the engine to overheat.

22 Examination and renovation: piston and piston rings

1   Attention to the piston and piston rings can be overlooked if a rebore is necessary, since new components will be fitted.

2   If a rebore is not necessary, examine the piston carefully. Reject the piston if it is scored or badly discoloured as the result of exhaust gases by-passing the rings.

3   Remove all carbon from the piston crown using a blunt scraper which will not damage the surface of the piston. A scraper made from soft aluminium alloy or hardwood is ideal; never use a hard metal scraper with sharp edges as this will almost certainly gouge the alloy surface of the piston. Clean away carbon deposits from the valve cutaways and finish off with metal polish so that a smooth, shining surface is achieved. Carbon will not adhere so readily to a polished surface.

4   Small high spots on the back and front areas of the piston can be carefully eased back with a fine swiss file. Dipping the file in methylated spirits or rubbing its teeth with chalk will prevent the file clogging and eventually scoring the piston. Only very small quantities of material should be removed, and never enough to interfere with the correct tolerances. Never use emery paper or cloth to clean the piston skirt; the fine particles of emery are inclined to embed themselves in the soft aluminium and accelerate the rate of wear between bore and piston.

5   The piston outside diameter is measured at right angles to the gudgeon pin axis, at a point 7 - 10 mm (0.3 - 0.4 in) above the base of the piston skirt. The piston/cylinder clearance can be calculated by subtracting the piston diameter from the maximum bore measurement; if the clearance figure derived is outside the tolerances given, the barrel must be rebored and an oversize piston fitted.

6   Check that the gudgeon pin is a tight press fit in the piston; if any slackness is apparent, compare the gudgeon pin with a new item. Renew the piston or the gudgeon pin (or both), depending on which is worn.

7   Discard the gudgeon pin circlips; these should never be re-used once they have been disturbed. Obtain new ones to be fitted on reassembly.

8   The piston ring/piston groove clearance must be checked, to ensure that the piston compression rings do not have excessive sidefloat. Measure the clearance with the rings fitted to the piston, using feeler gauges as shown in the accompanying photograph. If this clearance is greater than the service limit given in the Specifications Section of this Chapter, determine by careful measurement and comparison with the figures given which component is worn; if either the piston or the rings are worn to beyond the set service limits, they must be renewed.

9   Finally, check that the gudgeon pin circlip grooves are undamaged and that the piston rings and piston grooves are free from carbon; a short length of old piston ring ground to a chisel profile and fitted with a handle is ideal for scraping carbon deposits from piston ring grooves.

10 Piston ring wear is checked by measuring the end gap. Insert each ring in turn into the cylinder bore having previously established that the bore is within the specified wear limits (see Section 21); the test results will not be accurate if the test is carried out in an excessively worn cylinder bore. Use the piston crown to position each ring squarely in the bore at about 20 mm (0.8 in) from the bottom. Using feeler gauges, measure the ring installed end gap which must not exceed the limits given; if the end gap is excessive the piston rings must be renewed.

11 It is considered by many good practice to renew the rings as a matter of course, regardless of their apparent condition; this course is recommended, particularly if the machine has covered a high mileage. When ordering a new piston or rings, note that if the cylinder has been rebored, the oversize will be indicated by markings stamped on the piston crown, while oversize compression rings are stamped with a number on their upper edge adjacent to the end gap. Oversize oil ring spacers are identified by the following colour codes:

Brown denotes 1st oversize (+ 0.25 mm, 0.01 in)
Blue denotes 2nd oversize (+ 0.50 mm, 0.02 in)
Black denotes 3rd oversize (+ 0.75 mm, 0.03 in)
Yellow denotes 4th oversize (+ 1.00 mm, 0.04 in)

12 Do not assume when fitting new rings that their end gaps will be correct; the installed end gap must be measured as described above to ensure that it is within the specified tolerances; if the gap is too wide another piston ring set must be obtained (having checked again that the bore is within specified wear limits), but if the gap is too narrow it must be widened by the careful use of a fine file.

23 Examination and renovation: crankshaft assembly

1   The most likely areas of crankshaft failure are main bearing failure, accompanied by a low rumbling noise as the engine is running, or big-end bearing failure, accompanied by a pronounced click or knock from the crankcases. In both cases the noise will increase gradually and will be accompanied by increasingly severe levels of vibration which will be felt through the frame and footrests. Excessive wear in the small-end bearing is revealed by an annoying light metallic rattle. Crankshaft wear is unlikely to take place until a very high mileage has been covered, or unless routine maintenance, in the form of regular oil and filter changes, has been neglected.

2   Wash off the crankshaft to remove all traces of oil, then make a close visual inspection of the assembly, using a magnifying glass if necessary. If any obvious signs of damage are encountered, for example bent or distorted mainshafts or connecting rod, cracks or nicks in the connecting rod, damaged mainshaft threads, worn keyways or damaged cam chain sprocket teeth, take the assembly to a good Yamaha Service Agent for his advice; some damage may be reclaimed whereas in other cases the only solution will be the renewal of the crankshaft assembly.

3   Check for wear in the big-end bearing by arranging the connecting rod in the TDC position and by pushing and pulling the connecting rod. No discernible movement will be evident in an unworn bearing, but care must be taken not to confuse end float, which is normal, and

bearing wear. If a dial gauge is readily available, a further test may be carried out by setting the gauge pointer so that it abuts against the upper edge of the periphery of the small-end eye. Measurement may then be taken of the amount of side-to-side deflection of the connecting rod. If this measurement exceeds the service limit of 2.0 mm (0.08 in) then the big-end bearing must be renewed. Check also the big-end side clearance; while a certain amount is intentional, it should not exceed 0.7 mm (0.03 in).

4   Any measurement of crankshaft deflection can only be made with the crankshaft assembly removed from the crankcase and set up on V-blocks which themselves have been positioned on a completely flat surface. The amount of deflection should be measured with a dial gauge at a point just inboard of the threaded portion of the left-hand mainshaft. If the amount of deflection shown by the gauge needle exceeds the service limit of 0.03 mm (0.001 in), the assembly must be replaced with a serviceable item.

5   Check that the gudgeon pin is a tight press fit in the connecting rod small-end eye. If any play is detected compare the gudgeon pin with a new item and renew the pin or the crankshaft assembly (or both), whichever is found to be worn.

6   If any fault is found or suspected in any of the components comprising the crankshaft assembly, it is recommended that the complete crankshaft assembly is taken to a Yamaha Service Agent, who will be able to confirm the worst, and supply a new or service-exchange assembly. The task of dismantling and reconditioning the big-end assembly is a specialist task, and is beyond the scope and facilities of the average owner.

22.5 Measuring piston outside diameter

22.8 Measuring piston ring/groove clearance

23.3 Measuring big-end side clearance (axial clearance)

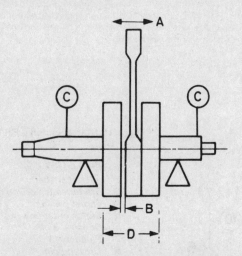

Fig. 1.14 Crankshaft measurement points

A   Big-end radial clearance   D   Crankshaft width
B   Big-end axial clearance   across flywheels
C   Crankshaft runout

24 Examination and renovation: cam chain and tensioner components

1   Examine the chain closely, looking for signs of wear or damage such as cracked, broken, or missing rollers, fractured sideplates, and links that are either stiff or unduly sloppy in action; any such damage will mean that the chain must be renewed. Note also that if the chain was rattling before the engine was dismantled and could not be quietened by tensioner adjustment, or if the tensioner was found to be near the limit of its adjustment range, the chain should be renewed regardless of its apparent condition. It is considered by many a worthwhile precaution to renew the chain as a matter of course, especially if a high mileage has been covered.
2   Renew the camshaft sprocket if its teeth are hooked, chipped or otherwise worn, and examine closely the sprocket retaining bolt and lock washer. The bolt threads must be clean and in good condition, and the lock washer must be renewed if weakened by excessive use.
3   The chain tensioner, like the chain, normally lives a trouble-free life. The mechanism should not, however, be neglected. Check the tensioner blade and the guide blade for wear and for separation of the rubber coating from the backing piece. No specifications are laid down for acceptable blade wear, but it is suggested that the components are

renewed if wear has reduced the thickness of rubber to less than 50%. If the rubber has begun to separate from the blade, the component should be renewed as a matter of course.
4   Examine closely all the components of the tensioner adjusting mechanism; all threads must be clean and undamaged, and the pushrod should be able to slide easily within the adjuster body. Polish away any burns or corrosion which might prevent this. The sealing O-rings should be renewed as a matter of course. Check the condition of the two springs and of the rubber damper between them; these must be renewed if there is the slightest doubt about their efficiency. Note that there is one spring only on all 1982 models, all 1983 models having a secondary smaller spring fitted.

25 Examination and renovation: starter clutch and drive components – SR125 only

1   To check whether the starter clutch is operating correctly, fit the driven gear to the rear of the clutch and rotor. When rotated in a clockwise direction, as viewed from the gear side, the clutch should lock immediately, allowing power to be transmitted from the gear to the crankshaft. When rotated anti-clockwise, the gear should be free to run smoothly. If the movement is unsatisfactory, remove the gear from the clutch. The gear boss should be smooth, scoring or damage to the surface indicates that the rollers are similarly marked and require further inspection.
2   The rollers, springs and plungers may be removed for examination with the clutch still attached to the rear of the rotor. Using a small, flat-bladed screwdriver, carefully push each plunger back against spring pressure until the roller can be removed. Then remove the springs and plungers. Signs of wear will be obvious and will necessitate renewal of the worn or damaged parts.
3   To dismantle the clutch further, the three Allen bolts must be removed. The clutch outer unit and the three dowel pins can now be removed from the rear of the rotor. Examine the clutch outer unit for wear in the form of elongation or scoring of the roller housing. If badly worn, the clutch outer unit must be renewed. Check the condition of the bearing in the centre of the gear boss by refitting the gear to the crankshaft and feeling for free play; if any is felt, the gear must be renewed. Similarly check the fit of the idler gear on its shaft, and the fit of the shaft in the crankcase. Check also that the teeth of the drive gear, idler gear and driven gear are undamaged and in good condition.
4   On reassembly, refit the dowels and clutch outer unit to the rear of the rotor, ensuring that each is located correctly. Thoroughly degrease the threads of the three Allen bolts, apply a few drops of thread locking compound to each, then refit the screws, tightening them securely. Refit the springs, plungers and rollers, using the reverse of the dismantling procedure, then refit the driven gear to the rear of the rotor, rotating it as necessary to engage the rollers on the gear boss. Keep the rotor/clutch assembly and gear together to avoid losing the springs, plungers and rollers.

25.4a First insert coil spring ...

25.4b ... then refit plunger

25.4c Press plunger back to insert clutch roller

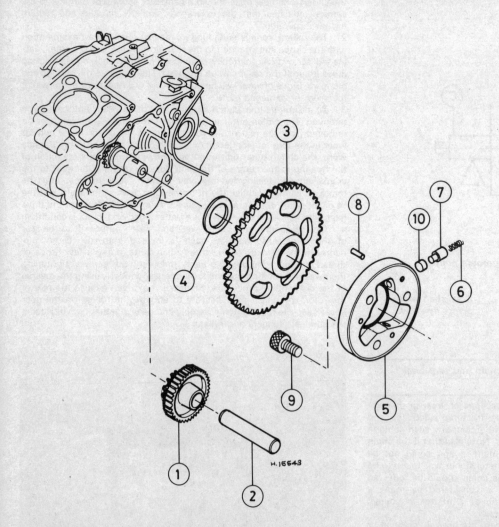

H.16643

Fig. 1.15 Starter clutch – SR125 only

1   Starter idler gear
2   Idler gear shaft
3   Starter clutch driven gear
4   Thrust washer
5   Clutch outer unit
6   Spring – 3 off
7   Plunger – 3 off
8   Locating pin – 3 off
9   Allen bolt – 3 off
10 Roller – 3 off

26 Examination and renovation: primary drive and balancer drive gears

1   The primary driven gear pinion is riveted to the rear of the clutch outer drum and incorporates six small damper units to act as a transmission shock absorber. Check the condition of the dampers by attempting to rotate the clutch outer drum while holding steady the primary driven gear pinion; if movement is excessive or sloppy, the complete assembly must be renewed.

2   Examine the primary drive gears looking for chipped, broken, or worn teeth. If such damage is found the gears must be renewed, but note that matched gears must be renewed always as a pair to avoid the excessive wear and noise that would result from running a part-worn gear with a new component.

3   The above also applies to the balancer shaft drive and driven

gears. Note however that while the balancer drive gear shock absorber can be tested as described above, the components in this case can be renewed if found to be damaged or worn. Place the complete gear pinion in a plastic bag to prevent the loss of any of the springs or dowel pins, then use a small screwdriver to displace the springs, so that the pinion inner and outer halves can be pressed apart. Renew any component which shows signs of wear or damage.

4   Reassembly is the reverse of the above, but note that the assembly can only be rebuilt successfully if the dots on the pinion inner and outer halves are aligned as shown in the accompanying photograph.

27 Examination and renovation: clutch assembly

1   The plain and friction plates should all be given a thorough wash in a petrol/paraffin mix to remove all traces of friction material debris and oil sludge; follow this by cleaning the inside of the clutch drum in a similar manner.

2   The obvious sign of the clutch friction plates having worn beyond their service limit is clutch slip. To check the degree of wear present on the friction plates, measure the thickness of each plate across the faces of the bonded linings and compare the measurement obtained with the information given in the Specifications Section of this Chapter. If any plate has worn below the service limit of 2.6 mm (0.10 in), then the plates must be renewed as a complete set.

3   Check the condition of the tongues around the outer edge of each friction plate, at the same time checking the slots in the clutch drum wall. In an extreme case, clutch chatter may have caused the plate tongues to make indentations in the slots; these indentations will trap the plates as they are freed, impairing clutch action. If the damage is only slight, the indentations can be removed by careful work with a fine file and any burrs removed from the plate tongues in a similar fashion. More extensive damage will necessitate renewal of the parts concerned. Note that there is a definite limit to the amount of material that can be removed from each plate tongue.

4   Check the clutch plain plates for any signs of warpage. This can be achieved by laying each plate on a completely flat surface, such as a sheet of plate glass, and attempting to pass a feeler gauge between the plate and the surface. Both the plate and the surface must be cleaned of all contamination. The maximum allowable warpage for each plain plate is 0.05 mm (0.002 in).

5   The plain plates should be free from scoring and any signs of overheating, which will be apparent in the form of blueing. Check the condition of both the tongues in the inner edge of each plain plate and the slots of the clutch centre. Any slight damage found on either of

these components should be removed by using a method similar to that described for the friction plates and clutch drum. The final check for the plain plates is to measure each plate for thickness.

6   Examine the clutch pressure plate, clutch centre, and the clutch outer drum for wear or damage of any sort. The likelihood of major components such as these wearing to any great extent is unlikely, but the possibility must be borne in mind in order not to overlook a fault. The only remedy for damage or wear is the renewal of the part concerned.

7   The clutch springs do not wear, but over an extended mileage will lose tension and settle to a shorter length, thus reducing the pressure on the plates and promoting clutch slip. Measure the free length of each spring. If any has settled to a length of 33.9 mm (1.34 in) or less, the springs must all be renewed as a complete set.

8   The clutch release mechanism components should be examined for signs of wear, particularly if clutch engagement and disengagement feel rough or jerky. The pushrod must be straight and its ends must be unworn with no signs of excessive heat (blueing), and the clutch release shaft must be unworn and free from corrosion. Renew any component that is worn or damaged.

26.4 Dots must align before inner and outer halves can be reassembled

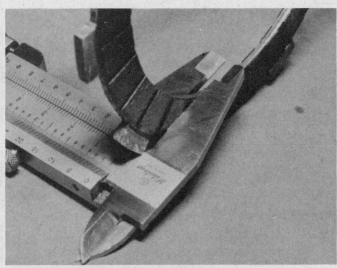

27.2 Measuring clutch friction plate thickness

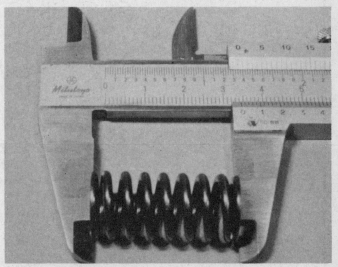

27.7 Measuring clutch spring free length

28 Examination and renovation: kickstart mechanism – XT125 only

1   The kickstart mechanism is a robust assembly and should not normally require attention. Apart from obvious defects such as a broken return spring, the friction clip is the only component likely to cause problems if it becomes worn or weakened. The clip is intended to apply a known amount of drag on the kickstart pinion, causing the latter to run up its quick thread and into engagement when the kickstarter lever is operated.

2   The clip can be checked using a spring balance. Hook one end of the balance onto the looped end of the friction clip. Pull on the free end of the balance and note the reading at the point where pressure overcomes the clip's resistance. This should normally be 1.0 kg (2.2 lb). If the reading is higher or lower than this and the mechanism has been malfunctioning, renew the clip as a precaution. Do not attempt to adjust a worn clip by bending it.

3   Examine the kickstart pinion for wear or damage, remembering to check it in conjunction with the output shaft-mounted idler pinion. In view of the fact that these components are not subject to continuous use, a significant amount of wear or damage is unlikely to be found.

29 Examination and renovation: gearbox components

1   Give the gearbox components a close visual inspection for signs of wear or damage such as broken or chipped teeth, worn dogs, damaged or worn splines and bent selectors. Replace any parts found unserviceable because they cannot be reclaimed in a satisfactory manner.

2   The gearbox shafts are unlikely to sustain damage unless the lubricating oil has been run low or the engine has seized and placed an unusually high loading on the gearbox. Check the surfaces of the shafts, especially where a pinion turns on them, and renew the shafts if they are scored or have picked up. The shafts can be checked for trueness

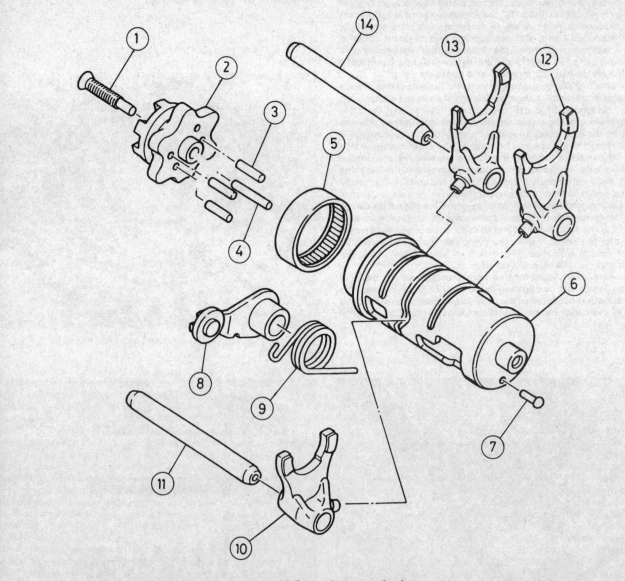

Fig. 1.16 Gear selector mechanism

1 Torx screw	5 Bearing	8 Detent roller arm	12 Selector fork
2 Selector cam	6 Selector drum	9 Return spring	13 Selector fork
3 Pin – 3 off	7 Neutral indicator switch	10 Selector fork	14 Selector fork shaft
4 Pin	contact	11 Selector fork shaft	

by setting them up in V-blocks and measuring any bending with a dial gauge. The procedure for dismantling and rebuilding the gearbox shaft assemblies is given in Section 30 of this Chapter.

3   Examine the gear selector claw assembly noting that worn or rounded ends on the claw can lead to imprecise gear selection. The springs in the selector mechanism and the detent or stopper arm should be unbroken and not distorted or bent in any way.

4   Examine the selector forks carefully, ensuring that there is no sign of scoring on the bearing surface of either their claw ends, their bores or their selector drum guide pins. Check for any signs of cracking around the edges of the bores or at the base of the fork arms.

5   Check each selector fork shaft for straightness by rolling it on a sheet of plate glass and checking for any clearance between the shaft and the glass with feeler gauges. A bent shaft will cause difficulty in selecting gears. There should be no sign of any scoring on the bearing surface of the shaft or any discernible play between each shaft and its selector fork(s).

6   The tracks in the selector drum should not shown signs of undue wear or damage. Check also that the selector drum bearing surfaces are unworn, renew the drum if it is worn or damaged.

7   Note that certain pinions have a bush fitted within their centres. If any one of these bushes appears to be over-worn or in any way damaged, then the pinion should be returned to a Yamaha service agent, who will be able to advise which course of action to take as to its renewal.

8   Finally, carefully inspect the splines of both shafts and pinions for any signs of wear, hairline cracks or breaking down of the hardened surface finish. If any one of these defects is apparent, then the offending component must be renewed. It should be noted that damage and wear rarely occur in a gearbox which has been properly used and correctly lubricated, unless very high mileages have been covered.

9   Clean the gearbox sprocket thoroughly and examine it closely, paying particular attention to the condition of the teeth. The sprocket should be renewed if the teeth are hooked, chipped, broken or badly worn. It is considered bad practice to renew one sprocket on its own; both drive sprockets should be renewed as a pair, preferably with a new final drive chain. Examine the splined centre of the sprocket for signs of wear. If any wear is found, renew the sprocket as slight wear between the sprocket and shaft will rapidly increase due to the torsional forces involved. Remember that as the output shaft will probably wear in unison with the sprocket, it is therefore necessary to carry out a close inspection of the shaft splines.

10   Carefully examine the gear selector components. Any obvious signs of damage, such as cracks, will mean that the part concerned must be renewed. Check that the springs are not weak or damaged and examine all points of contact, eg. selector cam and selector stop arm, for signs of excessive wear. If doubt arises about the condition of any component it must be compared with a new part to assess the amount of wear that has taken place, and renewed if found to be damaged or excessively worn. Do not forget to check the pins set in the selector cam; these must be renewed if bent or worn.

30 Gearbox shafts: dismantling and reassembly

Dismantling – general

1   The gearbox clusters should not be disturbed needlessly, and need only be stripped when careful examination of the whole assembly fails to resolve the source of a problem or where obvious damage, such as stripped or chipped teeth is discovered.

2   The input and output shaft components should be kept separate to avoid confusion during reassembly. Using circlip pliers, remove the circlip and plain washer which retain each part. As each item is removed, place it in order on a clean surface so that the reassembly sequence is self-evident and the risk of parts being fitted the wrong way round or in the wrong sequence is avoided. Care should be exercised when removing circlips to avoid straining or bending them excessively. The clips must be opened just sufficiently to allow them to be slid off the shaft. Note that a loose or distorted circlip might fail in service, and any dubious items must be renewed as a precautionary measure. The same applies to worn or distorted thrust washers.

3   If dismantling of the input shaft assembly proves to be necessary the 2nd gear pinion will have to be pressed from position by using an hydraulic press; no other method of removal is possible. As it is

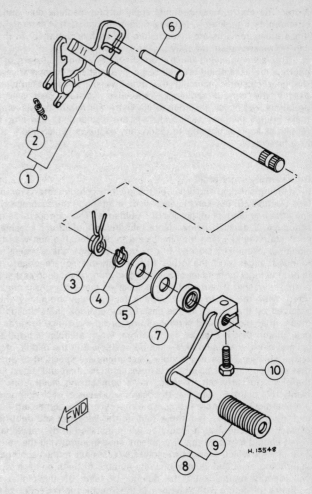

Fig. 1.17 Gearchange shaft

1	Gearchange shaft	6	Return spring anchor
2	Spring	7	Oil seal
3	Return spring	8	Gearchange lever
4	Circlip	9	Rubber
5	Washer	10	Pinch bolt

unlikely that this type of tool will be readily available, it is recommended that the complete shaft assembly be returned to a Yamaha service agent who will be able to remove the pinion, renew any worn or damaged components and return the shaft assembly complete.

4   If an hydraulic press is available and it is decided to attempt removal of the 2nd gear pinion from the input shaft, it is very important to realise fully the dangers involved when using such a tool. Both the tool and the shaft assembly must be set up so that there is no danger of either item slipping. The tool must be correctly assembled in accordance with the maker's instructions as the force exerted by the tool is considerable and perfectly capable of stripping any threads from holding studs or inflicting other damage upon itself and the shaft. Always wear proper eye protection in case a component should fail and shatter before it becomes free, as may happen if the component is flawed. **Before** removing the 2nd gear pinion, measure carefully the distance between the outer faces of the 1st and 2nd gear pinions, as shown in the accompanying photograph, then measure with feeler gauges the clearance between the 4th gear pinion boss and the input shaft splined shoulder; again this is shown in the accompanying photographs. These measurements will vary from machine to machine, but as a guide the measurement made on the machine stripped for the photographs in this Manual were as follows:

Input shaft 1st – 2nd gear width – 90.72 mm (3.57 in)
4th gear pinion/shaft shoulder clearance – 0.203 mm (0.008 in)

Note: The above measurements apply to one machine only and are intended as a guide only, not as a recommendation; it is essential that these measurements are made before the shaft is disturbed, so that it can be reassembled correctly.

5　The accompanying illustration shows how both clusters of the gearbox are assembled on their respective shafts. It is imperative that the gear clusters, including the thrust washers, are assembled in exactly the correct sequence, otherwise constant gear selection problems will occur. In order to eliminate the risk of misplacement, make rough sketches as the clusters are dismantled. Also strip and rebuild as soon as possible to reduce any confusion which might occur at a later date.

Reassembly – general

6　Having checked and renewed the gearbox components as required (see Section 29) reassemble each shaft, referring to the accompanying line drawing and photographs for guidance. The correct assembly sequence is detailed below. Note that the manufacturer specifies a particular way in which the circlips are to be fitted. If a non-wire type circlip is examined closely, it can be seen that one surfaces has rounded edges and the other has sharply-cut square edges, this feature being a by-product of any stamped component such as a circlip or thrust washer. The manufacturer specifies that each circlip must be fitted with the sharp-edged surface facing away from any thrust received by that circlip. In the case of the gearbox shaft circlips this means that the rounded surface of any circlip must face towards the gear pinion that it secures. Furthermore, when a circlip is fitted to a splined shaft, the circlip ears must be positioned in the middle of one of the splines. These two simple precautions are specified to ensure that each circlip is as secure as is possible on its shaft and is best able, therefore, to carry out its task. The accompanying illustrations will clarify this point. Ensure that the bearing surfaces of each component are liberally oiled before fitting. Note that where the terms 'left-hand' and 'right-hand' are used, these refer to the left-hand and right-hand of each component as it would be when installed in the machine.

7　It should be noted that if problems arise in identifying the various gear pinions which cannot be resolved by reference to the accompanying photographs and illustrations, the number of teeth on each pinion will identify them. Count the number of teeth on the pinion and compare this figure with that given in the Specifications Section of this Chapter, remembering that the output shaft pinions are listed first, followed by those on the input shaft. The problem of identification of the various components should not arise, however, if the instructions given in paragraph 2 of this Section are followed carefully.

Input shaft

8　The input shaft is readily identified by its integral 1st gear pinion. Slide the 5th gear pinion into position with the selector dogs facing away from the 1st gear, followed by a splined thrust washer.

9　Ensuring that the circlip is positioned correctly as described above, slide the circlip down the length of the shaft to secure the 5th gear pinion. This is followed by the 3rd gear pinion, which is fitted with its selector fork groove next to 5th gear, and the 4th gear pinion which is fitted with the selector dogs facing towards 3rd gear and is slid down the shaft to butt against the shaft splined shoulder. The 2nd gear pinion must now be fitted.

10　Thoroughly degrease both the input shaft left-hand end and the 2nd gear pinion. Apply a locking compound, such as Loctite Bearing Fit, to the internal surface of the pinion and push it as far as possible over the shaft end and down the length of the shaft. The pinion must be fitted so that the protruding shoulder faces to the right. A means must now be found of pressing the pinion on to the shaft to a precise position. While this can be achieved, using a hammer and a long tubular drift, the method employed in practice was as follows. A vice with a jaw opening of at least 8 inches must be found. Place a soft alloy or wooden cover over one of the vice jaws and place the threaded right-hand end of the shaft against this cover. Slip a socket or tubular drift of suitable length and diameter over the left-hand end of the shaft and position this against the other vice jaw. With the socket or tubular drift bearing only on the surface of the pinion, tighten the vice until the outer faces of the 1st and 2nd gear pinions are precisely the previously measured distance apart; this can be confirmed by measuring the clearance between the 4th gear pinion and the shaft shoulder. Check the measurement frequently as the vice is tightened, using a micrometer or vernier gauge for absolute accuracy.

11　Spin the 4th gear pinion by hand; it is essential that it is free to rotate easily. If the pinion does become locked, whether by contact with the 2nd gear pinion or by the action of the locking compound, the 2nd gear pinion must be removed again for all components to be cleaned, checked, and refitted correctly.

Output shaft

12　Hold the output shaft by its splined left-hand end and place the 3rd gear pinion over the shaft right-hand end with its selector dogs facing to the right. Slide the pinion down to butt against the shaft shoulder, fit a splined thrust washer to locate it and secure both components with a circlip.

13　Slide the 5th gear pinion into place so that its selector fork groove is next to the 3rd gear pinion. The 1st gear pinion is fitted with its recessed face towards the left, and is followed by a plain thrust washer. On XT125 models secure all components by refitting the circlip, but on SR125 models an elastic band must be tightened around the shaft end to prevent the loss of any components.

14　Holding the shaft by its right-hand end, place the 4th gear pinion over the shaft left-hand end, then slide the pinion down so that its selector fork groove butts against the 3rd gear pinion. This is followed by the 2nd gear pinion, which is fitted with its flat surface to the left. The last item to be fitted is a plain thrust washer. Tighten an elastic band over the shaft end.

30.4 Measure input shaft 1st-2nd gear width as shown before disturbing 2nd gear pinion

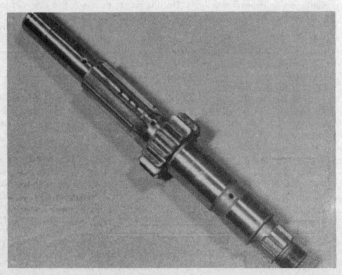

30.8a Input shaft is identified by integral 1st gear pinion

30.8b Fit 5th gear pinion as shown ...

30.8c ... followed by splined thrust washer ...

30.9a ... and secured by a circlip

30.9b 3rd gear pinion is fitted as shown ...

30.9c ... and is followed by 4th gear pinion

30.9d 2nd gear pinion must be pressed into place

30.10 Measuring 4th gear pinion/shaft shoulder clearance – note careful use of vice

30.12a The output shaft

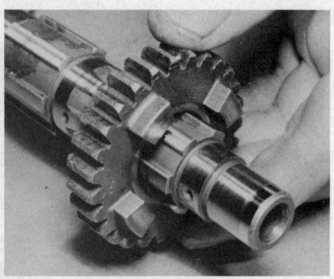

30.12b 3rd gear pinion is fitted as shown over shaft right-hand end ...

30.12c ... and is followed by a splined thrust washer ...

30.12d ... and a circlip

30.13a 5th gear pinion is fitted as shown

30.13b 1st gear pinion recessed face must be to the left, as shown

30.13c Do not omit thrust washer from shaft right-hand end

30.14a 4th gear pinion is fitted as shown over shaft left-hand end ...

30.14b ... and is followed by 2nd gear pinion, as shown, and by ...

30.14c ... the thrust washer. Note precautions taken to prevent oil seal damage (see Section 34)

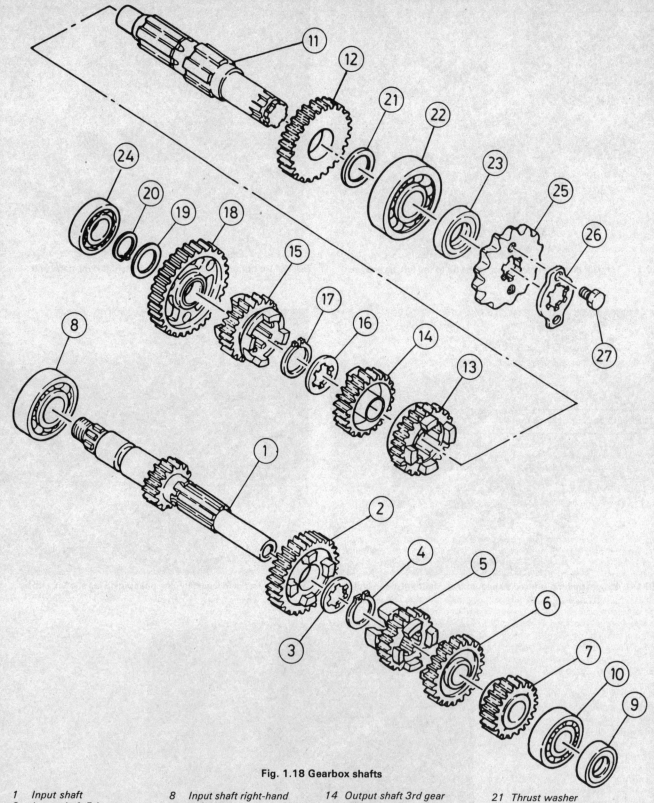

Fig. 1.18 Gearbox shafts

1	Input shaft	8	Input shaft right-hand bearing
2	Input shaft 5th gear pinion	9	Oil seal
3	Splined thrust washer	10	Input shaft left-hand bearing
4	Circlip	11	Output shaft
5	Input shaft 3rd gear pinion	12	Output shaft 2nd gear pinion
6	Input shaft 4th gear pinion	13	Output shaft 4th gear pinion
7	Input shaft 2nd gear pinion		

14	Output shaft 3rd gear pinion	21	Thrust washer
15	Output shaft 5th gear pinion	22	Output shaft left-hand bearing
16	Splined thrust washer	23	Oil seal
17	Circlip	24	Output shaft right-hand bearing
18	Output shaft 1st gear pinion	25	Gearbox sprocket
19	Thrust washer	26	Sprocket retaining plate
20	Circlip – XT model only	27	Bolt – 2 off

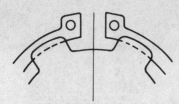

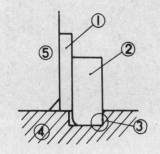

Fig. 1.19 Correct fitting of a circlip to a splined shaft

1   *Thrust washer*   4   *Shaft*
2   *Circlip*   5   *Gear pinion*
3   *Square edge*

31 Engine reassembly: general

1   Before reassembly of the engine/gearbox unit is commenced, the various component parts should be cleaned thoroughly and placed on a sheet of clean paper, close to the working area.

2   Make sure all traces of old gaskets have been removed and that the mating surfaces are clean and undamaged. Great care should be taken when removing old gasket compound not to damage the mating surface. Most gasket compounds can be softened using a suitable solvent such as methylated spirits, acetone or cellulose thinner. The type of solvent required will depend on the type of compound used. Gasket compound of the non-hardening type can be removed using a soft brass-wire brush of the type used for cleaning suede shoes. A considerable amount of scrubbing can take place without fear of harming the mating surfaces. Some difficulty may be encountered when attempting to remove gaskets of the self-vulcanising type, the use of which is becoming widespread, particularly as cylinder head and base gaskets. The gasket should be pared from the mating surface using a scalpel or a small chisel with a finely honed edge. Do not, however, resort to scraping with a sharp instrument.

3   Gather together all the necessary tools and have available an oil can filled with clean engine oil. Make sure that all new gaskets and oil seals are to hand, also all replacement parts required. Nothing is more frustrating than having to stop in the middle of a reassembly sequence because a vital gasket or replacement has been overlooked. As a general rule each moving engine component should be lubricated thoroughly as it is fitted into position.

4   Make sure that the reassembly area is clean and that there is adequate working space. Refer to the torque and clearance setting whenever they are given. Many of the smaller bolts are easily sheared if overtightened. Always use the correct size screwdriver bit for the cross-head screws and never an ordinary screwdriver or punch. If the existing screws show evidence of maltreatment in the past, it is advisable to renew them as a complete set.

32 Reassembling the engine/gearbox unit: preparing the crankcases

1   At this stage the crankcase castings should be clean and dry with any damage, such as worn threads, repaired. If any bearings are to be refitted, the crankcase casting must be heated first as described in Section 15.

2   Place the heated casting on a wooden surface, fully supported around the bearing housing. When refitting the input shaft left-hand bearing, remember to insert first the oil seal into the bearing housing. Position the bearing on the casting, ensuring that it is absolutely square to its housing then tap it fully into place using a hammer and a tubular drift such as a socket spanner which bears only on the bearing outer race. Be careful to ensure that the bearing is kept absolutely square to its housing at all times.

3   Oil seals are fitted into a cold casing in a similar manner. Apply a thin smear of grease to the seal circumference to aid the task, then tap the seal into its housing using a hammer and a tubular drift which bears only on the hard outer edge of the seal, thus avoiding any risk of the seal's being distorted. Tap each seal into place until its flat outer surface is just flush with the surrounding crankcase.

4   Where retaining plates are employed to secure bearings or oil seals, thoroughly degrease the threads of the mounting screws, apply a few drops of thread locking compound to them, and tighten them securely.

5   When all bearings and oil seals have been fitted and secured, lightly lubricate the bearings with clean engine oil and apply a thin smear of grease to the sealing lips of each seal.

6   Support the crankcase right-hand half on two wooden blocks placed on the work surface; there must be sufficient clearance to permit the crankshaft and input shaft to be fitted.

32.2 Keep bearing square to its housing as it is refitted. Note that drift bears only on bearing outer race

32.3a Smear grease over seals to assist refitting

32.3b Ensure seal is just flush with surrounding housing, as shown

33.1 Excessive force will not be required to fit crankshaft

33 Reassembling the engine/gearbox unit: refitting the crankshaft and gearbox components

1   Refit temporarily the rotor retaining bolt to the crankshaft left-hand end and screw the bolt in as far as possible to prevent damage or distortion during crankshaft fitting. Push the crankshaft as far as possible into the right-hand main bearing, using a smear of oil to ease the task, check that it is absolutely square to the crankcase, and tap it fully into place using only a soft-faced mallet. Remove the protecting bolt.

2   Excessive force will not be required to fit the crankshaft; a few firm taps should be sufficient. If any difficulty is encountered do not risk damaging the crankshaft by resorting to excessive force, take the components to a Yamaha Service Agent for the crankshaft to be drawn into place using the correct service tool.

3   Fit the assembled gear clusters together, ensuring that all pinions are correctly meshed, and lower the assembly as a single unit into the crankcase half. Use a soft-faced mallet to tap the input shaft into its bearing, noting that force will not be necessary. Check that both shafts are fully in place and free to rotate. Do not forget to remove any elastic bands.

33.3 Fit gear clusters as a single unit

4   Engage the selector fork on the input shaft 3rd gear pinion, using the marks or notes made on dismantling to identify the fork and placing it so that its marked surface faces to the left.

5   The selector forks can be identified, if necessary by the numbers cast in their left-hand faces; fork number '1' fits on the input shaft 3rd gear pinion, number '2' fits on the output shaft 5th gear pinion, and number '3' fits on the output shaft 4th gear pinion.

6   Swing the selector fork away from the drum so that the drum can be inserted into its bearing. Check that the neutral indicator switch contact is firmly fixed in the drum left-hand end, then rotate the drum so that the contact is in the 6 o'clock position (if the input shaft is at 12 o'clock), thus assembling the transmission in neutral. Swing the selector fork across until its guide pin locates in the drum centre track, then lubricate the selector fork shaft and push it through the fork bore fully into its crankcase housing.

7   Using the marks made of dismantling, identify the two remaining selector forks and engage each in turn on its correct respective output shaft pinion and selector drum track; position each fork so that its marked surface faces to the left. Lubricate the selector fork shaft and press it firmly through both fork bores and into its crankcase housing.

8   Insert the balancer shaft into its bearing and tap it into place, using only a soft-faced mallet.

9   Make a final check that all components have been correctly fitted, that all bearing surfaces are well lubricated, and that all shafts are free to rotate. Rotate the selector drum to check that all gears can be selected, then return the drum to the neutral position.

33.4 Fit single selector fork, then swing away ...

33.6a ... so that selector drum can be refitted, then swing back ...

33.6b ... so that selector fork shaft can be inserted

33.7a Identify forks and refit number '2' fork as shown ...

33.7b ... followed by number '3' fork ...

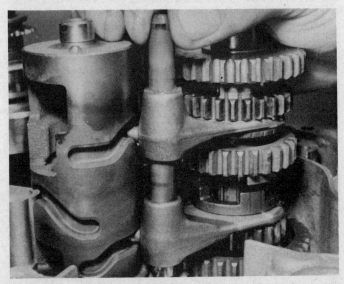

33.7c ... then refit selector fork shaft

33.8 Do not forget to refit balancer shaft

34 Reassembling the engine/gearbox unit: joining the crankcase halves

1   Apply a thin film of sealing compound to the gasket surface of the crankcase right-hand half, then press the two locating dowels firmly into their recesses in the crankcase mating surface. Make a final check that all components are in position and that all bearings and bearing surfaces are lubricated and remove the rubber band from the output shaft end. To prevent any risk of damage to the output shaft oil seal as the shaft splines pass through it, temporarily fit a spare O-ring to the groove machined in the shaft end, and smear a liberal quantity of grease over it.
2   Lower the crankcase left-hand half into position, using firm hand pressure only to push it home. It may be necessary to give a few gentle taps with a soft-faced mallet to drive the casing fully into place. Do not use excessive force, instead be careful to check that all shafts and dowels are correctly fitted and accurately aligned, and that the crankcase halves are exactly square to each other. If necessary, pull away the crankcase left-hand half to rectify the problem before starting again.
3   When the two halves have joined correctly and without strain, refit the crankcase retaining screws using the cardboard template to position each screw correctly. Working in a diagonal sequence from the centre outwards, progressively tighten the screws until all are securely and evenly fastened; the recommended torque setting is 0.7 kgf m (5 lbf ft).
4   Wipe away any excess sealing compound from around the joint area, then check the free running and operation of the crankshaft and gearbox components. If a particular shaft is stiff to rotate, a smart tap on each end using a soft-faced mallet, will centralise the shaft in its bearing. If this does not work, or if any other problem is encountered, the crankcases must be separated again to find and rectify the fault. If this suggestion was employed, do not forget to remove the O-ring from the output shaft end and to wipe away any surplus grease. Pack clean rag into the crankcase mouth to prevent the entry of dirt, then refit the crankcase drain plug, not forgetting its filter gauze and coil spring. Tighten the drain plug to a torque setting of 4.3 kgf m (31 lbf ft).

34.1 Apply sealing compound to gasket surface – do not forget locating dowel

35 Reassembling the engine/gearbox unit: refitting the gear selector external components

1   Insert the four pins into the rear face of the selector cam. The single longer pin fits into the drilling with a punch mark next to it,

nearest to the neutral detent cut-out in the cam. The remaining three pins are refitted as shown in the accompanying illustration.
2   Refit the cam on the selector drum right-hand end, taking care not to dislodge any pins and noting that the cam is located by the engagement of its central boss in the drum end, but that the cam is aligned by the longer pin fitting into a drilling in the drum. Degrease the threads of the cam retaining Torx screw, apply a few drops of thread locking compound and refit the screw, tightening it to a torque setting of 1.2 kgf m (9 lbf ft).
3   Refit the gearchange shaft return spring to the shaft, ensuring that the spring ends are correctly engaged as shown in the accompanying photograph, then refit the circlip to retain the spring. This is followed by a large plain washer, the detent roller arm and its return spring, and a second plain washer. Refer to the accompanying photograph to ensure that all components are correctly refitted.
4   To protect the lips of the shaft oil seal as the shaft is refitted, wrap a thin layer of insulating tape around the splines or smear a liberal quantity of grease over them. Refit the shaft assembly but slide it only partly into place, as shown in the accompanying photographs. Slide the detent arm only down the shaft, check that its return spring is correctly located, then press it into place on the selector cam, where it should engage in the neutral position cut-out. Swing the selector claw arm into line with the drum.
5   Press the gearchange arm fully into place, ensuring that its return spring free ends locate one on each side of the crankcase stop and that the claw arm engages correctly with the pins set in the selector cam.
6   Temporarily refit the gearchange lever to the shaft splines and check that all gears can be selected, rotating the input shaft to assist selection. While a certain amount of difficulty is inevitable, it should be possible to select all gears with relative ease, whether changing up or down. If any undue difficulty is encountered, the cause must be found and rectified before reassembly work can proceed.

36 Reassembling the engine/gearbox unit: refitting the kickstart shaft and idler gear – XT125 only

1   Refit the circlip on the innermost of the two grooves machined in the output shaft right-hand end. Place a thrust washer over the shaft end, followed by the kickstart idler gear; note that one side of the idler gear has a protruding boss while the other side is heavily chamfered around its edge. The chamfered side must face outwards. Secure the idler gear with the second thrust washer and a circlip.
2   If the kickstart assembly was dismantled for repair work, it must now be rebuilt and offered up to the crankcase as a single unit. Place the kickstart pinion on the workbench with its flat surface downwards and install the friction clip so that its looped end points upwards. Place the kickstart pinion over the end of the kickstart shaft with the friction clip pointing inwards, towards the shaft left-hand end, and slide the pinion down the shaft to engage with the large diameter splines, then refit the large plain washer which locates against the shaft shoulder. Place the kickstart return spring over the shaft with both spring ends facing inwards, towards the large diameter splines, and insert the spring short inner end into its locating hole in the kickstart shaft. Refit the white nylon spring guide onto the shaft, ensuring that the cut-out on one end is facing inwards and engages with the spring inner end, then refit the circlip and the two thrust washers.
3   Lubricate all bearing surfaces of the kickstart assembly and insert the assembly into the crankcase. As the end of the shaft fits into its housing in the crankcase wall, ensure that the large shaft stopper arm locates correctly against the stop cast in the crankcase wall, and that the friction clip looped end fits into the recess provided for it. Make a quick check to ensure that the kickstart assembly is operating correctly by rotating the shaft as far as possible anti-clockwise. The shaft should rotate smoothly and easily until the stopper arm comes into contact with its second stop, and the kickstart pinion should move easily up its shaft splines to engage with the teeth of the idler gear. Return the shaft to its normal position by rotating it clockwise and use a suitable pair of pliers to bring the return spring long hooked end around so that it can be engaged on the long stop dowel protruding from crankcase wall. Take care at this point to ensure that the spring end is hooked firmly around the stop, as the spring will be under quite heavy pressure. Since the gearchange shaft and kickstart mechanism return springs share the same stop, be careful to ensure that neither fouls the correct operation of the other.

35.1 Ensure selector pins are correctly refitted in cam, as shown

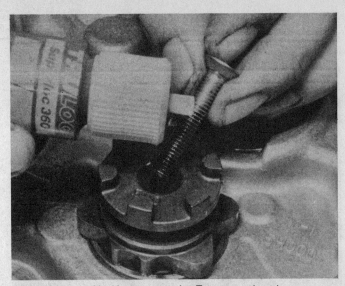

35.2 Apply thread locking compound to Torx screw threads

35.3a Gearchange shaft return spring must be fitted as shown and secured by circlip

35.3b Fit first plain washer against circlip ...

35.3c ... followed by detent roller arm and return spring

35.3d Do not omit second plain washer

35.4a First engage detent roller arm on selector cam ...

35.4b ... then refit selector claw arm, as shown

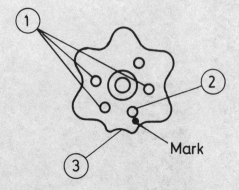

Fig. 1.20 Arrangement of pins in selector cam

1   Short pins – 3 off   3   Neutral position
2   Long pin

37 Reassembling the engine/gearbox unit: refitting the oil pump and the primary and balance shaft drive gears

1   Place its coil spring over the oil feed quill and insert both into the crankshaft right-hand end, maintaining finger pressure while the pin is refitted fully into the crankshaft cross-drilling to retain the two. Check that the feed quill is free to move in and out against spring pressure.

2   Place the first thick washer over the crankshaft end, sliding it down to rest against the bearing. This washer has no cut-out for the Woodruff key. Refit the balancer drive gear, marked face to the right, aligning its Woodruff key cut-out exactly with the crankshaft keyway. Insert the Woodruff key, ensuring that it covers the end of the oil feed quill retaining pin. Refit the thick washer aligning its keyway with the Woodruff key.

3   Refit the primary drive gear followed by the retaining nut and its lock washer, so that the lock washer inner tab engages with the gear keyway. Lock the crankshaft by the method used on dismantling and tighten the retaining nut to a torque setting of 5.0 kgf m (36 lbf ft), then retain it securely by bending up one of the lock washer tabs against a flat of the nut.

4   Refit its Woodruff key to the balancer shaft, then refit the balancer driven gear, rotating both crankshaft and balancer shaft so that as the driven gear engages the Woodruff key, its teeth mesh with those of the drive gear, with the timing marks aligned exactly. This is shown in the photographs accompanying the text and is essential to ensure that the balancer shaft is positioned accurately in relation to the crankshaft. Severe vibration will result if the balancer shaft is not accurately timed.

5   Refit the balancer driven gear retaining nut and its lock washer, engaging the lock washer inner tab with the gear keyway. Lock the balancer drive gears by the method used on dismantling and tighten the retaining nut to a torque setting of 5.0 kgf m (36 lbf ft), then retain it securely by bending up one of the lock washer tabs against one flat of the nut.

6   Fit a new oil pump gasket to the crankcase wall and liberally oil the pump, ensuring that all its passages are well lubricated. Rotate the pump nylon driven gear until the mounting screw holes are revealed by the three apertures in the gear. Refit the pump, rotating the crankshaft to ensure that the gear teeth mesh correctly. Apply a few drops of thread locking compound to the threads of each of the retaining screws then refit all three screws, tightening them evenly to a torque setting of 0.7 kgf m (5 lbf ft). Rotate the crankshaft to check that the pump rotates easily, then clip the pump driven gear metal cover into place.

37.1a First thick washer has no cutout for Woodruff key

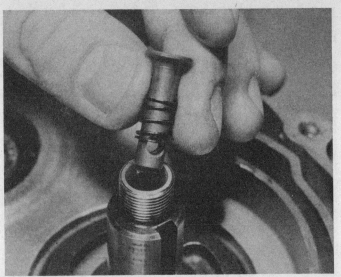

37.1b Insert oil feed quill and spring into crankshaft end ...

37.1c ... and secure by refitting pin

37.1d Balancer drive gear marked face must be visible – align keyways as shown ...

37.1e ... then refit Woodruff key so that pin end is covered

37.1f Second thick washer will engage Woodruff key – refit as shown

37.3a Refit primary drive gear

37.3b Lock washer inner tab engages with gear keyway

37.3c Note method used to lock crankshaft while retaining nut is fastened

37.3d Use lock washer to secure nut as shown – repeat for balancer shaft

37.4 Balancer timing marks (arrowed) must align exactly

37.6a Apply thread locking compound to pump retaining screw threads ...

37.6b ... and tighten screws securely

37.6c Do not forget to refit pump driven gear cover

38 Reassembling the engine/gearbox unit: refitting the clutch

1   Liberally grease the clutch release shaft, refit its return spring, then insert the shaft fully into the crankcase ensuring that the return spring is correctly engaged and that the shaft is rotated to the correct position, as shown in the accompanying photographs. Fit a new sealing washer to the shaft retaining screw, apply thread locking compound to its threads and refit the screw, tightening it securely to a torque setting of 1.2 kgf m (9 lbf ft).

2   Liberally oil the clutch pushrod and insert it into the input shaft, using the wear marks on each end to ensure that the pushrod is refitted the right way round. Refit the steel ball.

3   Oil the bush at its centre, then refit the clutch outer drum, ensuring that its teeth mesh correctly with the primary drive gear and (on XT125 models only) the kickstart idler gear. Refit the thick thrust washer and the clutch centre.

4   Refit the retaining nut lock washer, noting that its smaller tab must engage with the slot in the clutch centre boss. Refit the nut, lock the clutch centre by the method used on dismantling, and tighten the nut to a torque setting of 5.0 kgf m (36 lbf ft). Secure the nut by bending up against one of its flats one of the lock washer tabs and check that the clutch centre and outer drum are free to rotate independently of each other.

5   If new clutch friction plates are to be fitted, they should be coated first with a film of oil. Starting with a friction plate followed by a plain plate, build up the plates alternately to finish with a friction plate.

6   Temporarily insert the short pushrod into the input shaft to check that the release shaft is correctly engaged. Rotate the release shaft to the front of the engine and feel for pressure on the end of the short pushrod, then release the shaft and press in the short pushrod. If the movement seems rough or jerky, the cause must be found. If all is well, remove the pushrod and screw on to it the hexagon-headed release plate. Insert the two into the pressure plate, ensuring that the hexagon of the release plate is engaged with that of the pressure plate, then refit the adjuster locknut. Check that the O-ring is fitted securely to the short pushrod left-hand end then refit the pushrod/pressure plate assembly, ensuring that the pushrod enters the input shaft and that the pressure plate engages correctly on the spring posts and teeth of the clutch centre.

7   Holding the pressure plate firmly, unscrew fully the release adjuster mechanism. Refit the clutch springs and their retaining bolts. Working progressively and in a diagonal sequence, tighten the retaining bolts securely to a torque setting of 0.6 kgf m (4 lbf ft).

8   The clutch release mechanism must now be adjusted. Slacken, if necessary, the adjuster locknut and rotate the release shaft by pushing the operating arm as far as possible towards the front of the engine by hand. Maintain hand pressure and screw in (or out) the adjuster until the pointed end of the operating arm aligns exactly with the index mark, a protrusion cast in the crankcase top surface, as shown in the accompanying photograph. Hold the adjuster so that it cannot rotate and tighten securely the locknut. Do not overtighten the nut; the recommended torque setting is 0.8 kgf m (6 lbf ft).

9   Check the clutch adjustment. With the cable disconnected, the operating lever pointed end should return under spring pressure to a small distance behind the crankcase index mark. If the lever is pushed forwards, a small amount of free play should be felt before firm resistance is encountered exactly when the lever pointed end aligns with the index mark.

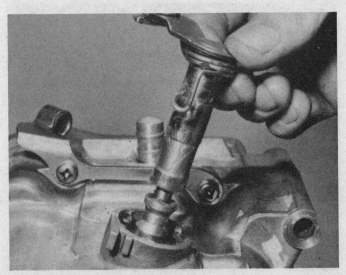

38.1a Grease thoroughly release shaft before refitting

38.1b Ensure that return spring is correctly engaged

38.1c Tighten securely shaft retaining screw

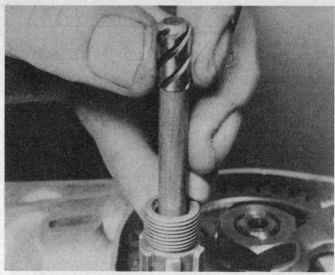

38.2a First refit clutch pushrod ...

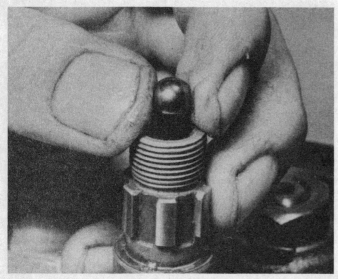

38.2b ... then insert steel ball

38.3a Clutch outer drum is fitted over input shaft end

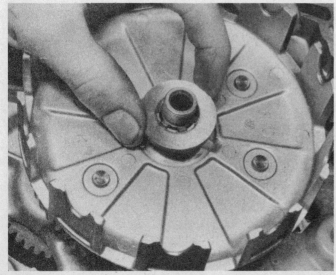

38.3b Do not forget the thick thrust washer ...

38.3c ... before refitting the clutch centre

38.4a Note tool fabricated to hold clutch centre while retaining nut is tightened (or slackened)

38.4b Use lock washer to secure retaining nut as shown

38.5a Fit clutch plain and ...

38.5b ... friction plates alternately

38.6a Clutch short pushrod is assembled as shown ...

38.6b ... and engages with centre of pressure plate

38.7 Tighten securely clutch spring retaining bolts

38.8a Use release mechanism adjuster as shown ...

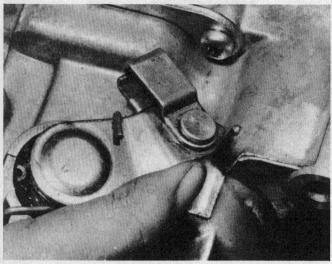

38.8b ... so that operating arm pointed end aligns exactly with crankcase index mark

39 Reassembling the engine/gearbox unit: refitting the crankcase right-hand cover

1   On SR125 models only, do not forget to fit the starter motor before refitting the crankcase cover. Refer to Section 40, paragraph 3.
2   Check that all components are correctly fitted and secured, and that all bearing surfaces are lubricated. Refit the two locating dowels into their recesses in the crankcase gasket surface and fit a new gasket, using a smear of grease to stick it in place.
3   If the kickstart shaft oil seal was removed, it must now be refitted. Smear grease over the sealing lips of the seal.
4   Lower the cover into position, using only firm hand pressure to press it home and ensuring that it is aligned correctly on the crankshaft and on the locating dowels. It may be necessary to give a few taps with a soft-faced mallet to seat the cover, but do not force it into position if resistance is encountered, remove instead the cover and rectify the problem before starting again.
5   Refit the cover retaining bolts, using the cardboard template to position correctly each screw and not forgetting to renew the sealing washer under the head of the bolt above and to the right of the filler plug orifice. Working progressively and in a diagonal sequence from the centre outwards, tighten securely the cover retaining bolts to a torque setting of 0.7 kgf m (5 lbf ft).
6   Renew the two O-rings fitted in the oil filter chamber and cap, using a smear of grease to stick them in place. Insert the filter into the chamber, refit the chamber cap, then refit and tighten securely the cap retaining screws to a torque setting of 0.7 kgf m (5 lbf ft) and the filter chamber drain plug to a torque setting of 1.0 kgf m (7 lbf ft).

40 Reassembling the engine/gearbox unit: refitting the cam chain, the starter motor and drive components, the generator and ignition components, the neutral indicator switch and the crankcase left-hand cover

1   Loop the cam chain over the crankshaft left-hand end, engage it on the drive sprocket and feed the remainder up through the crankcase tunnel. Secure the chain to prevent it from dropping into the crankcase. Lower the tensioner blade through the crankcase tunnel and engage it on its bottom mountings. Apply thread locking compound to their threads and refit the two mounting bolts, tightening each to a torque setting of 0.8 kgf m (6 lbf ft). Check that the tensioner blade is free to move on its pivot.
Note: if the cylinder head and barrel are to be refitted, it is best to do this now, so that the camshaft can be set with the crankshaft aligned in the TDC position according to the more accurate timing marks stamped on the crankshaft sprocket and cast in the crankcase wall (see accompanying photograph). Alternatively, the generator rotor and crankcase left-hand cover can be refitted so that the timing marks stamped in the rotor rim and cast in the rim of the upper inspection aperture can be used. Refer to Section 41, paragraph 12.
2   On SR125 models only, refit the thrust washer against the crankshaft sprocket, followed by the starter clutch driven gear. On all models, refit the Woodruff key in the crankshaft keyway, then refit the generator rotor, aligning its keyway with the key. On SR125 models, ensure that the starter clutch rollers engage correctly. Refit the rotor retaining bolt and its lock washers, hold the rotor by applying an open-ended spanner to the flats of its centre boss and tighten the bolt to a torque setting of 5.0 kgf m (36 lbf ft).
3   On SR125 models only, refit the starter motor and drive components. Renew the O-ring set in the motor mounting boss, smear it with grease and offer up the motor, ensuring that it is correctly aligned. Tighten the two mounting screws securely. Position the starter idler gear between the motor shaft and the driven gear, then secure it by pushing the shaft through the gear and into its crankcase housing. Ensure that the starter motor lead is routed correctly through the channel formed by projections cast in the crankcase and that it is

retained by the clamp at the crankcase joint underneath the rear of the unit.

4   On all models, fit a new sealing washer to the neutral indicator switch and refit the switch. Do not overtighten it.

5   Refit the two locating dowels to the crankcase gasket surface and place a new gasket over them, using a smear of grease to stick it in place. If the alternator and ignition source and pulser coils were removed, they must now be refitted. Refit first the coils, then the wiring clamps ensuring that the wiring of each component is correctly routed and cannot be trapped or pinched, then press the sealing grommet into its recess in the cover wall. Apply a few drops of thread locking compound to the threads of each of the screws, then refit and tighten securely the screws.

6   Lower the cover into place, ensuring that the wiring is correctly routed, and tap it home using a soft-faced mallet. Refit the retaining screws using the cardboard template to position them correctly. Working progressively and in a diagonal sequence from the centre outwards tighten securely all eight screws to a torque setting of 0.7 kgf m (5 lbf ft).

7   Route carefully the neutral indicator switch lead. It may be necessary to trim the gasket to enable the lead to fit into its channel. Then connect the lead to the switch. Do not overtighten the switch terminal screw.

39.1 SR125 only – starter motor must be refitted before crankcase right-hand cover

39.2 Always use a new gasket – note two locating dowels (arrowed)

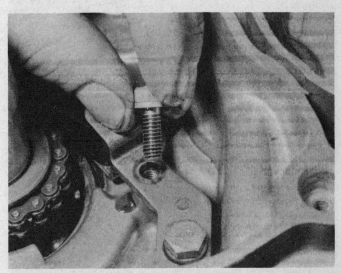

40.1a Apply thread locking compound to threads of tensioner bottom mounting bolts

40.1b Crankshaft and crankcase timing marks (arrowed) can be aligned to set crankshaft at TDC

40.2a SR125 only – refit thrust washer against crankshaft sprocket ...

40.2b ... followed by starter clutch driven gear

40.2c Engage rollers of starter clutch when refitting rotor

40.2d Hold rotor as shown while tightening retaining bolt

40.3a Refit starter idler gear and shaft ...

40.3b ... and route carefully starter motor lead, as shown – SR125 only

40.5 Always use a new gasket – note two locating dowels arrowed

40.7 Press neutral lead into channel so that it does not foul sprocket cover

---

41 Reassembling the engine/gearbox unit: refitting the piston, cylinder barrel and cylinder head

1   Refit the piston rings to the piston, using the method employed on removal. The first component to be fitted is the oil control ring central spacer, followed by its two side rails which are fitted one on each side of the spacer; while none of these component have a specific top or bottom surface when new, if part-worn components are being reused the wear marks will reveal which way up they were originally fitted. Always refit part-worn components in their exact original locations, to prevent excessive wear.

2   The top surface of each compression ring is marked; refer to the accompanying illustration to identify the top and second compression rings, then refit them. Rotate the rings so that their end gaps are aligned as shown in the next illustration.

3   Fit a new circlip to the groove in one of the piston bosses, then insert the gudgeon pin from the opposite side of the piston. If the gudgeon pin is a very tight fit, heat the piston as described in Section 6 of this Chapter. Do not allow the gudgeon pin to project beyond the inside of the boss.

4   Bring the connecting rod to the top of its stroke and lubricate the small-end eye and gudgeon pin. Pack the crankcase mouth and cam chain tunnel with clean rag. Place the piston over the connecting rod ensuring that the arrow embossed on the piston crown is facing to the front of the engine unit, then push through the gudgeon pin. Secure the gudgeon pin by fitting the second circlip and ensure that both circlips are correctly located in their grooves. Never re-use old circlips; new ones should be used always.

5   Refit both locating dowels in their recesses around the left-hand pair of larger diameter cylinder retaining bolts, then fit a new cylinder base gasket, using a smear of grease to stick it in place. Place a new O-ring in the recess around the right-hand rear retaining bolt thread and around the base of the barrel spigot. Oil the piston rings, piston and bore liberally, then refit the cylinder barrel.

6   If a piston ring compressor is not available, insert the piston crown into the cylinder bore, ensuring that the piston is absolutely square to the bore, and compress by hand each ring in turn while pressing the barrel down with a gentle twisting motion to help the rings enter the bore. While a generous lead-in is provided to help this task, great care must be taken or the piston rings will break.

7   Pull the barrel down until the entire piston is in the cylinder bore, then hold the barrel in that position while the rag is removed and the cam chain is passed up through the tunnel in the barrel casting. Keeping the cam chain taut, slide the barrel down to rest on the gasket surface, then refit and tighten, by hand only, the barrel retaining Allen bolts, not forgetting the clutch cable adjuster (XT125 only). Secure the cam chain to prevent it from dropping into the crankcase.

8   Insert the cam chain guide blade into the front of the cam chain tunnel, using a torch to ensure that the blade bottom end locates correctly in its recess in the crankcase wall. Fit the blade upper locating projections into the recesses in the cylinder barrel. Refit the three locating dowels to their recesses around the cylinder studs and position a new cylinder head gasket on the gasket surface. A tubular rubber seal is fitted around the right-hand rear locating dowel.

9   Keeping the cam chain taut, hook a length of stiff wire to its upper end. Pass the wire up through the cylinder head cam chain tunnel, lower the cylinder head over the wire and cam chain to rest on the cylinder head gasket. Secure the cam chain.

10   Check that the cylinder head is seated correctly, then refit the four long bolts and their washers, and the two Allen screws. Tighten all six fasteners by hand only at first.

11   The tightening sequence is shown in the accompanying photographs. Working progressively, by about one turn at a time, and in the sequence shown, tighten the cylinder head and barrel fasteners to the following torque settings:

Cylinder head 8 mm flange bolts	2.2 kgf m (16 lbf ft)
Cylinder head 8 mm Allen screws	2.0 kgf m (14.5 lbf ft)
Cylinder barrel 6 mm Allen screws	1.0 kgf m (7 lbf ft)

12   Rotate the crankshaft until it is exactly at TDC. If the crankcase left-hand cover and generator rotor are removed, this position is found by aligning the dot stamped in the crankshaft sprocket with the arrow cast in the crankcase wall. If the crankcase cover and the rotor are in position, TDC is found as described under setting the valve clearances in Routine Maintenance. Whichever set of marks is used, it is essential

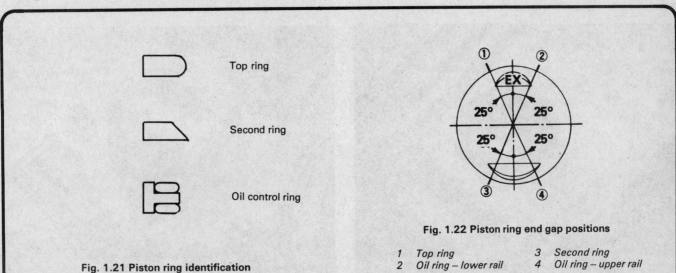

Fig. 1.21 Piston ring identification

Top ring

Second ring

Oil control ring

Fig. 1.22 Piston ring end gap positions

1   Top ring   3   Second ring
2   Oil ring – lower rail   4   Oil ring – upper rail

that the crankshaft is aligned with absolute accuracy and is not disturbed while the camshaft is refitted; check frequently that this is the case.

13 The camshaft should be in the 'compression' position. This is found by checking that both rockers have free play when the sprocket locating pin is in the 12 o'clock position (see accompanying photographs).

14 Without disturbing the crankshaft setting, engage the sprocket on the cam chain (note that one face of the sprocket has a timing mark stamped on it; this surface must face outwards, to the left) so that when the chain front run is absolutely taut the sprocket will fit correctly on the camshaft and its locating pin, with the pin and sprocket timing mark aligned exactly with the pointer cast in the upper rim of the sprocket aperture. This is shown in the accompanying photograph. Press the sprocket on to the camshaft, then refit the retaining bolt and washer.

15 Great care and some patience is required when carrying out the above task, but absolute accuracy is necessary if the valve timing is to be correct. If the valve timing is incorrect, the engine will lose power and run roughly, and there is a real risk of serious engine damage. The essential requirement is that with both sets of timing marks accurately aligned, the chain front run is taut.

16 Lock the crankshaft by applying a spanner to the rotor retaining bolt, then tighten the camshaft sprocket retaining bolt to a torque setting of 6.0 kgf m (43 lbf ft).

17 Refit the long coil spring to the tensioner pushrod, followed by the rubber damper and (on 1983 on models only) the smaller coil spring. Fit new O-rings to the tensioner locknut and cap, insert the pushrod assembly into the adjuster body and screw the body into the rear of the cylinder barrel. Screw it in until the body end is flush with the pushrod rear end, then refit the adjuster locknut, but do not tighten it until the setting has been checked with the engine running. Leave off the tensioner cap, as a reminder.

18 Turn the engine over several times to check that all components have been refitted correctly and are functioning properly, then set it to TDC on the compression stroke and check that the timing marks still align exactly. If necessary, remove the cam chain tensioner and repeat the procedure from paragraph 14 onwards.

19 Refit the cam sprocket cover, ensuring that a new O-ring is fitted if necessary and that the tachometer drive (1983 XT125 models only) engages correctly. Tighten the cover screws to a torque setting of 0.7 kgf m (5 lbf ft).

20 Following the procedure given in Routine Maintenance check, and adjust if necessary the valve clearances. Oil all components in the cylinder head liberally and refit the inspection covers, renewing if necessary their O-rings and tightening the retaining Allen screws to a torque setting of 1.0 kgf m (7 lbf ft).

21 Check that the spark plug is clean and correctly gapped and refit it, tightening it by hand only at first until it is correctly seated, then apply a suitable box spanner and tighten the plug by a further $\frac{1}{4}$ turn, or to a torque setting of 2.0 kgf m (14.5 lbf ft). Refit the two inspection caps set in the crankcase left hand cover.

41.4a Arrow cast in piston crown must face to front of engine

41.4b Insert gudgeon pin to retain piston ...

41.4c ... and secure with circlip as shown

41.5 Always use a new gasket – note location of dowels and O-ring

41.7 Keep cam chain taut while refitting cylinder barrel

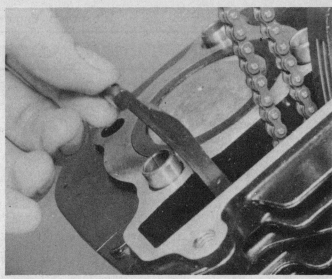

41.8a Insert cam chain guide into chain tunnel ...

41.8b ... ensuring that guide bottom end locates correctly in crankcase recess

41.8c Note locations of dowel pins and rubber seal

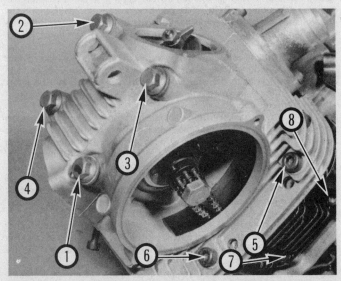

41.11 Cylinder head and barrel retaining bolt tightening sequence – reverse to slacken

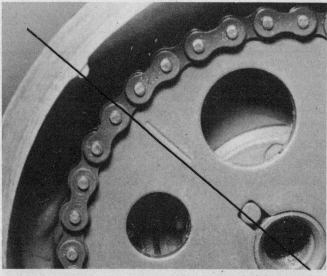

41.14 Align timing marks as shown to position camshaft and sprocket

41.17a Tensioner spring fits over pushrod

41.17b Do not forget rubber damper

41.20 Adjust valve clearances as in Routine Maintenance

42 Refitting the engine/gearbox unit in the frame

1   If this was removed, refit the engine top mounting plate/cylinder head steady, but do not tighten its mounting bolts fully. Have ready the single engine top mounting bolt. On XT125 models, refit the two thick washers, one on each side of the crankcase rear mounting lug; these washers should be stuck in place with grease or even glue to avoid their loss. Pack grease into the crankcase lug and into both subframe pivot bearings.

2   Being careful to avoid damage by manoeuvring it past the footrests and brake pedal, lift the engine/gearbox unit into the frame and retain it by refitting the top mounting bolt and its nut. On XT125 models be careful that the crankcase rear lug passes between the subframe pivot lugs. Align the crankcase lug with the pivot lugs and tap the sub-frame pivot bolt through the crankcase lug, the opposite pivot lug and through the frame, displacing the dummy bolt as it goes. Refit the pivot bolt retaining nut and the engine lower rear mounting bolt and nut. On SR125 models, refit the engine upper and lower rear mounting bolts and their nuts.

3   Refit the engine front mounting plate (XT125) or plates (SR125) with the four retaining bolts and their nuts. Check that the

engine/gearbox unit is aligned correctly and is held securely and without strain. Check also that no components are trapped. On XT125 models only, tighten the sub-frame pivot bolt to a torque setting of 8.0 kgf m (58 lbf ft). On all models, tighten all engine mounting bolts to a torque setting of 3.3 kgf m (24 lbf ft).

4   On XT125 models only, refit the left-hand footrest, tightening its retaining bolt to a torque setting of 4.3 kgf m (31 lbf ft). Refit the crankcase bashplate, tightening securely its mounting bolt.

5   On all models, refit the carburettor, tightening its hose clamps securely and ensuring that the throttle cable is properly routed and correctly adjusted (see Routine Maintenance). Engage the clutch cable on the adjuster bracket, connect it to the operating lever and bend up the small tang to retain the cable end nipple. Adjust the clutch cable as described in Routine Maintenance. Refit the breather pipe to its crankcase stub and secure it with its wire clip.

6   Engage the gearbox sprocket on the chain, refit the sprocket on the output shaft end, and install the sprocket retaining plate. Apply a few drops of thread locking compound to their threads and refit the sprocket retaining bolts, tightening them to a torque setting of 1.0 kgf m (7 lbf ft). As described in Routine Maintenance, check the chain tension and adjust it, if necessary. Remember to reset the rear brake adjustment and stop lamp rear switch setting if the chain tension needs adjustment. Refit the gearbox sprocket cover and the gearchange pedal, tightening the sprocket cover screws securely. The gearchange lever pinch bolt is tightened to a torque setting of 1.0 kgf m (7 lbf ft).

7   Routing them carefully, and securing them with any clamps that are provided, connect the electrical leads to the main loom and the starter motor lead to the starter relay (SR125 only). Refit the spark plug cap to the spark plug and, on 1983 on XT125 models only, refit the tachometer cable.

8   Place a new gasket in the exhaust port, using a smear of grease to stick it in place, then refit the exhaust system (SR125) or exhaust pipe (XT125). Tighten the exhaust pipe/cylinder head Allen bolts to a torque setting of 1.2 kgf m (9 lbf ft), then secure the exhaust rear mountings to the torque settings specified. On SR125 models, remember to adjust the rear brake. On XT125 models it may be necessary to slacken the silencer mounting bolts so that the exhaust pipe and silencer can be aligned correctly; tighten the pipe/silencer clamp bolt to a torque setting of 2.0 kgf m (14.5 lbf ft).

9   Connect the battery again, switch on the ignition, and check that all circuits are operating correctly. Refit the fuel tank, the seat and the sidepanels. Switch on the fuel tap to fill the float chamber; check for fuel leaks.

10 Check that both oil drain plugs are refitted and securely fastened, then fill the crankcase with 1.3 litre (2.3 pint) of good quality SAE 20W40SE engine oil. Refit the filler plug and remember to check the oil level after the engine has been run for the first time.

42.2 Lift engine into frame and hang from top mounting bolt

42.8a Always fit a new exhaust gasket ...

42.8b ... and tighten exhaust front mountings first ...

42.8c ... then the rear mountings

42.10 Fill crankcase with 1.3 litres of oil – remember to check oil level

43 Starting and running the rebuilt engine

1   Attempt to start the engine using the usual procedure adopted for a cold engine. Do not be disillusioned if there is no sign of life initially. A certain amount of perseverance may prove necessary to coax the engine into activity even if new parts have not been fitted. Should the engine persist in not starting, check that the spark plug has not become fouled by the oil used during re-assembly. Failing this, go through the fault finding charts and work out what the problem is methodically.

2   When the engine does start, keep it running as slowly as possible to allow the oil to circulate. Use the oil delivery checking bolt, as described in Routine Maintenance, to check that the oil is circulating correctly; oil should appear after 2-3 minutes of running at idle speed. Tighten the check bolt. Open the choke as soon as the engine will run without it. During the initial running, a certain amount of smoke may be in evidence due to the oil used in the reassembly sequence being burnt away. The resulting smoke should gradually subside.

3   Check the engine for blowing gaskets and oil leaks. Before using the machine on the road, check that all the gears select properly, and that the controls function correctly. Working as described in Routine Maintenance check that the cam chain tensioner setting is satisfactory. Tighten the adjuster locknut and cap to the torque settings given.

4   As soon as the engine has warmed up to its normal operating temperature, allow it to idle and check the carburettor idle speed adjustment as described in Chapter 2 of this Manual. If any repair work has been carried out and new components have been fitted, carburettor adjustment will almost certainly be required. Once the engine is ticking over smoothly at its correct speed, check and reset if necessary the throttle cable adjustment.

5   Stop the engine and allow the oil level to settle for one or two minutes, then check the oil level. With the machine standing upright on level ground the oil level should be between the marks adjacent to the level window set in the crankcase right-hand cover. Remove the filler plug and add oil if necessary to bring the level up to the mark.

44 Taking the rebuilt machine on the road

1   Any rebuilt machine will need time to settle down, even if the parts have been replaced in their original order. For this reason it is highly advisable to treat the machine gently for the first few miles to ensure oil has circulated throughout the lubrication system and that any new parts have begun to bed down.

2   Even greater care is necessary if the engine has been rebored or if a new crankshaft has been fitted. In the case of a rebore, the engine will have to be run-in again, as if the machine were new. This means greater use of the gearbox and a restraining hand on the throttle until at least 500 miles have been covered. There is no point in keeping to any set speed limit; the main requirement is to keep a light loading on the engine and to gradually work up performance until the 500 mile mark is reached. These recommendations can be lessened to an extent when only a new crankshaft is fitted. Experience is the best guide since it is easy to tell when an engine is running freely.

3   If at any time a lubrication failure is suspected, stop the engine immediately, and investigate the cause. If any engine is run without oil, even for a short period, irreparable engine damage is inevitable.

4   When the engine has cooled down completely after the initial run, recheck the various settings, especially the valve clearances. During the run most of the engine components will have settled into their normal working locations. Check the various oil levels, particularly that of the engine as it may have dropped slightly now that the various passages and recesses have filled.

Chapter 2 Fuel system and lubrication

Contents

Specifications

Fuel tank capacity

	SR125	XT125
Overall	10.0 litre (2.2 gal)	7.3 litre (1.6 gal)
Reserve	N/Av	1.7 litre (3.0 pint)

Carburettor

	SR125	XT125
Manufacturer	Teikei	Teikei
Type	Y24P	Y24P
Choke size	24 mm (0.95 in)	24 mm (0.95 in)
ID number	5N000	12V00
Main jet	108	118
Main air jet:		
1982 model	1.3	1.8
1983 on model	1.3	1.4
Jet needle	4C95	4B91
Clip position – grooves from top	3rd	3rd
Needle jet	T00	2.600
Throttle valve cutaway	2.25	2.25
Pilot jet	38	40
Pilot air jet	1.0	1.2
Pilot mixture screw – turns out	$1-1\frac{1}{2}$	$1\frac{1}{4}$
Float valve seat	2.0	2.0
Starter jet 1	60	60
Starter jet 2	64	60
Fuel level	7.5 ± 1.0 mm (0.30 ± 0.04 in)	3.5 ± 1.0 mm (0.14 ± 0.04 in)
Float height	26.5 ± 1.0 mm (1.04 ± 0.04 in)	25.0 ± 1.0 mm (0.98 ± 0.04 in)
Idle speed	1250 - 1350 rpm	1250 - 1350 rpm

Lubrication system

All models

Type	Wet sump, 2 gauze filters
Recommended oil	Good quality, SAE 20W40SE engine oil
Oil capacity:	
At filter cleaning or overhaul	1.3 litre (2.29 pint)
At oil change	1.0 litre (1.76 pint)

Oil pump

Type	Trochoid
Rotor width	6 mm (0.2362 in)
Inner rotor/outer rotor clearance	0.15 mm (0.0059 in)
Service limit	0.35 mm (0.0138 in)
Outer rotor/housing clearance	0.15 mm (0.0059 in)
Service limit	0.35 mm (0.0138 in)
End cover/rotor clearance	0.03 - 0.09 mm (0.0012 - 0.0035 in)
Service limit	0.14 mm (0.0055 in)

Torque settings

Component	kgf m	lbf ft
Inlet stub Allen screws	1.2	9.0
Carburettor hose clamp screws	0.2	1.5
Air filter cover retaining screws	0.5	3.5
Air filter casing mounting screws	0.7	5.0
Exhaust pipe/cylinder head Allen bolts	1.2	9.0
Exhaust mounting bolts:		
SR125	2.0	14.5
XT125	2.7	19.5
Exhaust pipe/silencer clamp bolt – XT125	2.0	14.5
Exhaust head shield mounting screws – XT125	0.7	5.0
Oil feed checking plug	0.7	5.0
Oil pump mounting screws	0.7	5.0
Engine oil drain plug	4.3	31.0
Filter chamber drain plug	1.0	7.0
Oil filter cover retaining screws	0.7	5.0

1 General description

The fuel system comprises a tank from which fuel is fed by gravity to the carburettor float chamber via a tap which has 'Off', 'On' and 'Reserve' positions. The latter position provides a reserve supply of fuel. Air is drawn into the carburettor via an oil-impregnated polyurethane foam filter element which is contained in a housing to the rear of the cylinder barrel.

Engine lubrication is of the wet sump type, the oil contained in the reservoir formed by the crankcase castings being drawn through a gauze filter by an oil pump. The pump is of the Eaton trochoid type and is driven by gears from the crankshaft; the oil is forced through a full-flow gauze oil filter 'element' and then to the crankshaft, the camshaft and the two gearbox shafts. All components not provided with a direct supply of oil are lubricated by splash, whereupon the oil drains back into the crankcase reservoir. A by-pass valve is fitted to maintain full oil flow if the filter should become so clogged as to restrict the flow.

The exhaust system fitted to SR125 models is a single unit comprising the exhaust pipe and silencer welded together. The unit is chrome plated. The XT125 exhaust system is similar but incorporates a second separate silencer assembly and is routed upwards over the engine/gearbox unit to pass down the right-hand side of the machine at a high level in keeping with the trail bike styling of the machine. It is finished in a matt-black heat resistant coating.

2 Fuel tank: removal, examination and refitting

1   If it is necessary to remove the fuel tank for repairs the following points should be noted. Fuel tank repair, whether necessitated by accident damage or by fuel leaks, is a task for the professional. Welding or brazing is not recommended unless the tank is purged of all fuel vapour, which is a difficult condition to achieve. Resin-based tank sealing compounds are a much more satisfactory method of curing leaks, and are now available through suppliers who advertise regularly in the motorcycle press. Accident damage repairs will inevitably involve re-painting the tank; matching of modern paint finishes, especially metallic ones, is a very difficult task not to be lightly undertaken by the average owner. It is therefore recommended that the tank be removed by the owner, and taken for professional attention.

2   Carefully detach the sidepanels and remove the dual seat, then turn the petrol tap to the 'Off' position. Use a pair of pliers to release the wire petrol pipe retaining clip and pull the pipe off the stub at the rear of the tap. Careful use of a small screwdriver may be necessary to ease the pipe off the stub. Allow any fuel in the pipe to drain into a small clean container. The tank may now be detached from the frame by unscrewing the retaining bolt at the rear of the tank and pulling the tank up and rearwards off its front mounting rubbers. Place the tank mounting components in a safe place ready for refitting. Inspect the mounting rubbers for signs of damage or deterioration and if necessary renew them before refitting of the tank is due to take place.

3   Store the tank in a safe place whilst it is removed from the machine, well away from any naked lights or flames. It will otherwise represent a considerable fire or explosion hazard. Check that the tap is not leaking and that it cannot be accidentally knocked into the 'On' position. Placing the tank on a soft protected surface and covering it

with a protective cloth or mat may well avoid damage being caused to the finish by dirt, grit, dropped tools, etc.

4   To refit the tank, reverse the procedure adopted for its removal. Move it from side to side before it is fully home, so that the rubber buffers engage with the guide channels correctly. If difficulty is encountered in engaging the front of the tank with the rubber buffers, apply a small amount of petrol to the buffers to ease location. Secure the tank with the retaining bolt whilst ensuring that the mounting components are correctly located and that there is no metal to metal contact between the tank and frame.

5   Finally, always carry out a leak check on the fuel pipe connections after fitting the tank and turning the tap lever to the 'On' position. Any leaks found must be cured; as well as wasting fuel, any petrol dropping onto hot engine castings may result in a fire or explosion.

2.2 Fuel tank is retained by a single bolt at the rear

3 Fuel tap: removal, examination and refitting

1   The fuel tap assembly is secured to the underside of the tank by two screws, the joint being sealed by an O-ring.

2   Always take careful precautions against the risk of fire; for example, never smoke or use a naked light to illuminate the work surface. Always use a soft bristled brush such as an old toothbrush when cleaning to avoid damage to the delicate filter gauze. Some form of eye protection is recommended against the drops of fuel which will inevitably be flying around during cleaning operations. If work is being carried out to cure fuel leaks, ensure that all retaining fasteners are tight but not overtightened. The tap components are delicate and

easily distorted; overtightening will merely increase any leaks. If the components are correctly fastened and the leaks persist, the tap must be stripped and the relevant seal renewed.

3   Petrol tap removal must be preceded by draining the petrol remaining in the tank. Remove the petrol feed pipe from the carburettor, switch the tap to the 'Res' position and allow all the fuel to drain into a clean, dry container of suitable size. Note that this container must be constructed of metal and clearly marked if the petrol is to be stored for any length of time. Alternatively, the tank can be removed, as described in the preceding Section, and placed on one side so that the petrol level is below that of the tap. Take care not to damage the tank paintwork if this method is employed, and ensure that petrol does not leak from the filler cap.

4   Unscrew the filter bowl by using a close-fitting ring spanner on the moulded square end of the bowl. Pick out the sealing O-ring. Unscrew the two bolts which retain the tap to the underside of the tank and carefully withdraw the tap assembly. The filter gauze can then be removed for cleaning. The tap lever is retained by a grub screw threaded into the underside of the tap body (SR125) or two screws in the body side (XT125). Remove the screw(s), then withdraw the tap lever. It may be necessary to pad the jaws of a suitable pair of pliers with cloth or tape and to pull the lever out as it is sealed by a tight-fitting O-ring. Pick out the small spring and the shaped plug behind it.

5   Thoroughly clean and inspect all the tap components, renewing any parts that are worn or damaged. Again, pay particular attention to the fibre sealing washers beneath the heads of the two tap mounting bolts and to the large O-ring set in the tap mating flange surface. It is recommended that these components are renewed whenever the tap is disturbed as their condition is critical to the prevention of persistent petrol leaks.

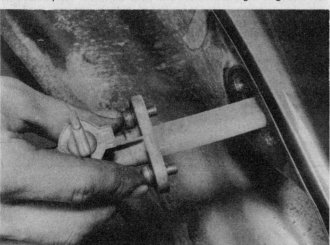

3.1 Fuel tap is retained by two screws – remove to clean filter gauze

3.4 Remove grub screw to release tap lever (SR125) – note what happens to carelessly handled filter bowls

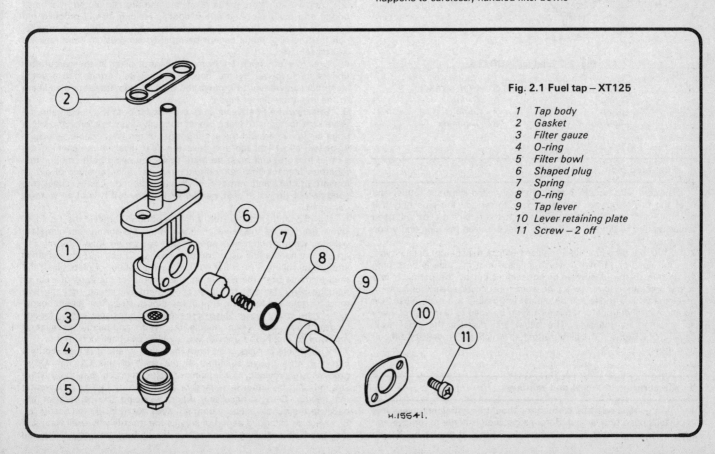

Fig. 2.1 Fuel tap – XT125

1   Tap body
2   Gasket
3   Filter gauze
4   O-ring
5   Filter bowl
6   Shaped plug
7   Spring
8   O-ring
9   Tap lever
10 Lever retaining plate
11 Screw – 2 off

H.15541.

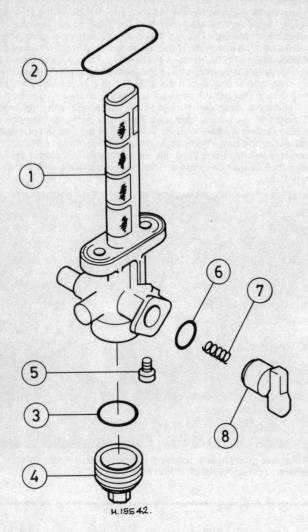

H.155 42.

Fig. 2.2 Fuel tap – SR125

1	Tap body	5	Grub screw
2	O-ring	6	O-ring
3	O-ring	7	Spring
4	Filter bowl	8	Tap lever

4 Fuel feed pipe: examination

1   The fuel feed pipe is made from thin walled synthetic rubber and is of the push-on type. It is necessary to replace the pipe only if it becomes hard or splits. It is unlikely that the retaining clips will need replacing due to fatigue as the main seal between the pipe and union is the interference fit.

2   If the fuel pipe has been replaced with a transparent plastic type, look for signs of yellowing which indicate that the pipe is becoming brittle due to the plasticiser being leached out by the petrol. It is a sound precaution to renew a pipe when this occurs, as any subsequent breakage whilst in use will be almost impossible to repair. **Note:** On no account should natural rubber tubing be used to carry petrol, even as a temporary measure. The petrol will dissolve the inner wall, causing blockages in the carburettor jets which will prove very difficult to remove.

5 Carburettor: removal and refitting

1   As a general rule, the carburettor should be left alone unless it is in obvious need of overhaul. Before a decision is made to remove and dismantle, ensure that all other possible sources of trouble have been

eliminated. This includes the more obvious faults such as fouled spark plug, a dirty air filter element or damaged exhaust system. If a fault has been traced back to the carburettor, proceed as follows.

2   Make sure that the petrol tap is turned off, then prise off the petrol feed pipe at the carburettor union.

3   Slacken the screws of the clips which secure the carburettor to its inlet stub and air filter hose so that the carburettor can be twisted free and partially removed. The threaded carburettor top should then be unscrewed to allow the throttle valve assembly to be withdrawn. It is not usually necessary to remove this from the cable and it can be left attached and taped clear of the engine. If removal is necessary, however, proceed as follows.

4   Holding the carburettor top, compress the throttle return spring against it and hold it in position against the cap so that the cable can be pushed down and slid out of its locating groove. The various parts can now be removed and should be placed with the carburettor..

5   The carburettor is refitted by reversing the removal sequence. Note that it is important that the instrument is mounted vertically to ensure that the fuel level in the float bowl is correct. A locating tab is fitted to provide a good guide to alignment but it is worthwhile checking this for accuracy. Once refitted, check the carburettor adjustments as described later in this Chapter.

6   **Note:** If the carburettor is to be set up from scratch it is important to check jet and float level settings prior to installaiton. Refer to Sections 7 and 8 before the carburettor is refitted.

6 Carburettor: dismantling, examination and reassembly

1   Invert the carburettor and remove the float chamber by withdrawing the four retaining screws. The float chamber bowl will lift away, exposing the float assembly, hinge and float needle. There is a gasket between the float chamber bowl and the carburettor body which need not be disturbed unless it is leaking.

2   With a pair of thin-nose pliers, withdraw the float pivot pin to free the floats and the float needle. Check that neither of the floats has punctured and that the float needle and seating are both clean and in good condition. If the needle has a ridge, it should be renewed in conjunction with its seating.

3   The two floats are made of plastic and are connected by a brass bridge and pivot piece. If either float is leaking, it will produce the wrong fuel level in the float chamber, leading to flooding and an over-rich mixture. The floats cannot be repaired successfully, and renewal will be required.

4   Unscrew the main jet from the central pillar in the carburettor underside, followed by the needle jet and its O-ring. Use a small electrical screwdriver to remove the pilot jet from its seating adjacent to the main/needle jet holder.

5   Unscrew the float valve seat and inspect both the needle and the valve seat for signs of wear, which normally takes the form of a slight ridge or groove around the seating taper of the float needle. Any such wear will allow leakage and raise the float level, thus richening the air/fuel mixture, and must be rectified by renewing both components together. Inspect both components very carefully for signs of dirt or foreign matter, and remove any that is found. Lastly, check the condition of the valve seat washer and renew it if it is at all worn or damaged.

6   To dismantle the throttle valve assembly, remove the retaining screw from inside the valve, then withdraw the spring seat complete with the white nylon needle support and coil spring. Invert the valve to tip out the needle and its supporting washer. Check that the needle is straight by rolling it on a flat surface such as sheet of plate glass and then examine both the needle and the needle jet for signs of wear or damage. Any damage to either component will mean that the two must be renewed together. Do not attempt to straighten a bent needle as they are easily broken; also, if the machine has been running for any length of time with a bent needle, the needle and needle jet must be renewed to rectify the uneven wear which will have occurred.

7   The needle is suspended from the valve, where it is retained by a circlip in the groove specified at the front of this Chapter. Other grooves are provided as a means of adjustment so that the mixture strength can be either increased or decreased by raising or lowering the needle. Care is necessary when replacing the carburettor top because the needle is easily bent if it does not fit inside the needle jet.

8   After an extended period of service the throttle valve will wear and may produce a clicking sound within the carburettor body. Wear will

be evident from inspection, usually at the base of the slide and in the locating groove. A worn slide should be replaced as soon as possible because it will give rise to air leaks which will upset the carburation.

9   The manually operated choke is unlikely to require attention during the normal service life of the machine. The plunger assembly is removed by unscrewing the large brass securing nut. Check that the brass plunger itself is unworn, that the plunger seating is clean and undamaged and that the plunger is operating smoothly. Any fault will mean that the complete assembly must be renewed as repairs are not possible and the assembly is available only as a single unit. Check that the plunger housing and the various passages in the carburettor body are clean and free from any particles of foreign matter.

10 If removal of the throttle stop and pilot mixture adjustment screw is required, screw each one carefully in until it seats lightly, counting and recording the number of turns required, and then unscrew each, complete with its spring and O-ring. Remove any dirt or corrosion and check for signs of wear or damage, renewing any component which needs it. When refitting the adjustment screws, ensure that the sealing O-rings are fitted first, then the screw retaining springs, and the screw itself. Tighten the screws carefully until they seat lightly, then unscrew

each one by the number of turns counted on removal to return it to its original position; this will serve as a basis for subsequent adjustments.

11 Before the carburettor is reassembled, using the reversed dismantling procedure, it should be cleaned out thoroughly, preferably by the use of compressed air. Avoid using a rag because there is always risk of fine particles of lint obstructing the internal air passages or the jet orifices. Check carefully the condition of the carburettor body and float chamber, looking for distorted or damaged mating surfaces or any other signs of wear. If severe damage or wear is found, the carburettor assembly will have to be renewed. Check the condition of all O-rings and gaskets, renewing any that are worn or distorted.

12 Never use a piece of wire or sharp metal object to clear a blocked jet. It is only too easy to enlarge the jet under these circumstances and increase the rate of petrol consumption. Always use compressed air to clear a blockage; a tyre pump makes an admirable substitute when a compressed air line is not available.

13 Do not use excessive force when reassembling the carburettor because it is quite easy to shear the small jets or some of the smaller screws. Before attaching the air cleaner hose, check that the throttle slide rises smoothly when the throttle is opened.

5.3 Carburettor top can be unscrewed to withdraw throttle valve assembly

6.6a Needle and clip are supported by metal washer inside throttle valve ...

6.6b ... and retained by spring-loaded nylon support set in spring seat

6.6c Spring seat fitted as shown inside throttle valve

6.9 Unscrew brass nut to release choke plunger assembly

6.10a Do not disturb throttle stop screw unnecessarily – same applies to ...

6.10b ... pilot mixture screw (see text) – note arrangement of O-rings and springs

6.11a Check drain plug seals are in good condition to prevent fuel leaks

6.11b Vacuum take-off plug sealing washer must be in good condition to prevent induction leaks

6.13a Renew float valve seat washer if worn or damaged – essential to maintain fuel level

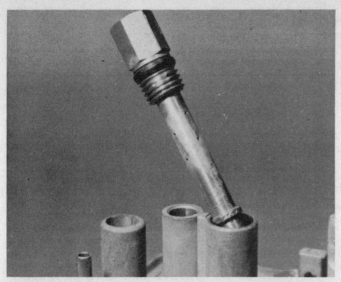

6.13b Note position of O-ring around needle jet – do not omit

6.13c Main jet screws into base of needle jet – tighten securely

6.13d Pilot jet screws into location shown – do not overtighten

6.13e Refit float needle to valve seat ...

6.13f ... then refit floats and secure with pivot pin

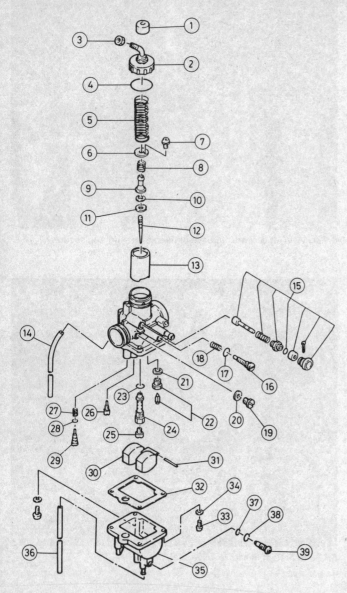

Fig. 2.3 Carburettor

1 Cap	21 Sealing washer
2 Carburettor top	22 Float needle valve
3 Cable adjusting nut	assembly
4 O-ring	23 O-ring
5 Return spring	24 Needle jet
6 Spring seat	25 Main jet
7 Screw	26 Pilot jet
8 Spring	27 Spring
9 Nylon needle support	28 O-ring
10 Needle clip	29 Mixture screw
11 Washer	30 Float
12 Jet needle	31 Float pivot pin
13 Throttle valve	32 Float chamber gasket
14 Breather pipe	33 Screw – 4 off
15 Choke assembly	34 Spring washer – 4 off
16 Throttle stop screw	35 Float chamber
17 O-ring	36 Drain pipe
18 Spring	37 O-ring
19 Vacuum take-off plug	38 O-ring
20 Sealing washer	39 Drain plug

7 Carburettor: checking the settings

1 The various jet sizes, throttle valve cutaway (on slide type carburettors) and needle position are predetermined by the manufacturer and should not require modification. Check with the Specifications list at the beginning of this Chapter if there is any doubt about the types fitted. If a change appears necessary it can often be attributed to a developing engine fault unconnected with the carburettor. Although carburettors do wear in service, this process occurs slowly over an extended length of time and hence wear of the carburettor is unlikely to cause sudden or extreme malfunction. If a fault does occur, check first other main systems, in which a fault may give similar symptoms, before proceeding with carburettor examination or modification.

2 Where non-standard items, such as exhaust systems, air filters or camshafts have been fitted to a machine, some alterations to carburation may be required. Arriving at the correct settings often requires trial and error. In many cases the manufacturer of the non-standard equipment will be able to advise on correct carburation changes.

3 As a rough guide, up to $\frac{1}{8}$ throttle is controlled by the pilot jet, $\frac{1}{8}$ to $\frac{1}{4}$ by the throttle valve cutaway, $\frac{1}{4}$ to $\frac{3}{4}$ throttle by the needle position and from $\frac{3}{4}$ to full by the size of the main jet. These are only approximate divisions, which are by no means clear cut. There is a certain amount of overlap between the various stages.

4 If alterations to the carburation must be made, always err on the side of a slightly rich mixture. A weak mixture will cause the engine to overheat which may cause engine seizure. Reference to the colour page in Routine Maintenance will show how, after some experience has been gained, the condition of the spark plug electrodes can be interpreted as a reliable guide to mixture strength.

8 Carburettor: adjustment

1 Before any dismantling or adjustment is undertaken, eliminate all other possible causes of running problems, checking in particular the spark plug, ignition timing, air cleaner, valve clearances and the exhaust. Checking and cleaning these items will often resolve a mysterious flat spot or misfire.

2 The first step in carburettor adjustment is to ensure that the jet sizes, needle position and float height are correct, which will require the removal and dismantling of the carburettor as described in Sections 5 and 6 of this Chapter.

3 If the carburettor has been removed for the purpose of checking jet sizes, the float level should be measured at the same time. It is unlikely that once this is set up correctly there will be a significant amount of variation, unless the float needle or seat have worn. These should be checked and renewed, if necessary, as described in Section 6.

4 Remove the float bowl from the carburettor body and very carefully peel away the float chamber gasket. Check that the gasket surface of the carburettor body is clean and smooth once the gasket is removed. Hold the carburettor body so that the venturi is now vertical with the air filter side upwards and the floats are hanging from their pivot pin. Carefully tilt the carburettor to an angle of about 60° – 70° from the vertical so that the tang of the float pivot is resting firmly on the float needle and the float valve is therefore closed, but also so that the spring-loaded pin set in the float needle itself is not compressed. Measure the distance between the gasket face and the bottom of one float with an accurate ruler or a vernier caliper; the distance should be 25.0 mm (0.98 in) on XT125 models, and 26.5 mm (1.04 in) on SR125 models. A tolerance is permissible of 1.0 mm (0.04 in) above or below the set figure but note that the more accurate the setting is, the better the engine's performance, economy and reliability will be.

5 If adjustment is required, remove the float assembly and bend by a very small amount the small tang which acts on the float needle pin. Reassemble the float and measure the height again. Repeat the process until the measurement is correct, then check that the other float is exactly the same height as the first. Bend the pivot very carefully and gently if any difference is found between the heights of the two floats.

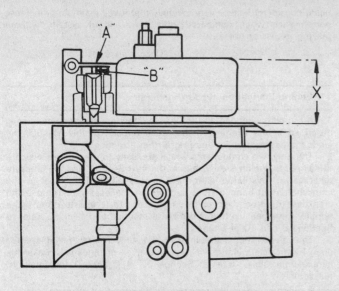

Fig. 2.4 Measuring the float height

A   Float tang   X   Float height
B   Float needle

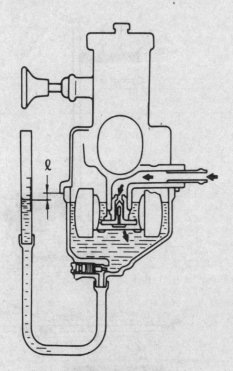

Fig. 2.5 Measuring the fuel level

ℓ Fuel level

6   When the jet sizes have been checked and reset as necessary, reassemble the carburettor and refit it to the machine as described in Sections 5 and 6 of this Chapter. Note that a fuel level is also given. This is measured with the carburettor on the machine and is thus quicker in that respect, but if the level is found to be faulty, the carburettor must still be removed from the machine for the float height to be altered. Since, however, it is arguably more accurate to use the fuel level as the guide, the procedure is given below.

7   The machine must be standing absolutely upright on level ground, as the slightest tilt will make the test inaccurate. Remove the breather tube from the spigot at the base of the float bowl and connect to it a length of clear plastic tubing that has an internal diameter of exactly 6 mm (0.24 in), then bring this up the side of the carburettor body, next to the throttle stop screw, and tape it in place, thus forming a U-tube as shown in the accompanying illustration. Switch the fuel tap on and unscrew the float chamber drain plug by just enough to allow petrol into the tube. Start the engine and allow it to run for a few minutes, to find the correct fuel level, then stop the engine. Measure the distance between the carburettor body bottom edge and the level of fuel in the tube. This should be 7.5 mm (0.30 in) on SR125 models or 3.5 mm (0.14 in) on XT125 models. Note that a tolerance of 1 mm (0.04 in) is allowable above or below this figure.

8   Whichever method is used, once the float height/fuel level is known to be accurate and the carburettor is refitted to the machine, start the engine and allow it to warm up to normal operating temperature, preferably by taking the machine on a short journey. Stop the engine and screw the pilot mixture screw in until it seats lightly, then unscrew it by the number of turns shown in the Specifications Section for the particular model. Start the engine and set the machine to its specified idle speed by rotating the throttle stop screw as necessary. Try turning the pilot screw inwards by about $\frac{1}{4}$ turn at a time, noting its effect on the idling speed, then repeat the process, this time turning the screw outwards.

9   The pilot mixture screw should be set in the position which gives the fastest consistent tickover. The tickover speed may be reduced further, if necessary, by unscrewing the throttle stop screw the required amount. Check that the engine does not falter and stop after the throttle twistgrip has been opened and closed a few times.

10   Throttle cable adjustment should be checked at regular intervals and after any work is done to the carburettor or to the cable itself. The amount of free play specified for the throttle cable is 2 - 5 mm (0.08 - 0.2 in); use the adjuster on the carburettor top, followed if necessary by the adjuster below the twistgrip, to achieve the correct setting. Tighten securely the adjuster locknuts and replace the rubber sleeves over the adjusters.

11   For XT125 owners only, some machines have been difficult to start, or idle poorly, when very hot. While this generally only occurs when a machine is brand new, the problem disappearing by the time the machine has covered 5 - 600 miles, a solution can be found in persistent cases by altering two of the basic settings. These are:

1   Pilot mixture screw now 1 full turn out, not $1\frac{1}{4}$
2   Needle clip position now 4th groove from top, not 3rd

Note that the modified settings are only to be used if the problem is encountered.

9   Air filter: general

The air filter will require no attention other than the regular cleaning and re-oiling described in the Routine Maintenance Chapter of this Manual.

10   Exhaust system: general

1   Exhaust systems fitted to four-stroke machines do not become clogged with carbon deposits as a general rule. The most common cause of problems will be corrosion, which will attack the components from inside as well as outside.

2   Check at regular intervals that the exhaust is securely fastened and that there are no leaks at any of the joints: leaks caused by damaged gaskets must be cured by the renewal of the gasket. Check that the system components are intact and have not been rotted away by corrosion; the only cure is the renewal of the affected component.

3   The matt-black painted finish is cheaper to renovate but less durable than a conventional chrome-plated system. It is inevitable that the original finish will deteriorate to the point where the system must be removed from the machine and repainted. Reference to the advertisements in the national motorcycle press, or to a local Yamaha agent and to the owners of machines with similarly-finished exhausts will help in selecting the most effective finish. The best are those which require the paint to be baked on, although some aerosol sprays are almost as effective.

4   On SR125 models the exhaust system is retained by two Allen bolts to the cylinder head and by a single bolt to the pillion footrest mounting; removal and refitting is a straightforward task requiring no

preliminary dismantling. On XT125 models, the system is fastened to the cylinder head by two Allen bolts and to the rear of the frame by two bolts, the two parts of the system being secured by a clamp bolt. Heatshields are screwed both to the exhaust pipe and to the silencer tailpipe; these can be removed to permit thorough cleaning and repainting.

5   To remove the system on XT125 models, detach carefully the right-hand sidepanel, remove the two screws securing the exhaust pipe to the cylinder head then slacken fully the clamp bolt and tap forwards the pipe using a soft-faced mallet. Remove the two mounting bolts which secure the silencer to the frame and manoeuvre the silencer clear of the machine.

6   Refit the exhaust system by reversing the removal sequence. Always renew the exhaust gaskets to prevent leaks, and refit the system, tightening the fasteners only by hand at first. When the system is correctly aligned on its mounting, tighten the mounting bolts securely working from the front backwards. The recommended torque settings for all exhaust system fasteners are given in the Specifications Section of this Chapter.

7   Do not at any time attempt to modify the exhaust system in any way. The exhaust system is designed to give the maximum power possible consistent with legal requirements and yet to produce the minimum noise level possible. If an aftermarket accessory system is being considered, check very carefully that it will maintain or increase performance when compared with the standard system, without making excessive noise.

11 Engine lubrication system: general

1   If the oil is changed and the gauze filters are cleaned regularly as described in the Routine Maintenance Section of this Manual, the lubrication system will require no further attention.

2   The only two components which are likely to wear in any way are the oil pump, which is described in the next Section, and the pressure relief valve. This latter is formed by the oil feed quill set in the crankshaft right-hand end; it is therefore necessary to remove the crankcase right-hand cover to gain access to it, and to remove the primary drive gear so that it can be dismantled and cleaned. Refer to Sections 8 and 10 of Chapter 1.

3   The valve is such a simple device it is only likely to 'fail' if jammed open by an accumulation of dirt; regular oil changes will make this almost impossible. Refer to Section 37 of Chapter 1 for details of reassembly.

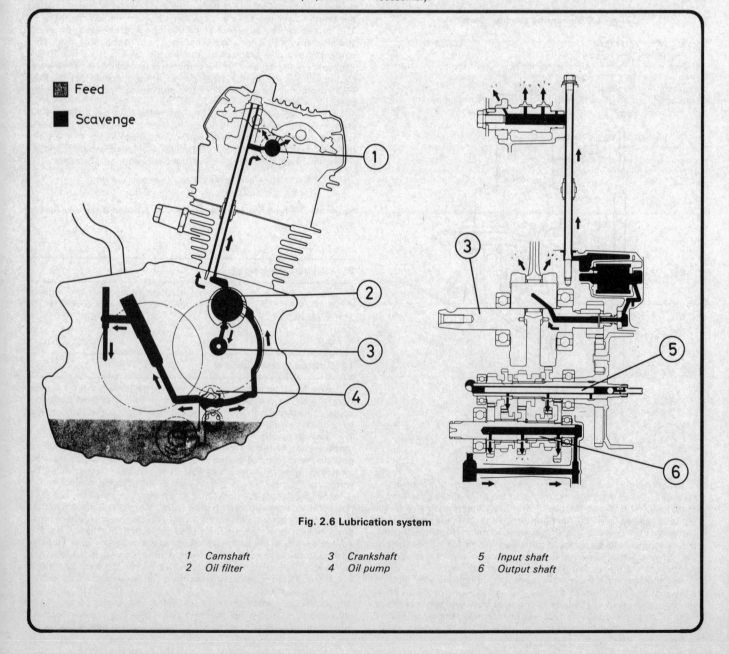

■ Feed

■ Scavenge

Fig. 2.6 Lubrication system

1	Camshaft	3	Crankshaft	5	Input shaft
2	Oil filter	4	Oil pump	6	Output shaft

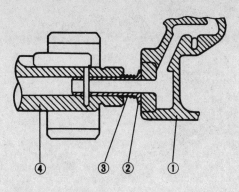

Fig. 2.7 Pressure release valve

1	Crankcase cover	3	Spring
2	Oil feed quill	4	Crankshaft

12 Oil pump: dismantling, examination and reassembly

1   It is necessary to carry out some preliminary dismantling work, depending on the model being worked on, to drain the engine oil and to remove the crankcase right-hand cover before the oil pump can be removed. The work necessary is described in Section 8 and 10 of Chapter 1.

2   On refitting, have ready a new oil pump/crankcase gasket and a new crankcase cover gasket; these are essential to prevent loss of oil pressure or oil leaks. Refer to Sections 37 and 39 of Chapter 1.

3   To dismantle the pump, use an impact driver (if necessary) to remove the fourth countersunk screw, then pull apart both halves of the pump body, noting the two locating dowel pins. Press the drive pin out of the driven gear shaft and withdraw the shaft, then shake the rotors out of the pump body.

4   Wash all the oil pump components with petrol and allow them to dry before carrying out a full examination. Before part reassembling the pump for the various measurements to be made, check the castings for cracks or other damage, especially the pump end cover. Examine all the components, especially the rotors, for signs of scuffing and wear, or for signs of scoring, chipping or other surface damage which will occur if metallic particles find their way into the oil pump assembly. Renewal of the affected parts is the only remedy under these circumstances, bearing in mind that the rotors must always be renewed as a matched pair. Check first with a Yamaha Service Agent; it would appear that individual pump components are available for SR125 models only, while it is necessary to renew the complete pump assembly on XT125 models. The pumps would appear to be the same, but their components may not be interchangeable.

5   Reassemble the pump rotors and measure the clearance between the outer rotor and the pump body, using a feeler gauge. If the measurement exceeds the service limit of 0.35 mm (0.014 in) the rotor or the body must be renewed, whichever is worn. Measure the clearance between the outer rotor and the inner rotor, using a feeler gauge. If the clearance exceeds 0.35 mm (0.014 in) the rotors must be renewed as a set. With the pump rotors installed in the pump body, lay a straight edge across the mating surface of the pump body. Again with a feeler gauge measure the clearance between the rotor faces and the straight edge. If the clearance exceeds 0.14 mm (0.006 in) the rotors should be renewed as a set.

6   Reassemble the pump by reversing the dismantling procedure. Both rotors have a punch mark stamped in one face; insert them into the pump body with the marked face uppermost, as shown in the accompanying photograph. Refit the drive gear to the pump end cover, insert the drive pin through the gear shaft and refit the two locating dowels. Place the pump end cover assembly on to the pump body, being careful to align the driveshaft and pin with the slot in the inner rotor, and to align the dowels with their respective holes. Press together the two parts of the pump and spin the nylon gear pinion to check that the pump rotates without stiffness.

7   Apply thread locking compound to its threads and refit the countersunk screw, tightening it securely. Oil the pump liberally, filling all its passages, before refitting it to the machine.

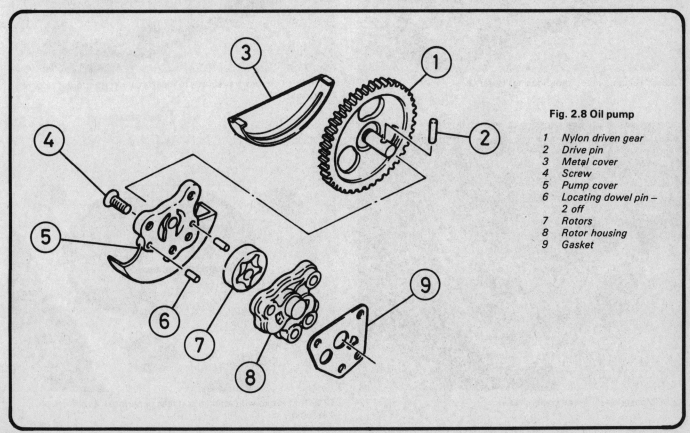

Fig. 2.8 Oil pump

1   Nylon driven gear
2   Drive pin
3   Metal cover
4   Screw
5   Pump cover
6   Locating dowel pin –
        2 off
7   Rotors
8   Rotor housing
9   Gasket

12.3a Remove countersunk screw to dismantle pump

12.3b Press out drive pin to release driven gear and shaft

12.5a Measuring outer rotor/housing clearance

12.5b Position rotors as shown to measure inner rotor/outer rotor clearance

12.5c Measuring rotor/end cover clearance

12.6 Refit rotors with marked surfaces uppermost, as shown, on reassembly

Chapter 3 Ignition system

Contents

Specifications

Ignition system type
SR125	Transistor-controlled (TCI)
XT125	Capacitor discharge (CDI)

Ignition timing – BTDC
Initial	9° @ 1300 rpm
Full advance:	
SR125	29° @ 5500 rpm
XT125	29° @ 6000 rpm

Flywheel generator
Source coil resistance:	
SR125	White-White 0.52 ohm ± 10%
XT125	Brown-Red 450 ohm ± 10%
Pulser coil resistance:	
SR125	Green-Brown, Yellow-White 230 ohm ± 10%
XT125	Green-White 265 ohm ± 10%

Ignition HT coil
Minimum spark gap	6 mm (0.24 in)
Primary winding resistance:	
SR125	2.75 ohm ± 10%
XT125	1.60 ohm ± 10%
Secondary winding resistance:	
SR125	7.9 K ohm ± 20%
XT125	6.6 K ohm ± 20%

Spark plug
Make	NGK
Type	D8EA
Gap	0.6 - 0.7 mm (0.024 - 0.028 in)

1 General description

Since the ignition system is fully electronic there are no mechanical components which can wear out, and no need, therefore, for regular checking and adjustment.

Apart from the ignition and engine kill switches, the HT coil and spark plug and the relevant wiring, the transistor-controlled system of the SR125 model comprises only two pulser or pickup coils mounted on the crankcase left-hand cover and the ignitor unit mounted under the seat, while the capacitor discharge system fitted to the XT125 model comprises a source coil and a pulser coil mounted on the generator stator and the CDI unit mounted behind the steering head.

2 Ignition system: fault diagnosis

1 As no means of adjustment is available, any failure of the system can be traced to the failure of a system component or a simple wiring fault. Of the two possibilities, the latter is by far the most likely. In the event of failure, check the system in a logical fashion, as described below.

2 Remove the spark plug, giving it a quick visual check, noting any obvious signs of flooding or oiling. Fit the plug into the plug cap and rest it on the cylinder head so that the metal body of the plug is in good contact with the cylinder head metal. The electrode end of the plug should be positioned so that sparking can be checked as the engine is spun over.

3 *Important note.* The energy levels in electronic systems can be very high. On no account should the ignition be switched on whilst the plug or plug cap is being held. Shocks from the HT circuit can be most unpleasant. Secondly, it is vital that the plug is in position and soundly earthed when the system is checked for sparking. The ignition components can be **seriously damaged** if the HT circuit becomes isolated.

4 Having observed the above precautions, turn the ignition and engine kill switches to 'On' and kick the engine over. If the system is in good condition a regular, fat blue spark should be evident at the plug electrodes. If the spark appears thin or yellowish, or is non-existent, further investigation will be necessary. Before proceeding further, turn the ignition off and remove the key as a safety measure.

5 Ignition faults can be divided into two categories, namely those where the ignition system has failed completely and those which are due to a partial failure. The likely faults are listed below, starting with the most probable source of failure. Work through the list systematically, referring to the subsequent sections for full details of the necessary checks and tests.

a) Defective spark plug or spark plug cap
b) Loose, corroded or damaged wiring connections, broken or shorted wiring between any of the component parts of the ignition system
c) Faulty ignition switch or engine kill switch
d) Faulty ignition coil
e) Faulty ignitor unit (SR125 model) or CDI unit (XT125)
f) Faulty source coil (XT125 only) or pulser coil (all models)

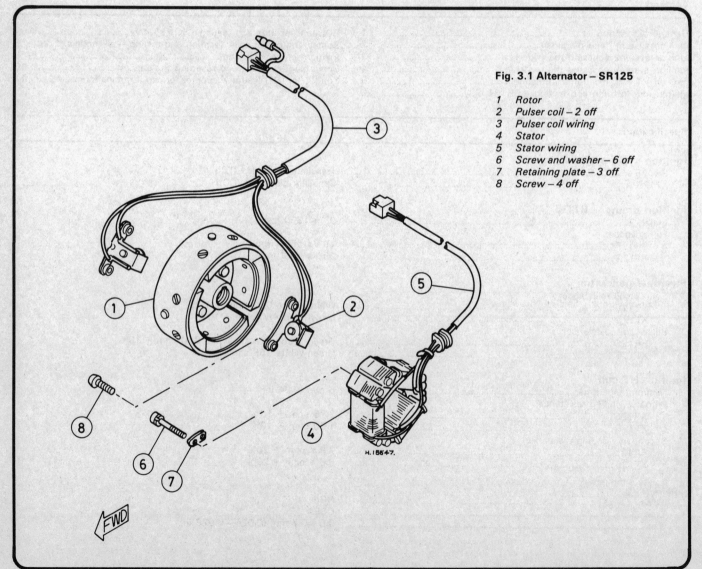

Fig. 3.1 Alternator – SR125

1 Rotor
2 Pulser coil – 2 off
3 Pulser coil wiring
4 Stator
5 Stator wiring
6 Screw and washer – 6 off
7 Retaining plate – 3 off
8 Screw – 4 off

H.15547.

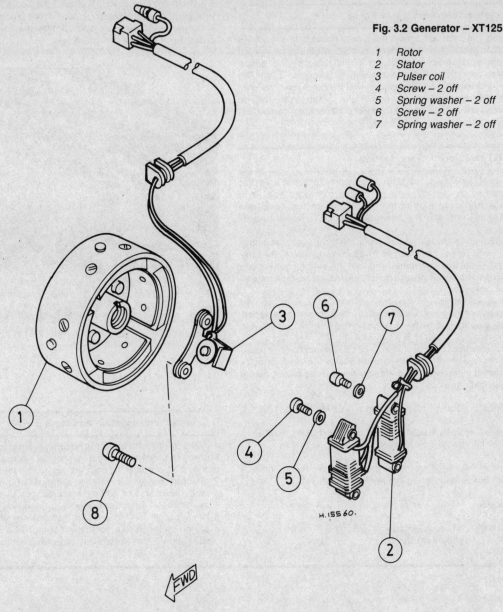

Fig. 3.2 Generator – XT125

1 Rotor
2 Stator
3 Pulser coil
4 Screw – 2 off
5 Spring washer – 2 off
6 Screw – 2 off
7 Spring washer – 2 off

3 Ignition system: checking the wiring

1 The wiring should be checked visually, noting any signs of corrosion around the various terminals and connectors. If the fault has developed in wet conditions, water may have entered any of the connectors or switches, causing a short circuit. A temporary cure can be effected by spraying the relevant area with one of the proprietary de-watering aerosols, such as WD40 or similar. A more permanent solution is to dismantle the switch or connector and coat the exposed parts with silicone grease to prevent the ingress of water. The exposed backs of connectors can be sealed off using a silicone rubber sealant.

2 Light corrosion can normally be cured by scraping or sanding the affected area, though in serious cases it may prove necessary to renew the switch or connector affected. Check the wiring for chafing or breakage, particularly where it passes close to part of the frame or its fittings. As a temporary measure, damaged insulation can be repaired with PVC tape, but the wire concerned should be renewed at the earliest opportunity.

3 Using the wiring diagram at the end of the manual, check each wire for breakage or short circuits using a multimeter set on the resistance scale or a dry battery and bulb wired as shown in the accompanying illustration. In each case, there should be continuity between the ends of each wire.

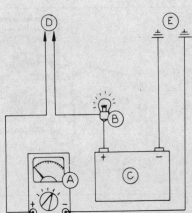

Fig. 3.3 Simple testing arrangement for checking the wiring

A Multimeter
B Bulb
C Battery
D Positive probe
E Negative probe

4   Ignition system: checking the switches

Again using the test equipment described above and the wiring diagram at the back of this Manual, check whether the switch connections are being made and broken as indicated by the switch diagrams which are part of the main wiring diagram. It will be necessary to remove the headlamp rim and reflector unit to gain access to the connectors of each switch. If any switch is found to be defective usually renewal will be required although nothing can be lost by attempting repair.

5   Ignition HT coil: location and testing

1   The ignition HT coil is a small black or grey plastic sealed unit that is readily identified by the HT lead protruding from one end. It is mounted on the frame top tube to the rear of the steering head; the sidepanels, the dual seat and the fuel tank must be removed to gain access to it.

2   Maintenance is restricted to ensuring that the coil mounting bracket/frame earth points are clean and free from corrosion, that the mounting bolts are securely tightened and that the wiring connections are in good order. If the coil proves defective it must be renewed as repairs are not possible.

3   If the coil is suspected of being faulty it should be removed and taken to a competent Yamaha Service Agent or auto-electrical expert for checking on a spark gap tester. A sound coil will produce a reliable spark across a minimum gap of 6 mm (0.24 in).

4   If a spark gap tester is not available, a basic test can be conducted using a multimeter with ohm and kilo ohm scales. The coil primary windings are tested by making the meter connections as shown below and noting the readings obtained:

SR125 model	Orange to Red/white leads	2.75 ohm ± 10%
XT125 model	Orange lead to earth (mounting bracket)	1.60 ohm ± 10%

The coil secondary windings are tested by making the meter connections as shown below and noting the readings obtained:

SR125 model	HT to Orange leads	7.9 K ohm ± .10%
XT125 model	HT lead to earth (mounting bracket)	6.6 K ohm ± 10%

5   If either of the readings obtained is appreciably above or below the set figure, the coil should be considered faulty and renewed, although since the set figures are approximate the coil should be taken to an expert for a more thorough check.

5.1 Location of ignition HT coil – SR125 (XT125 similar)

6   Ignitor unit: location and testing – SR125 only

1   The ignitor unit is a large square sealed unit rubber mounted to the frame, underneath the seat. It will be necessary to remove the side panels and the seat to gain access to the unit and its connectors.

2   Unfortunately no data is supplied with which the unit can be tested, the course of action recommended by the manufacturer being to eliminate all other components in the ignition system and then to fit a new ignitor unit. It is recommended, therefore, that the complete machine be taken to a competent Yamaha Service Agent for thorough testing before this somewhat expensive solution is adopted.

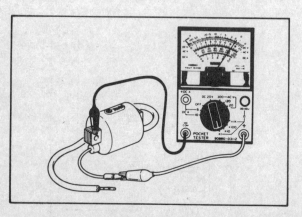

Primary coil test

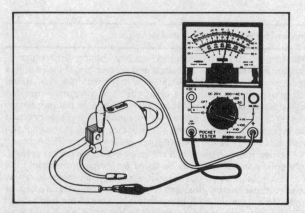

Secondary coil test

Fig. 3.4 Ignition HT coil resistance tests

6.1 Location of ignitor unit – SR125

7 CDI unit: location and testing – XT125 only

1   The CDI unit is a small square sealed unit bolted to the frame behind the steering head. It will be necessary to remove the seat, the side panels and the fuel tank to gain access to the unit and its connectors.
2   Unfortunately no data is supplied with which the unit can be tested, the course of action recommended by the manufacturer being to eliminate all other components in the ignition system and then to fit a new unit. It is recommended, therefore, that the complete machine be taken to a competent Yamaha Service Agent for thorough testing before this somewhat expensive solution is adopted.

7.1 Location of CDI unit – XT125

8 Source and pulser coils: location and testing – all models

1   The ignition pulser coil is mounted on the crankcase left-hand cover, while the ignition source coil (XT125 model) is incorporated in the alternator stator assembly. If any of these coils are found through testing to be faulty they must be renewed, although an auto-electrical

expert may be found who can attempt a repair; it should be noted that in some cases the coils cannot be purchased as a separate replacement part and can be obtained only as part of the stator assembly.
2   Removal and refitting of the coils themselves are described in Sections 7 and 40 of Chapter 1, but each coil can be tested in place; it will be necessary to remove the sidepanels, the seat and the fuel tank to gain access to the various connectors, and a good quality multimeter must be available.
3   To test the pulser (or pickup) coil, disconnect the wires from the ignitor or CDI unit at the multi-pin block connector, make the meter connections as shown below, and compare the readings obtained with those given.

Pulser coil resistance values

SR125 model	Green-Brown, Yellow-White	230 ohm ± 10%
XT125 model	Green-White	265 ohm ± 10%

4   To test the ignition source coil (XT125 model only) disconnect the various wires as described above and use the meter in the same way but making the connections shown below.

Source coil resistance value

Brown to Red leads	450 ohm ± 10%

5   If any of the readings obtained do not correspond with those given the coil must be considered faulty and renewed. It is worthwhile, however, to take the machine to a competent Yamaha Service Agent for accurate testing.

9 Ignition timing: checking

1   Although there is no provision for the adjustment of the ignition timing since there should be no need for it, it may prove necessary on occasion to check that the ignition timing is correct and that the components of the secondary advance circuit are functioning correctly. For example the generator stator or pulser coil (as appropriate) may have been disturbed during the course of other work on the engine/gearbox unit, in which case it would be advisable to check that it has been refitted correctly.
2   The ignition timing can be carried out using only a good quality 'strobe' timing lamp. It is recommended that one of the better quality xenon tube lamps is purchased, of the type which requires an external power source. The cheaper types may not produce enough light to be of any use, and may even produce an inaccurate reading.
3   Remove the inspection cap that is screwed into the top of the crankcase left-hand cover, then connect the strobe according to its manufacturer's instructions. It is useful to engage the aid of an assistant who can control the engine speed while the first person uses the timing lamp, and it is recommended that a piece of rag be placed over the inspection aperture, whenever the strobe is not being used to illuminate the timing mark, to reduce to a minimum the amount of oil that will be ejected as the engine rotates.
4   Start the engine and allow it to idle, then aim the lamp at the inspection aperture. The pointer in the rim of the inspection aperture should be between the two parallel lines which are stamped on the rotor rim to form the timing index mark. Increase engine speed slowly to no more than 5500 - 6000 rpm (as appropriate); the two lines should move smoothly out of sight and the full advance mark (a dot stamped in the rotor rim) should appear and move into alignment with the pointer. Stop the engine and disconnect the strobe, then refit the inspection plug and wash off all traces of oil from the engine. Do not forget to check the oil level and to top up if necessary.
5   If the timing marks were not in alignment, or if any doubts arise about the efficiency of the ignition advance the machine should be taken to a competent Yamaha Service Agent for an expert second opinion. If a discrepancy is encountered, the fault will be in the pulser coil or the ignitor/CDI unit; these must be tested and renewed if necessary as described in the relevant Sections of this Chapter. It is worth checking, however, that the alternator rotor and stator are correctly fitted and securely fastened (see Sections 7 and 40 of Chapter 1) before any components are condemned unnecessarily.

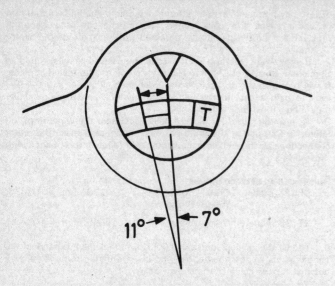

Fig. 3.5 Ignition timing index marks at idle speed

10 Spark plug: checking and resetting the gap

1   The spark plug supplied as original equipment is the NGK D8EA, which will prove satisfactory in most operating conditions; alternatives are available to allow for varying altitudes, climatic conditions and the use to which the machine is put. If the spark plug is suspected of being faulty it can be tested only by the substitution of a brand new (not second-hand) plug of the correct make, type, and heat range; always carry a spare on the machine.

2   Note that the advice of a competent Yamaha Service Agent or similar expert should be sought before the plug heat range is altered from standard. The use of too cold, or hard, a grade of plug will result in fouling and the use of too hot, or soft, a grade of plug will result in engine damage due to the excess heat being generated. If the correct grade of plug is fitted, however, it will be possible to use the condition of the spark plug electrodes to diagnose a fault in the engine or to decide whether the engine is operating efficiently or not. The series of photographs in Routine Maintenance will show this clearly.

3   It is advisable to carry a new spare sparking plug on the machine, having first set the electrodes to the correct gap. Whilst spark plugs do not fail often, a new replacement is well worth having if a breakdown does occur. Ensure that the spare is of the correct heat range and type.

4   The correct electrode gap is 0.6 - 0.7 mm (0.024 - 0.028 in). The gap can be assessed using feeler gauges. If necessary, alter the gap by bending the outer electrode, preferably using a proper electrode tool. **Never** bend the centre electrode, otherwise the porcelain insulator will crack, and may cause damage to the engine if particles break away whilst the engine is running.

5   Before refitting a spark plug into the cylinder head; coat the threads sparingly with a graphited grease to aid future removal. Use the correct size spanner when tightening the plug, otherwise the spanner may slip and damage the ceramic insulator. The plug should be tightened by hand only at first and then secured with a quarter turn of the spanner so that it seats firmly on its sealing ring. If a torque wrench is available, tighten the plug to a torque setting of 2.0 kgf m (14.5 lbf ft).

6   Never overtighten a spark plug otherwise there is risk of stripping the threads from the cylinder head, especially as it is cast in light alloy. A stripped thread can be repaired without having to scrap the cylinder head by using a 'Helicoil' thread insert. This is a low-cost service, operated by a number of dealers.

11 Spark plug (HT) lead and suppressor cap: examination

1   Erratic running faults and problems with the engine suddenly cutting out in wet weather can often be attributed to leakage from the high tension lead and spark plug cap. If this fault is present, it will often be possible to see tiny sparks around the lead and cap at night. One cause of this problem is the accumulation of mud and road grime around the lead, and the first thing to check is that the lead and cap is clean. It is often possible to cure the problem by cleaning the components and sealing them with an aerosol ignition sealer, which will leave an insulating coating on both components.

2   Water dispersant sprays are also highly recommended where the system has become swamped with water. Both these products are easily obtainable at most garages and accessory shops. Occasionally the suppressor cap or the lead itself may break down internally. If this is suspected, the components should be renewed.

3   When the HT lead is permanently attached to the ignition coil, it is recommended that the renewal of the HT lead be entrusted to an auto-electrician who will have the expertise to solder on a new lead without damaging the coil windings.

Chapter 4 Frame and forks

Refer to Chapter 7 for information relating to the 1991-on SR125 models

Contents

Specifications

Frame
Type .... Welded tubular steel

Front forks

	SR125	XT125
Type	Oil damped, coil sprung, telescopic	
Wheel travel	120 mm (4.7 in)	205 mm (8.1 in)
Spring free length	362 mm (14.25 in)	496.5 mm (19.55 in)
Fork oil capacity – per leg	184 cc (6.48 fl oz)	249 cc (8.77 fl oz)
Fork oil level	N/Av	174 mm (6.85 in)
Recommended fork oil	SAE 10W/30SE engine oil	SAE 10 fork oil or SAE 10W/30SE engine oil

Rear suspension

	SR125	XT125
Type	Pivoted fork, two coil spring oil damped shock absorbers	Cantilever (Yamaha Monocross)
Wheel travel	78 mm (3.1 in)	180 mm (7.1 in)
Suspension unit travel	78 mm (3.1 in)	92 mm (3.6 in)
Spring free length	178.5 mm (7.03 in)	265 mm (10.43 in)
Gas pressure	N/App	14 kg/cm^2 (199 psi)
Pivoted fork/subframe maximum endfloat	1.0 mm (0.039 in)	1.0 mm (0.039 in)
Pivoted fork/subframe maximum free play	1.0 mm (0.039 in)	1.0 mm (0.039 in)

Torque settings

Component	kgf m	lbf ft
Engine mounting bolts	3.3	24.0
Front wheel spindle nut:		
SR125	4.5	32.5
XT125	3.9	28.0
Handlebar clamp bolts	2.0	14.5
Steering stem crown bolt:		
SR125..	4.5	32.5
XT125	5.5	40.0
Fork cap bolts – SR125 only	4.5	32.5
Top yoke pinch bolts – XT125 only	2.0	14.5
Bottom yoke pinch bolts:		
SR125	3.2	23.0
XT125	3.8	27.5
Footrest mounting bolts – XT125 only:		
Left-hand (12 mm x 1)	4.3	31.0
Right-hand (10 mm x 2)	4.5	32.5
Swinging arm/sub-frame pivot bolt retaining nut:		
SR125	4.5	32.5
XT125	8.0	58.0
Suspension unit mountings:		
SR125	3.5	25.0
XT125	2.5	18.0
Suspensiom unit preload adjuster locknut – XT125 only	5.5	40.0
Rear wheel spindle nut:		
SR125	6.5	47.0
XT125	8.5	61.5

1   General description

A welded tubular steel frame is employed, the frame being of the open diamond type which uses the engine as a stressed member. The front forks are of the conventional coil sprung, hydraulically damped type, and on SR125 models the rear suspension is equally conventional, comprising two coil sprung, hydraulically damped suspension units acting on a tubular steel pivoted fork.

XT125 models are fitted with a cantilever rear suspension, Yamaha's original 'MonoCross' design. A sub-frame of square-section tubing pivots on plain bushes, its movement being controlled by a single suspension unit of De Carbon type. The unit is coil sprung, with hydraulic damping and a nitrogen-filled gas chamber to act as a supplementary springing medium.

2   Front fork legs: removal and refitting

1   Place the machine securely on its centre stand or on a stout wooden box or paddock stand so that the front wheel is clear of the ground. The front wheel can then be removed according to the instructions given in the relevant Section of Chapter 5.
2   Remove the four mudguard mounting bolts then carefully withdraw the mudguard, taking care not to damage the finish. Mudguard removal is not necessary on the XT125 model.
3   On SR125 models, the fork legs are retained in the top yoke by the fork top bolt. Remove the fork top bolts and the bottom yoke pinch bolts. It may be necessary to release the handlebars to gain access to the top bolts – see Section 5. It should then be possible to slide the fork leg down and away from the yoke. On the XT125 model, the fork legs are retained by pinch bolts in both top and bottom yokes. On these models slacken the pinch bolts and slide the fork legs down and out of the yokes. Note that the top bolts should be slackened first, if the forks are to be dismantled.
4   If the fork legs prove to be stuck in the yokes, apply penetrating fluid and attempt to rotate the legs by hand to free them. It may be necessary to completely remove the pinch bolts and to spring the clamps apart slightly with a large, flat-bladed screwdriver. Great care must be taken not to distort or to break the clamp, as this will necessitate renewal of the complete yoke. If the leg is still reluctant to move, push a metal bar of suitable diameter through the spindle lug in the fork lower leg and tap firmly downwards on the protruding end of the bar to drive the fork leg from the yokes.
5   Once the legs have been removed, put them to one side to await stripping and examination. If they are not to be dismantled, ensure that they remain upright so that no fork oil is lost.
6   Reassembly is a straightforward reversal of the removal sequence, noting the following points. On models fitted with a fork top bolt, the leg must be pushed up through the bottom yoke to the underside of the top yoke and retained there by firmly tightening the top bolt. On XT125 models push the fork leg up through both yokes until the top of the chromed stanchion tube is flush with the upper surface of the top yoke. It may be necessary to remove the rubber plug from the top of the fork leg to ease this task. Once in place, the fork legs should be retained by tightening the top yoke pinch bolts as lightly as possible. For both types of forks, refitting the legs will be made easier if a small amount of grease or oil is smeared over the upper length of the stanchion. Tighten the gaiter clips securely (where fitted).
7   When fitting the front mudguard and wheel back into the forks, tighten the spindle nut and other mounting bolts only lightly at first and take the machine off its centre stand or box. Apply the front brake and push down on the handlebars several times so that the operation of the fork legs settles each component in its correct place. Using a torque wrench, tighten all nuts and bolts from the wheel spindle upwards to the fork top bolt or top yoke pinch bolt, to the torque settings given in the Specifications Section of this Chapter. This will ensure that the fork components can operate freely and easily, with no undue strain imposed from an overtightened bolt or an awkwardly-positioned part.
8   Be very careful to check fork operation, front brake adjustment and that all nuts and bolts are securely fastened before taking the machine out on the road.

2.2 Mudguard is retained by two bolts to each fork leg

2.3a Remove fork top bolt ...

2.3b ... and slacken pinch bolt to release fork legs

3 Front fork legs: dismantling and reassembly

1 Dismantle and rebuild the fork legs separately so that there is no chance of exchanging components, thus promoting undue wear.

SR125 models

2 Remove the O-ring from the top of the fork stanchion and invert the leg over a container to drain the oil. Pump the leg several times to ensure that as much oil as possible is removed.

3 Displace the dust seal from the top of the fork lower leg and withdraw the circlip and the plain washer from the top of the lower leg, above the oil seal. Using soft jaws covers to prevent the alloy from being marked, clamp the fork lower leg wheel spindle lug in a vice and withdraw the stanchion with the seal and bushes. To do this, press the stanchion in as far as possible, then withdraw it sharply. This 'slide-hammer' action must be repeated several times before the stanchion will be released. In especially stubborn cases, take the fork leg to a Yamaha Service Agent who can dismantle it using a slide hammer 90890-01290 and adaptor 90890-01291. For those owners who have the facilities, a slide hammer arrangement can be devised as shown in the accompanying photograph.

4 With the oil seal released from the fork lower leg, withdraw the stanchion complete with the three bushes. Remove from inside the stanchion, the fork spring, noting carefully which way round it is fitted, the washer and the spacer. Invert the lower leg to tip out the damper rod.

5 Carefully clean the upper length of the stanchion, removing any dirt or corrosion, smear oil along its length and slide off the oil seal and the fork top bush. Note that since this will almost certainly damage the seal lips, in spite of the precautions described, the seals must be renewed whenever the forks are dismantled. The remaining bushes can be removed after their retaining circlips have been withdrawn.

6 On reassembly, it is assumed that all components are scrupulously clean. Refer to the photographs and illustrations accompanying the text when refitting the bushes to the stanchion. Ensure that all circlips are correctly seated and do not stand proud of their bushes. Oil the stanchion surface before refitting the top bush and a new oil seal.

7 Having refitted the spacer and washer inside the stanchion, use the notes made on dismantling to refit the fork spring the correct way up. If no notes were made, wear marks on the washer and on the damper rod might reveal which end of the spring bore against them. Insert the damper rod into the fork lower leg.

8 Smear oil over the bushes and insert the stanchion fully into the lower leg, then press the top bush down so that its shoulder locates in the recess in the lower leg. Smear grease over the outside of the fork seal and press it into the lower leg as far as possible by hand, ensuring that it enters squarely into its housing. Refit the plain washer on top of the seal.

9 The seal must be driven into the lower leg far enough to expose the circlip groove and no further. The Yamaha service tool 90890-01149 is a metal tube about 2 – 3 inches long and of the same inside and outside diameter as the seal, with two handles welded to it so that pressure can be applied. If this is not available a substitute could be fabricated; this is worthwhile if the forks are to be dismantled very often. Ensure that the surface which contacts the seal is free from burrs or sharp edges. The only alternative is to use a hammer and drift, tapping evenly all the way round the seal top surface; this is a method which requires care and patience if the seal is not to be damaged. Ensure that the drift bears only on the metal washer to avoid damage to the seal, and be very careful that the seal remains square in its housing.

10 Whichever method is used, as soon as the circlip groove is fully exposed above the metal washer, refit the seal retaining circlip, ensuring that it is correctly engaged in the groove. Pack the space above the seal with grease as additional protection against dirt and corrosion then refit the dust seal. Pump the fork several times to ensure that it is working smoothly and easily.

11 Refill the leg with 184 cc (6.48 fl oz) of the recommended grade of oil. Due to the small size of the filler orifice oil will have to be added using a cheap syringe, as shown, or poured in very slowly through a funnel. Be careful to put exactly the same amount of oil in both legs. Refit the O-ring in the recess at the top of the stanchion.

XT125 models

12 Displace the black plastic top plug and unscrew the fork top bolt. As mentioned in Section 2, it is easiest if the bolt is slackened while

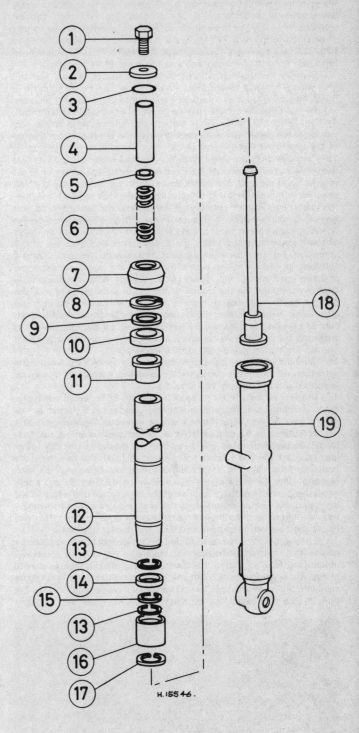

H.15546.

Fig. 4.1 Front fork – SR125

1	Top bolt	11	Top bush
2	Washer	12	Stanchion
3	O-ring	13	Circlip – 2 off
4	Spacer	14	Bush
5	Washer	15	Circlip
6	Fork spring	16	Bottom bush
7	Dust seal	17	Circlip
8	Circlip	18	Damper rod
9	Plain washer	19	Lower leg
10	Oil seal		

the stanchion is still clamped in the fork yokes. Alternatively, using soft jaw covers to avoid marking the chrome, the stanchion can be clamped in a vice. The top bolt has an internal hexagon, similar to that of an Allen screw; if a 17 mm key is not available an adaptor for use with ordinary spanners can be made by finding a spare bolt whose head will fit in the hexagon and welding a nut to its threads.

13 Remove the top bolt with its O-ring, the spacer, washer and the fork spring. Make a careful note of which way up the fork spring is fitted. Invert the leg over a suitable container to drain the oil. Pump the leg several times to ensure that as much oil as possible is removed.

14 On 1983 on models only, slacken the gaiter clamp screw and withdraw the gaiter. On all models, displace the dust seal from the top of the fork lower leg.

15 Carefully clamp, to avoid distortion, the fork lower leg in a vice and use an Allen key to unscrew the damper rod retaining bolt which is set in a recess in the base of the fork lower leg. In some cases the bolt will unscrew with ease, but it is more usual for the bolt to free itself from the lower leg and then rotate with the damper rod assembly, so that nothing useful is achieved. In such a case, obtain a length of wooden dowel, grind a coarse taper on one end which will engage in the head of the damper rod, and insert the dowel down into the bore of the stanchion. The services of an assistant will now be required. Clamp a self-locking wrench to the protruding end of the dowel and with the assistant preventing the dowel from turning and simultaneously applying pressure via the dowel to the head of the damper rod, the damper rod will be locked in place so that the retaining bolt can be unscrewed. When working alone, use a longer length of dowel which can be clamped in the vice. By pushing down on the fork lower leg with one hand it should be possible to lock the damper rod firmly enough for the retaining bolt to be unscrewed.

16 Carefully pull the stanchion out of the lower leg. Invert the stanchion to tip out the damper rod and spring, then invert the lower leg to tip out the damper rod seat.

17 The fork oil seal fitted to each leg should be renewed whenever the stanchion is removed and must be renewed if it is disturbed as the means used for removing the seal will almost certainly damage it. The seal is retained by a circlip which must be removed using a small, flat-bladed screwdriver to ease it away from its groove in the fork lower leg. Use a large flat-bladed screwdriver to lever the seal from its housing. Take care not to scratch the internal surface of the seal housing with the edge of the screwdriver blade, and do not apply excessive pressure or there is a risk of the upper edge of the fork lower leg being cracked or distorted. If the seal appears difficult to move, heat the leg by pouring boiling water over its outer surface. This will cause the alloy leg to expand sufficiently to loosen the seal.

18 On reassembly, it is assumed that all components are scrupulously clean. Refer to the illustration accompanying the text for additional guidance if needed. Clamp the lower leg securely in a vice by means of the wheel spindle boss. Coat the inner and outer diameters of the seal with the recommended fork oil and push the seal squarely into the bore of the fork lower leg by hand. Ensure that the seal is fitted

squarely, then tap it fully into position, using a hammer and a suitably sized drift such as a socket spanner. The drift should bear only on the harder, outer diameter of the seal, never on the sealing lips themselves, and should have a smooth undamaged surface when it comes into contact with the seal. Tap the seal into the bore of the lower leg just enough to expose the circlip groove. Refit the retaining circlip securely in its groove.

19 Slide the damper rod rebound spring into place under the head of the damper rod and insert the damper rod assembly into the stanchion. Push the damper rod down the length of the stanchion until it projects fully from the stanchion lower end. Refit the damper rod seat over the damper rod end, using a smear of grease to stick it in place.

20 Smear the sliding surface of the stanchion with a light coating of fork oil and carefully insert the stanchion into the lower leg, taking great care not to damage the sealing lips of the oil seal. Push a fork spring or the length of dowel used on dismantling down into the stanchion and apply pressure on this to ensure that the damper rod or its seat is pressed firmly into the base of the lower leg. Check that the threads of the damper rod bolt are clean and dry, apply a few drops of thread locking compound and fit the damper rod bolt. Do not forget the sealing washer fitted under the head of the bolt. Tighten the bolt only partially at first, using an Allen key of suitable size. Maintain pressure on the head of the damper rod and push the stanchion firmly as far down into the lower leg as possible to centralise the damper rod in the stanchion. The damper rod bolt can then be tightened firmly. Withdraw the spring or dowel from the stanchion.

21 Pack the space above the seal with grease as additional protection against dirt or corrosion, then refit the dust seal. On 1983 models only, smear grease over the stanchion upper length and refit the gaiter, but do not tighten its clamp until the fork leg has been refitted in the yokes.

22 Fill the leg with 249 cc (8.77 fl oz) of the recommended fork oil, using a finely graduated measuring vessel to ensure that exactly the same amount of oil is put in each leg. Very slowly pump the leg to distribute the oil, then check the oil level.

23 To measure the oil level in each leg, make up a dipstick from a piece of wire cut to the required length. Check that the fork spring has been removed and push the stanchion fully into the fork lower leg, then use the dipstick to check the level, which should be 174 mm (6.85 in) from the top of the stanchion. Add or remove oil as necessary. Once the correct oil level has been established the fork legs can be refilled to that level during routine maintenance when the forks are not completely dismantled. This will automatically allow for the presence of any residual fork oil which cannot be removed without fully dismantling the fork leg and will ensure smooth and consistent fork action.

24 When the fork oil has been poured in, and the level checked, pull the stanchion out of the leg as far as possible and insert the fork spring using the notes made on dismantling to ensure that it is fitted the correct way up. Refit the washer, the spacer and the top bolt, complete with its O-ring. Tighten securely the top bolt and refit the top plug.

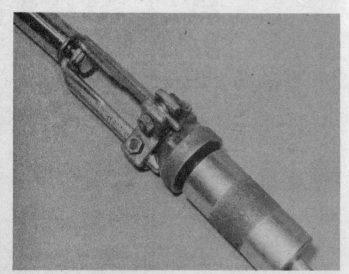

3.3 If available, slide hammer can be used as shown to dismantle fork leg

3.4 Note which way round fork spring was fitted before it is removed

3.6a Check circlips are correctly located in their grooves

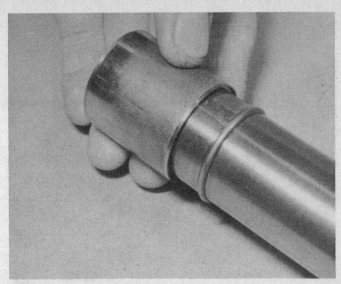
3.6b Oil bushes before refitting

3.6c Circlip must not project beyond bush

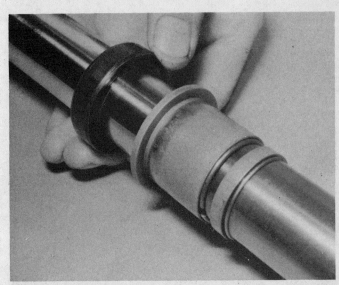
3.6d Refit oil seal and top bush over stanchion upper end – oil before refitting

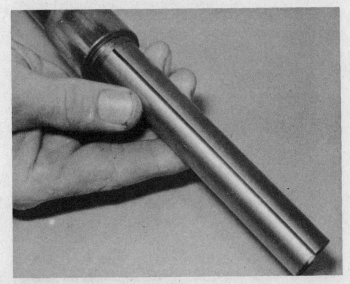
3.7a Insert spacer into fork stanchion ...

3.7b ... do not omit washer before refitting fork spring

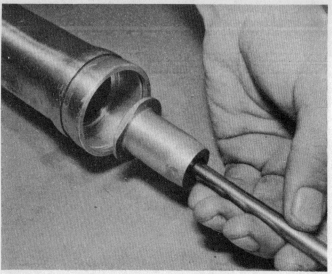

3.7c Damper rod is fitted as shown into lower leg

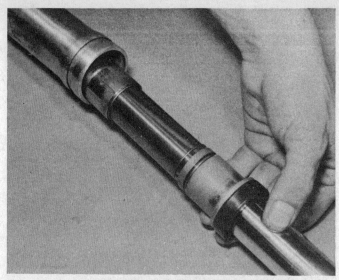

3.8a Oil bushes and seal before inserting stanchion into lower leg

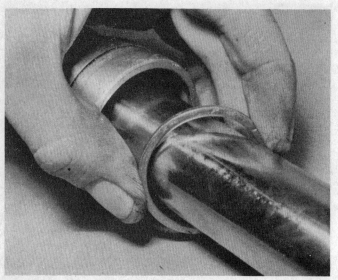

3.8b Plain washer will protect seal during refitting

3.10a Refit circlip as soon as groove is exposed ...

3.10b ... then refit dust seal

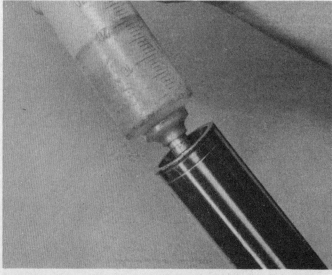

3.11a Pour correct amount of oil slowly into fork leg

3.11b Do not omit O-ring from top of fork leg

4 Front fork legs: examination and renovation

1   Carefully clean and dry all the components of the fork leg. Lay them out on a clean work surface and inspect each one, looking for excessive wear, cracks, or other damage. All traces of oil, dirt, and swarf should be removed, and any damaged or worn components renewed.

2   Examine the sliding surface of the stanchion or bushes, as applicable, and the internal surface of the lower leg, looking for signs of scuffing which will indicate that excessive wear has taken place. Slide the stanchion into the lower leg so that it seats fully. Any wear present will be easily found by attempting to move the stanchion backwards and forwards, and from side to side, in the bore of the lower leg. It is inevitable that a certain degree of slackness will be found, especially when the test is repeated at different points as the stanchion is gradually withdrawn from the lower leg, and it is largely a matter of experience accurately to assess the amount of wear necessary to justify renewal of either the stanchion, the bushes, or the lower leg. It is recommended that the two components be taken to a motorcycle dealer for an expert opinion to be given if there is any doubt about the degree of wear found. Note that while wear will only become a serious problem after a high mileage has been covered, it is essential that such wear is rectified by the renewal of the components concerned if the handling and stability of the machine are not to be impaired.

3   Check the outer surface of the stanchion for scratches or roughness; it is only too easy to damage the oil seal during the reassembly if these high spots are not eased down. The stanchions are unlikely to bend unless the machine is damaged in an accident. Any significant bend will be detected by eye, but if there is any doubt about straightness, roll down the stanchion tubes on a flat surface such as a sheet of plate glass. If the stanchions are bent, they must be renewed. Unless specialised repair equipment is available it is rarely practicable to effect a satisfactory repair to a damaged stanchion.

4   Check the stanchion sliding surface for pits caused by corrosion; if the gaiters are intact such damage will be rare. Such pits should be smoothed down with fine emery paper and filled, if necessary, with Araldite. Once the Araldite has set fully hard, use a fine file or emery paper to rub it down so that the original contour of the stanchion is restored.

5   After an extended period of service, the fork springs may take a permanent set. If the spring lengths are suspect, then they should be measured and the readings obtained compared with the lengths given in the Specifications Section of this Chapter. It is always advisable to fit new fork springs where the length of the original items has decreased by a significant amount. Always renew the springs as a set, never separately.

6   The piston ring fitted to the damper rod may wear if oil changes at the specified intervals are neglected. If damping has become

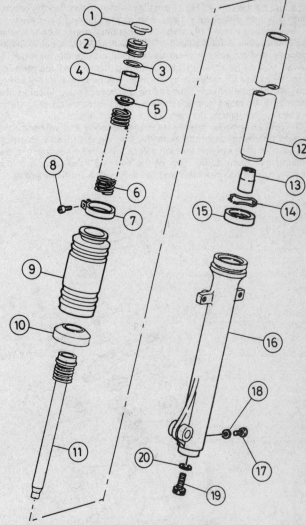

Fig. 4.2 Front fork – XT125

1 Top plug	11 Damper rod
2 Top bolt	12 Stanchion
3 O-ring	13 Damper rod seat
4 Spacer	14 Circlip
5 Washer	15 Oil seal
6 Fork spring	16 Lower leg
7 Gaiter clamp – 1983/84 model	17 Drain screw
8 Screw – 1983/84 model	18 Sealing washer
9 Gaiter – 1983/84 model	19 Allen bolt
10 Dust seal	20 Sealing washer

weakened and does not improve as a result of an oil change, the piston ring should be renewed. Check also that the oilways in the damper rod have not become obstructed.

7   Closely examine the gaiter or dust seal for splits or signs of deterioration. If found to be defective, it must be renewed as any ingress of dirt will rapidly accelerate wear of the oil seal and fork stanchion. It is advisable to renew any gasket washers fitted beneath bolt heads as a matter of course. The same applies to the O-rings fitted to the fork top bolts.

5 Steering head assembly: removal and refitting

1   Working as described in Section 2 of this Chapter, remove the front wheel, the mudguard (where applicable) and the front forks, then remove the seat, the sidepanels and the fuel tank.

2   Remove the handlebar clamp cover (SR125 only) then withdraw

the four handlebar clamp bolts and the handlebar clamps. Move the handlebars backwards as far as possible without straining the control cables or wiring and secure them clear of the steering head area.

3   The procedure from this stage onwards must depend on the work being undertaken. If the machine is being dismantled to repair accident damage, every component must be removed individually for repair or renewal, but if the steering head is being dismantled for greasing during the course of routine maintenance, it is permissible to avoid as much of the preliminary dismantling as possible by keeping the components in major sub-assemblies and by removing only those items which will hinder the removal of the fork yokes.

4   On SR125 models, release its mounting bolts and withdraw the complete headlamp assembly with the turn signals. If only electrical leads such as the horn and ignition switch wires are disconnected, the headlamp can hang down clear of the steering head area; it is not necessary to remove the horn and ignition switch from the yokes.

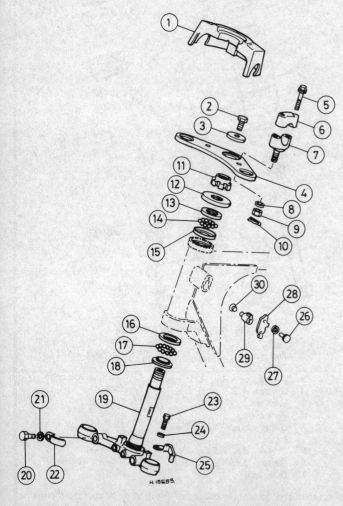

Fig. 4.3 Steering head assembly – SR125

1 Steering head cover	16 Bottom cup
2 Crown bolt	17 Steel ball – 19 off
3 Washer	18 Bottom cone
4 Top yoke	19 Bottom yoke
5 Bolt – 4 off	20 Bolt – 2 off
6 Handlebar clamp top half	21 Spring washer – 2 off
7 Handlebar clamp bottom half	22 Cable guide
8 Spring washer – 2 off	23 Bolt
9 Nut – 2 off	24 Spring washer
10 R-pin – 2 off	25 Cable guide
11 Bearing adjusting ring	26 Rivet
12 Dust excluder	27 Washer
13 Top cone	28 Steering lock cover
14 Steel ball – 22 off	29 Steering lock
15 Top cup	30 Conical spring

5   On XT125 models, disconnect the speedometer (and tachometer, where fitted) drive cables, unplug the instrument and warning lamp bulb holders and release the instrument panel by removing the two bolts which secure it to the fork top yoke. This will release the headlamp bracket; if the ignition switch wires only are disconnected, the complete assembly, including headlamp, turn signals and horn, can be allowed to hang down clear of the steering head area. There is no need to remove the front mudguard. Remove the front brake cable from its guides.

6   Remove the large chromium plated bolt from its location through the centre of the top yoke. Using a soft-faced hammer, give the top yoke a gentle tap to free it from the steering head and lift it from position. Carry out a final check around the bottom yoke to ensure that all components have been removed which might prevent its release.

7   Support the weight of the bottom yoke and, using a C-spanner of the correct size, remove the steering head bearing adjusting ring. If a C-spanner is not available, a soft metal drift may be used in conjunction with a hammer to slacken the ring.

8   Remove the dust excluder and the cone of the upper bearing. The bottom yoke, complete with steering stem, can now be lowered from position. Ensure that any balls that fall from the bearings as the bearing races separate are caught and retained. It is quite likely that only the balls from the lower bearing will drop free, since those of the upper bearing will remain seated in the bearing cup. Full details of examining and renovating the steering head bearings are given in Section 6 of this Chapter.

9   Fitting of the steering head assembly is a direct reversal of that procedure used for removal, whilst taking into account the following points. It is advisable to position all nineteen balls of the lower bearing around the bearing cone before inserting the steering stem fully into the steering head. Retain these balls in position with grease of the recommended type and fill both bearing cups with the same type of grease.

10   With the bottom yoke pressed fully home into the steering head, place the twenty-two balls into the upper bearing cup and fit the bearing cone followed by the dust excluder. Refit the adjusting ring and tighten it, finger-tight. The ring should now be tightened firmly to seat the bearings, using a C-spanner only; do not apply excessive force. Turn the bottom yoke from lock to lock five or six times to settle the balls, then slacken the adjusting ring until all pressure is removed.

11   To provide the initial setting for steering head bearing adjustment, tighten the adjusting ring carefully until resistance is felt then loosen it by $\frac{1}{8}$ to $\frac{1}{4}$ of a turn. Remember to check that the adjustment is correct, as described in Routine Maintenance, when the steering head assembly has been reassembled and the forks and front wheel refitted.

12   Finally, whilst refitting and reconnecting all disturbed components, take care to ensure that all control cables, drive cables, electrical leads, etc are correctly routed and that proper reference is made to the list of torque wrench settings given in the Specifications Section of this Chapter and of Chapter 5. Check that the headlamp beam height has not been disturbed and ensure that all controls and instruments function correctly before taking the machine on the public highway.

6   Steering head bearings: examination and renovation

1   Before commencing reassembly of the steering head component parts, take care to examine each of the steering head bearings. The ball bearing tracks of their respective cup and cone bearings should be polished and free from any indentations or cracks. If wear or damage is evident, then the cups and cones must be renewed as complete sets.

2   Carefully clean and examine the balls contained in each bearing assembly. These should also be polished and show no signs of surface cracks or blemishes. If any one ball is found to be defective, then the complete set should be renewed. Remember that a complete set of these balls is relatively cheap and it is not worth the risk of refitting items that are in doubtful condition. Note that two different sizes of ball are used, the upper bearing being fitted with $\frac{3}{16}$ in balls and the lower bearing with $\frac{1}{4}$ in items. Be careful at all times not to confuse the two sizes and ensure that each bearing is fitted with balls of the correct size.

3   Twenty-two balls are fitted in the top bearing and nineteen in the lower. This arrangement will leave a gap between any two balls but an extra ball must not be fitted, otherwise the balls will press against each

other thereby accelerating wear and causing the steering action to be stiff.

4 The bearing cups are a drive fit in the steering head and may be removed by passing a long drift through the inner bore of the steering head and drifting out the defective item from the opposite end. The drift must be moved progressively around the race to ensure that it leaves the steering head evenly and squarely.

5 The lower of the two cones fits over the steering stem and may be removed by carefully drifting it up the length of the stem with a flat-ended chisel or a similar tool. Again, take care to ensure that the cone is kept square to the stem. There is a rubber seal fitted beneath this

cone on XT125 models; the seal must be renewed if damaged or worn to prevent the entry of dirt into the bearing.

6 Fitting of the new cups and cone is a straightforward procedure whilst taking note of the following points. Ensure that the cup locations within the steering head are clean and free of rust; the same applies to the stem and head locations. Lightly grease the stem and head locations to aid fitting and drift each cup or cone into position whilst keeping it square to its location. Fitting of the cups into the steering head will be made easier if the opposite end of the head to which the cup is being fitted has a wooden block placed against it to absorb some of the shock as the drift strikes the cup.

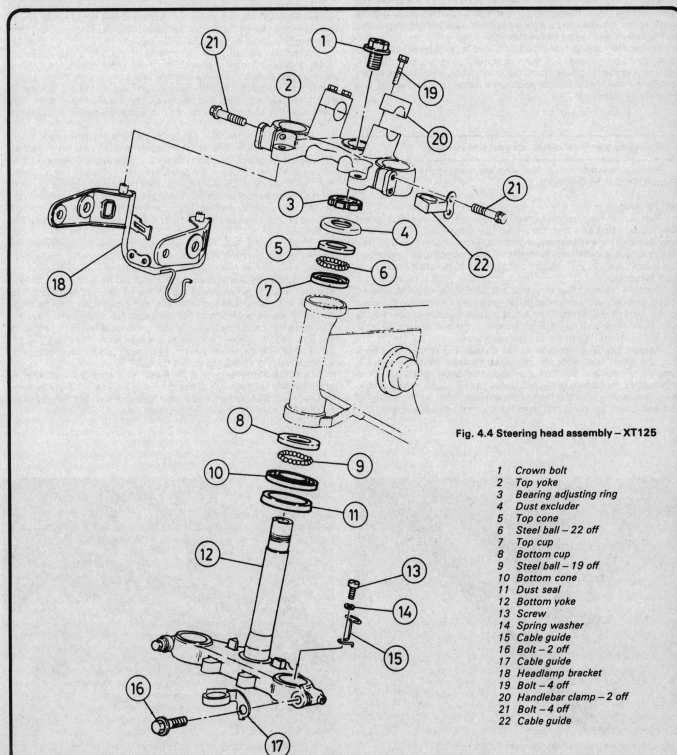

Fig. 4.4 Steering head assembly – XT125

1 Crown bolt
2 Top yoke
3 Bearing adjusting ring
4 Dust excluder
5 Top cone
6 Steel ball – 22 off
7 Top cup
8 Bottom cup
9 Steel ball – 19 off
10 Bottom cone
11 Dust seal
12 Bottom yoke
13 Screw
14 Spring washer
15 Cable guide
16 Bolt – 2 off
17 Cable guide
18 Headlamp bracket
19 Bolt – 4 off
20 Handlebar clamp – 2 off
21 Bolt – 4 off
22 Cable guide

7 Frame: examination and renovation

1   The frame is unlikely to require attention unless accident damage has occurred. In some cases, renewal of the frame is the only satisfactory remedy if the frame is badly out of alignment. Only a few frame specialists have the jigs and mandrels necessary for resetting the frame to the required standard of accuracy, and even then there is no easy means of assessing to what extent the frame may have been overstressed.

2   After the machine has covered a considerable mileage, it is advisable to examine the frame closely for signs of cracking or splitting at the welded joints. Rust corrosion can also cause weakness at these joints. Minor damage can be repaired by welding or brazing, depending on the extent and nature of the damage.

3   Remember that a frame which is out of alignment will cause handling problems and may even promote 'speed wobbles'. If mis-alignment is suspected, as a result of an accident, it will be necessary to strip the machine complete so that the frame can be checked, and if necessary, renewed.

8 Swinging arm/sub-frame: removal and refitting

1   Remove the rear wheel following the instructions given in the relevant Section of Chapter 5.

SR125 models

2   Remove, if required, the brake torque arm and the chainguard from the swinging arm, then slacken all four suspension unit mounting nuts. Remove the two suspension unit bottom mounting nuts and their washers, then pull the units sideways off their swinging arm mounting lugs. Note carefully the position and number of the plain washers at each mounting.

3   Remove the swinging arm pivot bolt securing nut and its washer, noting that this will release both footrests, then withdraw the pivot bolt. If the bolt proves stubborn, apply a good quantity of penetrating fluid, allow time for it to work, then displace the bolt using a hammer and a metal drift. Withdraw the swinging arm.

4   Reassembly is the reverse of the dismantling procedure. Check that the pivot bolt and the passages through which it fits are completely clean and free from corrosion, then apply liberal quantities of grease to the surface of the bolt and to the passages, not forgetting the inside diameter of the bushes themselves. Offer up the swinging arm and insert the pivot bolt from right to left, remembering to refit

correctly the footrests, then refit the retaining nut and its plain washer. Refit the suspension units, ensuring that the plain washers are correctly refitted, and tighten all four suspension unit mounting nuts or bolts to a torque setting of 3.5 kgf m (25 lbf ft), then tighten the pivot bolt retaining nut to 4.5 kgf m (32.5 lbf ft). Complete the remainder of the reassembly work.

5   Before taking the machine out on the road, check that all the nuts and bolts are securely fastened, and that the rear suspension, rear brake, and chain tension are adjusted correctly and working properly.

XT125 models

6   Remove the seat, the sidepanels and the fuel tank. Withdraw the suspension unit top mounting bolt and the single screw which passes through the frame immediately above the sub-frame pivot bolt retaining nut, then remove the retaining nut.

7   Withdraw the sub-frame pivot bolt. If the bolt proves stubborn, apply a good quantity of penetrating fluid, allow time for it to work, then displace the bolt using a hammer and a metal drift. Withdraw the sub-frame complete with the suspension unit, noting the position of the three sealing caps and the retaining plate on the pivot lugs. Separate the suspension unit from the sub-frame as described in Section 10.

8   Reassembly is the reverse of the dismantling procedure. Check that the pivot bolt and the passages through which it fits are completely clean and free from corrosion, then apply liberal quantities of grease to the surface of the bolt and to the passages, not forgetting the crankcase lug. Check that the two thick washers are correctly refitted in their recesses on each side of the crankcase lug and that the sealing caps, chain rubbing block and retaining plate are correctly refitted on the suspension lugs. Refit the suspension unit as described in Section 10.

9   Offer up the sub-frame ensuring that no components are displaced, and that the suspension unit passes correctly through the aperture in the rear mudguard. Push through the sub-frame pivot bolt from right to left and ensure that one of the flats on the bolt head engages with the small raised lug on the frame. Rotate the retaining plate to align its thread with the hole in the frame and refit its single screw. Push through from left to right the suspension unit top mounting bolt, ensuring that it is well greased, then refit its retaining nut and washer. Tighten the nut to a torque setting of 2.5 kgf m (18 lbf ft), then refit the sub-frame pivot bolt retaining nut, tightening it to a torque setting of 8.0 kgf m (58 lbf ft).

10 Complete the remainder of the reassembly work. Before taking the machine out on the road, check that all nuts and bolts are securely fastened and that the rear suspension, chain tension and rear brake are adjusted correctly and working properly.

8.4a Clean pivot bolt and apply grease before refitting

8.4b Do not forget to route chain correctly when refitting swinging arm

8.4c Refit suspension units to ensure swinging arm is correctly positioned ...

8.4d ... before pivot bolt is tightened

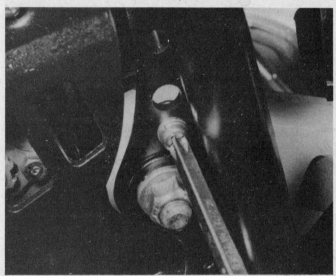

8.6a Single screw above pivot bolt retaining nut must be removed to release ...

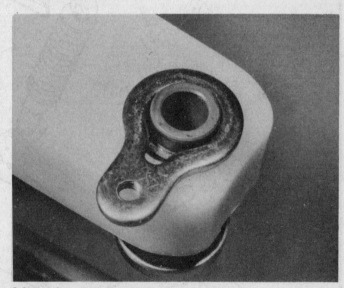

8.6b ... left-hand pivot inner sleeve retaining plate

8.9 Raised lug on frame must engage with flats of pivot bolt head

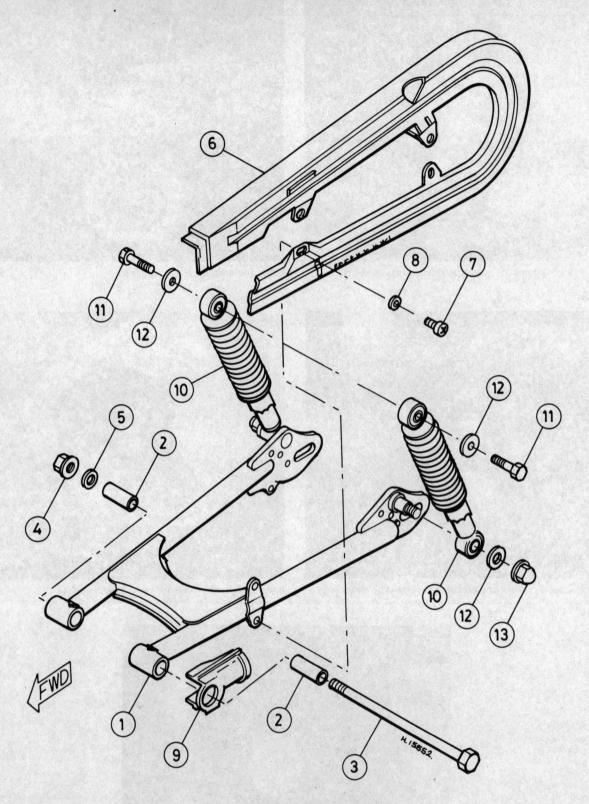

Fig. 4.5 Rear suspension – SR125

1	Swinging arm	5	Washer	8	Washer – 4 off	11	Bolt – 2 off
2	Bush – 2 off	6	Chainguard	9	Chain rubbing block	12	Washer – 4 off
3	Pivot bolt	7	Screw – 4 off	10	Suspension unit – 2 off	13	Nut
4	Nut						

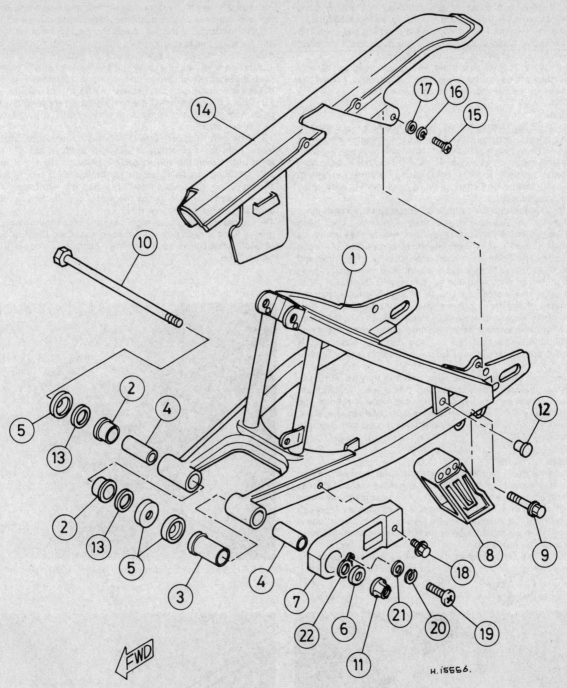

Fig. 4.6 Rear sub-frame – XT125

1	Sub-frame	7	Chain rubbing block
2	Bush – 2 off	8	Chain guide
3	Bush	9	Bolt – 2 off
4	Inner sleeve – 2 off	10	Pivot bolt
5	Sealing cap – 3 off	11	Nut
6	Oil seal	12	Plug – 2 off

13	Shim – as required	18	Bolt
14	Chainguard	19	Screw
15	Screw – 2 off	20	Spring washer
16	Spring washer – 2 off	21	Washer
17	Washer – 2 off	22	Inner sleeve retaining plate

9 Swinging arm/sub-frame: examination and renovation

1 Dismantle as far as possible all components, removing the sealing caps and pushing out the hardened metal inner sleeves and dust seals (where fitted) from each bearing. Thoroughly clean all components, removing all traces of dirt, corrosion and old grease.

2 Inspect closely all components looking for obvious signs of wear such as heavy scoring, or for damage such as cracks or distortion due to accidental impact. Any obviously damaged or worn component must be renewed. If the painted finish has deteriorated it is worth taking the opportunity to repaint the affected area, ensuring that the surface is correctly prepared beforehand.

3 Check the pivot bolt for wear. If the shank of the bolt is seen to be stepped or badly scored, then it must be renewed. Remove all traces of corrosion and hardened grease from the bolt before checking it for straightness by rolling it on a flat surface, such as a sheet of plate glass; if the bolt is not perfectly straight it must be renewed. Check

also that its threads and those of the retaining nut are in good condition; the nut must be renewed if it has lost its self-locking quality.

4   Detach the nylon buffer from the left-hand pivot lug and inspect it for signs of excessive wear. If the buffer no longer protects the pivot lug from the final drive chain, it must be renewed.

5   Since the two machines are fitted with pivot bearings of very different type, they are described in separate sub-sections. Follow the instructions relevant to the machine being worked on.

SR125 models

6   The bonded rubber bushes are an interference fit in the swinging arm mounting bosses, and are unlikely to wear or deteriorate until a high mileage has been covered, but wear may occur between the bush inner sleeves and the pivot, especially if the retaining nut has become loose. In normal service there should be no relative movement between the inner bushes and shaft; the fork movement is allowed by flexing of the bonded rubber.

7   Inspect the bush rubber for damage or separation from both inner and outer sleeves. Check also that the inner sleeves have not been moving on the shaft. If damage is evident the bushes must be renewed. Driving the bushes from position is unlikely to prove successful, particularly if they have been in position for a long time and corrosion has taken place. Removal is accomplished most easily using a fabricated puller as shown in the accompanying illustration. The puller sleeve should have an internal diameter slightly greater than the outside diameter of the bush outer sleeve. If possible, use a high tensile nut and bolt because these will be better able to take the strain during use. New bushes may be drawn into place using the same puller. If difficulty is encountered in removing old bushes it is recommended that the swinging arm be returned to a Yamaha Service Agent.

8   After fitting new bushes, the swinging arm fork may be refitted to the machine by reversing the dismantling procedure. No lubricant should be used on the bushes because they are made of rubber. The shaft should be lubricated to prevent corrosion between the shaft, bush inner bearings and frame members. A lithium soap-based grease is recommended.

XT125 models

9   The sub-frame pivot bearings consists of outer bushes pressed into each sub-frame pivot lug, bearing on inner hardened metal sleeves which are clamped in place by the pivot bolt. Any wear is usually found between inner sleeve and outer bushes and is checked, after thorough cleaning, by refitting the inner sleeve and feeling for free play. If any is found, or if serious wear marks such as scoring can be seen, the worn components must be renewed.

10   Only remove the outer bushes if renewal is required, since the method of removal will almost certainly damage the brittle material. If

necessary, they can be displaced by inserting a drift into each lug from the end opposite to the bush shoulder and tapping with a hammer.

11   On refitting the bushes, clean thoroughly the pivot lug, removing any burrs or traces of corrosion, then coat both surfaces with grease. Assemble a drawbolt arrangement as shown in the accompanying illustration and carefully draw the bush into position, being careful to keep it absolutely square to its housing at all times. Note that all outer bushes are fitted with their raised collars to the outside.

12   Check the condition of the sealing caps, renewing any that is worn or damaged. The caps must be in good condition to prevent the entry of dirt or water.

13   Note that shims are fitted underneath the sealing caps of the sub-frame right-hand pivot lug to eliminate endfloat along the axis of the pivot bolt. When the sub-frame is installed in the frame and the pivot bolt retaining nut is tightened to the specified torque setting, there should be no discernible free play when the sub-frame is pulled and pushed from side to side, but the arm should be free to move; add (or subtract) shims to achieve this.

14   On reassembly use a high-quality molybdenum disulphide based grease to pack each bearing. Smear grease over the inside and outside of each inner sleeve as it is refitted, and to the sealing lips of each sealing cap.

9.6 SR125 employs bonded rubber bushes at swinging-arm pivot

9.9 Check for wear between metal inner sleeve and outer bush – XT125

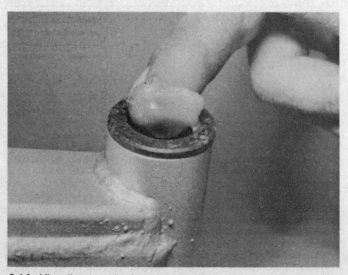

9.14a Liberally grease bushes on reassembly ...

9.14b ... do not forget sealing caps

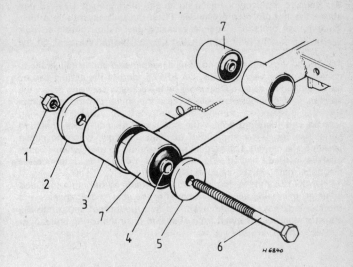

Fig. 4.7 Swinging arm bush removal tool – SR125

1 Nut	5 Thick washer
2 Thick washer	6 Bolt
3 Sleeve	7 Bush
4 Swinging arm	

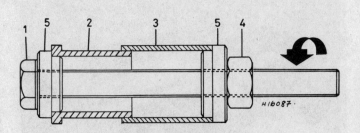

Fig. 4.8 Fitting the sub-frame pivot bushes – XT125

1 Drawbolt	4 Nut
2 Bush	5 Thick washer
3 Pivot lug	

10 Rear suspension unit(s): removal, examination and refitting

1   On SR125 models the suspension units are withdrawn by removing the four retaining cap nuts or bolts and plain washers, then pulling each unit sideways off its mounting lugs, noting that the pillion grab handle must be displaced first. Refitting is a straightforward reversal of the above, but care must be taken to refit correctly the plain washers. Tighten all four retaining nuts or bolts to a torque setting of 3.5 kgf m (25 lbf ft).

2   On XT125 models, remove the seat, the sidepanels and the fuel tank, then support the machine so that the rear wheel is clear of the ground and place a wooden block under the rear tyre so that the weight is taken off the sub-frame. Remove the suspension unit top mounting bolt, then withdraw the block and lower the rear wheel to the ground, to gain access to the unit bottom mounting. Remove the split-pin and plain washer, tap out the mounting pin and withdraw the suspension unit, noting the positions of the sealing caps on each side of its bottom mounting.

3   Refitting is the reverse of the above; thoroughly clean the mounting bolt, pin, and the bush inside diameters, removing all traces of dirt or corrosion, then apply a liberal smear of grease to each surface. Grease the sealing caps and refit them to the unit bottom mounting. Install the unit, push the mounting pin through from left to right and align one of the flats of its head with the small lug on the adjuster bracket. Refit the plain washer and insert a new split-pin, spreading its ends securely. Raise the rear wheel until the suspension unit top mounting aligns with its frame bracket, then push through

from left to right the mounting bolt. Refit its retaining nut and washer, then tighten the nut to a torque setting of 2.5 kgf m (18 lbf ft).

4   The suspension units fitted to SR125 models are sealed; if any wear or damage is found they must be renewed as a matched pair of complete units. Look for signs of oil leakage around the damper rod, worn mounting bushes, and any other signs of damage.

5   The XT125 suspension unit is examined in the same way and should be renewed if found to be damaged or worn; it is a sealed unit for which no replacement parts are available for repair or reconditioning. Only the mounting bushes can be renewed, if worn.

6   Displace the two inner sleeves and the sealing caps from the lower mounting eye, thoroughly clean all components then refit the sleeves and feel for traces of free play. Check also that the mounting bolts are a reasonably close fit in the sleeve. If any wear is discovered, the affected component must be renewed. The bonded rubber mounting bushes can be displaced using a version of the drawbolt arrangement described in the previous Section. Refit the bushes using a drawbolt, being careful to position each bush exactly in the centre of the mounting eye. Pack each bearing with high quality molybdenum disulphide based grease, and do not forget to renew the sealing caps if these are damaged or worn.

7   On XT125 models it is possible to remove the spring, if required. When removing a spring, note that it is under compression and no attempt should be made to disturb it unless a safe method of compressing it is available. The method employed is as follows. Slacken the adjuster locknut then unscrew fully the adjuster to reduce the pressure. Clamp the suspension unit in a vice by the mounting eye attached to the body of the damper itself, and not by the eye attached to the piston rod. The safest spring compressors are those used by car garages or sold at car accessory shops for use on the MacPherson struts fitted to the front suspension of many modern cars, particularly Fords. Following the manufacturer's instructions, clip the compressors on to the coils of the spring, one on each side as shown in the accompanying photograph, and tighten each one by equal amounts until the spring pressure is released safely and the two retaining collets can be picked out. The spring can then be pulled off the suspension unit and the pressure gradually released by unscrewing the compressors in stages. The spring is refitted by reversing the above process.

8   If the suspension unit causes handling problems due to the reduction in damping efficiency, or if signs of damage are visible, such as a bent piston rod, oil leakage, or a dented unit body, the complete assembly must be renewed. Do not throw the old unit away. It is first necessary to release the gas pressure by the following procedure.

9   Refer to the accompanying figure and mark a point 10 – 15 mm above the bottom of the cylinder. Place the unit securely in a vice. Wearing eye protection against escaping gas and/or metal particles, drill a 2 – 3 mm hole through the previously marked point on the cylinder.

10   The spring preload setting of each suspension unit is adjustable to compensate for varying loads. On SR125 models the setting can be easily altered by using a C-spanner on the adjuster cam ring below the springs. Turning clockwise will increase the spring tension and stiffen the rear suspension, turning anti-clockwise will lessen the spring tension and therefore soften the ride. As a general guide the third softest setting is recommended for road use only, when no pillion passenger is carried. The hardest setting should be used when a heavy load is carried, and during high-speed riding. The intermediate positions may be used as conditions dictate.

11   On XT125 models the adjustment is made by turning a threaded adjuster, this being accessible only after the seat, the sidepanels and the fuel tank have been removed. Slacken the locknut and rotate the adjuster clockwise (viewed from above) to raise the spring preload, or anti-clockwise to lower it. The operation is made easier if the special spanner is used. This has thin jaws and should be provided in the machine's toolkit but if not, a new one can be ordered as a separate item from a Yamaha dealer. The spring preload is altered by changing the installed length of the spring as described. The manufacturer has specified maximum and minimum lengths for the spring to act as guide-lines when setting up the suspension and to ensure maximum life for the spring and damper unit.

12   Using a ruler, measure the overall length of the spring from one collar to the other. The spring should be no more than 260 mm (10.2 in) long and no shorter than 245 mm (9.7 in). The standard length on delivery is 258 mm (10.1 in). Note that one full turn of the adjuster in either direction will alter spring length by 1 mm (0.039 in) and that adjustments should be made in increments of 2 mm (0.08 in) to produce any noticeable effect. When the adjustment is made, hold the adjuster and tighten securely the locknut to prevent any alteration in the setting. A torque setting of 5.5 kgf m (40 lbf ft) is given for the adjuster locknut, and this should be adhered to if the necessary equipment is available.

10.2 Seat and fuel tank must be removed to expose suspension unit top mounting and preload adjuster

10.3a Thoroughly clean and grease mounting pin before refitting

0.3b Flats of pin head must engage with raised lug as shown

10.3c Spread securely split-pin ends as shown – do not omit plain washer

10.6a Bonded rubber mounting bushes can be renewed if worn – XT125

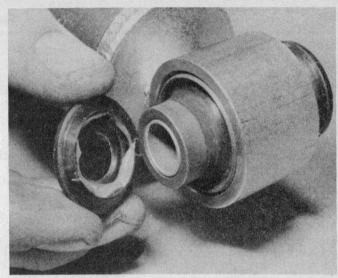

10.6b Grease liberally bearing sleeves and sealing caps on reassembly

10.7 Spring should be removed only if it can be compressed safely, as shown

10.11 Slacken locknut and rotate adjuster to alter spring preload

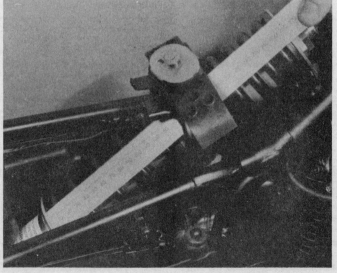

10.12 Preload is checked by measuring spring installed length as shown

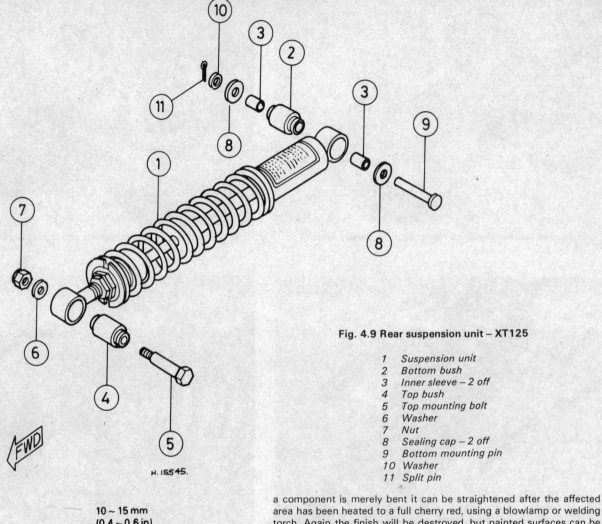

Fig. 4.9 Rear suspension unit – XT125

1   Suspension unit
2   Bottom bush
3   Inner sleeve – 2 off
4   Top bush
5   Top mounting bolt
6   Washer
7   Nut
8   Sealing cap – 2 off
9   Bottom mounting pin
10 Washer
11 Split pin

H. 15545.

10 ~ 15 mm
(0.4 ~ 0.6 in)

Ø 2 ~ 3 mm
(0.08 ~ 0.12 in)

Fig. 4.10 Position of drilling on rear suspension unit

11 Footrests, stands and controls: examination and renovation

1   At regular intervals all footrests and stands and the brake pedal and gearchange lever should be checked and lubricated. Check that all mounting nuts and bolts are securely fastened, using the recommended torque wrench settings where these are given. Check that any securing split-pins are correctly fitted.

2   Check that the bearing surfaces at all pivot points are well greased and unworn, renewing any component that is excessively worn. If lubrication is required, dismantle the assembly to ensure that grease can be packed fully into the bearing surface. Return springs, where fitted, must be in good condition with no traces of fatigue and must be securely mounted.

3   If accident damage is to be repaired, check that the damaged component is not cracked or broken. Such damage may be repaired by welding, if the pieces are taken to an expert, but since this will destroy the finish, renewal is usually the most satisfactory course of action. If

a component is merely bent it can be straightened after the affected area has been heated to a full cherry red, using a blowlamp or welding torch. Again the finish will be destroyed, but painted surfaces can be repainted easily, while chromed or plated surfaces can be only replated, if the cost is justified.

12 Speedometer and tachometer heads: removal, examination and refitting

1   These instruments must be carefully handled at all times and must never be dropped or held upside down. Dirt, oil, grease and water all have an equally adverse effect on them, and so a clean working area must be provided if they are to be removed.

2   The instrument heads are very delicate and should not be dismantled at home. In the event of a fault developing, the instrument should be entrusted to a specialist repairer or a new unit fitted. If a replacement unit is required, it is well worth trying to obtain a good secondhand item from a motorcycle breaker in view of the high cost of a new instrument.

3   Remember that a speedometer in correct working order is a statutory requirement in the UK. Apart from this legal necessity, reference to the odometer readings if the most satisfactory means of keeping pace with the maintenance schedules.

4   The instrument clusters are removed as a complete assembly as described in Section 5 of this Chapter. To remove them individually, it will be necessary on SR125 models to remove the headlamp reflector unit so that the instrument and warning lamp bulb holders can be unplugged and the instrument retaining nuts and washers removed. Unscrew its knurled retaining ring to release the drive cable and lift the instrument away.

5   On XT125 models, unplug the instrument and warning lamp bulb holders, disconnect the drive cable, withdraw the retaining R-clips and metal washers, then lift the instrument away.

13 Speedometer and tachometer drive cables: examination and renovation

1 It is advisable to detach the speedometer and tachometer drive cables from time to time in order to check whether they are adequately lubricated and whether the outer cables are compressed or damaged at any other point along their run. A jerky or sluggish movement at the instrument head can often be attributed to a cable fault.

2 To grease the cable, uncouple both ends and withdraw the inner cable. After removing any old grease, clean the inner cable with a petrol soaked rag and examine the cable for broken strands or other damage. Do not check the cable for broken strands by passing it through the fingers or palm of the hand, this may well cause a painful injury if a broken strand snags the skin. It is best to wrap a piece of rag around the cable and pull the cable through it, any broken strands will snag the rag.

3 Regrease the cable with high melting point grease, taking care not to grease the last six inches closest to the instrument head. If this precaution is not observed, grease will work into the instrument and immobilise the sensitive movement.

4 The cables on all models are secured at their upper ends by large knurled rings which must be tightened or slackened using a suitable pair of pliers. Do not overtighten the knurled rings, or they will crack necessitating renewal of the complete cable. The lower ends are pressed into housings in the front brake backplate or cam sprocket cover (as applicable) and secured by a wire circlip or a screw. Check that the sealing O-rings are in good condition.

5 When refitting drive cables, always ensure that they have smooth easy runs to minimise wear, and check that the cables are secured where necessary by any clamps or ties provided for the purpose of keeping the cables away from any hot or moving parts.

14 Speedometer and tachometer drives: location and examination

1 On both models the speedometer drive is located in the backplate of the front brake; it is therefore necessary to withdraw the front wheel from the machine in order to gain access to the drive components.

2 To dismantle the drive assembly, remove the retaining circlip from the centre of the backplate, then lift out the thrust washer, driveplate, drive gear and second thrust washer. Turn the backplate over and remove the worm gear supporting bush, which is screwed into the backplate and must be unscrewed using either a specially-fabricated peg spanner or a thin-nosed punch and a hammer. Withdraw the worm gear with the washer around its upper end. The oil seal should be renewed whenever it is disturbed in this way.

3 Carefully clean and inspect all the component parts. Any wear or damage will be immediately obvious and should be rectified by the renewal of the part concerned. The most likely areas of wear are on the tangs of the driveplate or on the teeth of either the drive gear or the drive pinion. If wear is encountered on the teeth of either of the latter components it is advisable to renew both together. Note also the condition of the large oil seal set in the backplate. If this seal shows any sign of damage or deterioration it must be renewed to prevent grease from the drive assembly working through to the brake linings.

4 Reassemble the speedometer drive assembly in the reverse order of dismantling. Lightly lubricate all components with a good quality high melting-point grease.

5 The tachometer drive mechanism fitted to 1983 on XT125 models only is contained within the cam sprocket cover and is therefore removed as described in Section 6 of Chapter 1. Wear is unlikely until a very high mileage has occurred, and if found, can be cured only by the renewal of the components concerned.

13.4a Instrument drive cables are retained by knurled rings at their upper ends

13.4b O-ring at cable lower ends should be renewed if damaged or worn

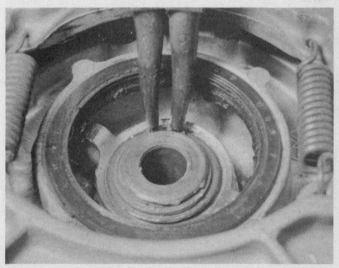

14.2 Displace circlip to release speedometer drive components

Chapter 5 Wheels, brakes and tyres

Refer to Chapter 7 for information relating to the 1991-on SR125 models

Contents

Specifications

Wheels

	SR125	XT125
Type	Steel rim, wire spoked	Steel rim, wire spoked
Size:		
Front	1.60 x 17	1.60 x 21
Rear	1.85 x 16	1.85 x 18
Rim maximum runout - radial and axial	2.0 mm (0.08 in)	2.0 mm (0.08 in)

Brakes

Type:	
Front	Single-leading shoe drum, cable operated
Rear	Single-leading shoe drum, rod operated
Front brake drum ID	130 mm (5.12 in)
Service limit:	
SR125	132 mm (5.20 in)
XT125	131 mm (5.16 in)
Rear brake drum ID	110 mm (4.33 in)
Service limit:	
SR125	112 mm (4.41 in)
XT125	111 mm (4.37 in)
Brake shoe friction material thickness	4 mm (0.16 in)
Service limit	2 mm (0.08 in)
Brake shoe return spring free length:	
Front	36.0 - 37.0 mm (1.42 - 1.46 in)
Rear	50.0 - 51.0 mm (1.97 - 2.01 in)

Tyres

	SR125	XT125
Type	Tubed	Tubed
Size:		
Front	3.00 x 17-4PR	2.75 x 21-4PR
Rear	3.50 x 16-4PR	4.10 x 18-4PR

Tyre pressures - cold

Note - loads given are total weight of rider, passenger and any accessories or luggage

	Front	Rear
SR125:		
Up to 198 lb (90 kg) - low speed	25 psi (1.72 kg/cm²)	28 psi (1.96 kg/cm²)
Up to 198 lb (90 kg) - high speed, 198-353 lb (90 - 160 kg)	25 psi (1.72 kg/cm²)	31 psi (2.20 kg/cm²)
XT125:		
Up to 254 lb (115 kg)	18 psi (1.27 kg/cm²)	21 psi (1.47 kg/cm²)
254-408 lb (115-185 kg)	18 psi (1.27 kg/cm²)	26 psi (1.77 kg/cm²)

For off-road riding only, tyre pressures should be reduced to approximately 14 psi (1.00 kg/cm²) – do not use lower pressures unless security bolts are fitted

Torque settings

Component	kgf m	lbf ft
Front wheel spindle nut:		
SR125	4.5	32.5
XT125	3.9	28.0
Rear wheel spindle nut:		
SR125	6.5	47.0
XT125	8.5	61.5
Rear sprocket retaining nuts:		
SR125	2.5	18.0
XT125	3.0	22.0

1 General description

Tyres of conventional tubed type are fitted on to chromed steel rims that are laced to light alloy full-width hubs. The SR125 employs an unusual spoke arrangement which means that only genuine Yamaha parts can be employed if the wheels are to be repaired or rebuilt.

The brakes are of the single-leading shoe drum type, the front being cable-operated while the rear is rod-operated.

2 Front wheel: examination and renovation

1   Spoked wheels can go out of true over periods of prolonged use and like any wheel, as the result of an impact. The condition of the hub, spokes and rim should therefore be checked at regular intervals.
2   When checking wheels, a wheel stand is invaluable, but failing this the wheel can be checked whilst in place on the machine after it has been raised clear of the ground. Make sure the machine is stable, if necessary using blocks beneath the crankcase as extra support. Spin

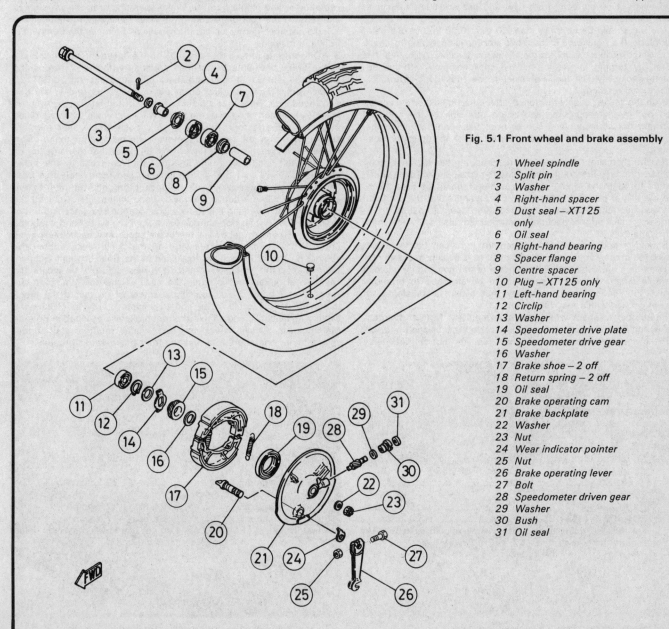

Fig. 5.1 Front wheel and brake assembly

1   Wheel spindle
2   Split pin
3   Washer
4   Right-hand spacer
5   Dust seal – XT125 only
6   Oil seal
7   Right-hand bearing
8   Spacer flange
9   Centre spacer
10 Plug – XT125 only
11 Left-hand bearing
12 Circlip
13 Washer
14 Speedometer drive plate
15 Speedometer drive gear
16 Washer
17 Brake shoe – 2 off
18 Return spring – 2 off
19 Oil seal
20 Brake operating cam
21 Brake backplate
22 Washer
23 Nut
24 Wear indicator pointer
25 Nut
26 Brake operating lever
27 Bolt
28 Speedometer driven gear
29 Washer
30 Bush
31 Oil seal

the wheel and ensure that there is no brake drag. If necessary, slacken the brake adjuster until the wheel turns freely. In the case of rear wheels it is advisable to remove the final drive chain.

3   Slowly rotate the wheel and examine the rim for signs of serious corrosion or impact damage. Slight deformities, as might be caused by running the wheel along a curb, can often be corrected by adjusting spoke tension. More serious damage may require a new rim to be fitted, and this is best left to an expert. Badly rusted steel rims should be renewed in the interests of safety as well as appearance.

4   If a new rim is required, some thought should be given to the size and type of the replacement. In some instances the problem of obtaining replacement tyres for an oddly sized original rim can be resolved by having a more common rim size fitted. Do check that this will not lead to other problems; fitting a new rim whose tyre fouls some other part of the machine could prove a costly error. Remember that changing the size of the rear wheel rim will alter the overall gearing.

5   Assuming the wheel to be undamaged, it will be necessary to check it for runout. This is best done by arranging a temporary wire pointer so that it runs close to the rim. The wheel can now be turned and any distortion noted. Check for lateral distortion and for radial distortion, noting that the latter is less likely to be encountered if the wheel was set up correctly from new and has not been subject to impact damage.

6   The rim should be no more than 2.0 mm (0.08 in) out of true in either plane. If a significant amount of distortion is encountered, check that the spokes are of approximately equal tension. Adjustment is effected by turning the square-headed spoke nipples with the appropriate spoke key. This tool is obtainable from most good motorcycle shops or tool retailers.

7   With the spokes evenly tensioned, any remaining distortion can be pulled out by tightening the spokes on one side of the hub and slackening the corresponding spokes from the opposite hub flange. This will allow the rim to be pulled across whilst maintaining spoke tension.

8   If more than slight adjustment is required, the tyre and inner tube should be removed first to give access to the spoke ends. Those which protrude through the nipple after adjustment should be filed flat to avoid the risk of puncturing the tube. It is essential that the rim band be in good condition as an added precaution against chafing. In an emergency, use a strip of duct tape; unprotected tubes will soon chafe on the nipples.

9   Should a spoke break, a replacement item can be fitted and retensioned in the normal way. Wheel removal is usually necessary for this operation, although complete removal of the tyre can be avoided if care is taken. A broken spoke should be attended to promptly because the load normally taken by that spoke is transferred to adjacent spokes which may fail in turn.

10 Remember to check wheel condition regularly. Normal maintenance is confined to keeping the spokes correctly tensioned and will avoid the costly and complicated wheel rebuilds that will inevitably result from neglect. When cleaning the machine do not neglect the wheels. If the rims are kept clean and well polished, many of the corrosion problems will be prevented.

3   Front wheel: removal and refitting

1   Support the machine securely on a strong wooden box placed underneath the engine/gearbox unit so that the front wheel is clear of the ground.

2   Remove the circlip which retains the lower end of the speedometer drive cable, then remove the cable by pulling it gently out of the recess in the brake backplate. Before the brake cable can be disconnected, enough free play must be gained for this to be possible. Starting at the handlebar end of the cable, pull back the rubber cover, slacken fully the adjuster locknut, and screw the adjuster fully in. Working at the cable lower end, slacken the adjuster lower nut and screw it down off the threaded length of the cable outer, displacing the grommet to permit this, then slacken the cable clamp at the top of the fork lower leg (XT125 only). Pull the cable outer straight up until the cable inner can be slipped out through the slot in the adjuster boss cast in the brake backplate. If insufficient free play exists for this to be possible, disconnect the cable at the handlebar end. Disengage the cable lower end nipple from the brake operating arm, then straighten and remove the split pin securing the wheel spindle nut. Remove the spindle nut, then gently tap out the spindle and remove the front wheel from the machine.

3   On refitting, ensure that the tabs on the speedometer drive piece in the brake backplate are aligned correctly with the corresponding slots in the wheel hub boss, and check that the spacer and, on XT125 models only, dust-excluding collar are correctly inserted in the hub right-hand side. Note that a plain washer is fitted into a recess in the wheel spindle lug of each of the fork lower legs; while these are glued in place at the factory, they may work loose. Check that they are secure whenever the wheel is removed and never omit them. Insert the wheel between the fork lower legs, ensuring that the large lug on the fork left-hand lower leg fits into the slot cast in the brake backplate. Check that the spindle is clean and completely free from corrosion, smear grease over it, and push it through from right to left. Refit the spindle nut and tighten it by hand only at first. Connect the brake cable by reversing the above disconnecting sequence and return the adjusters to their original positions. Spin the wheel and apply the brake lever hard to centralise the brake shoes and backplate on the drum. While keeping firm pressure on the brake lever, tighten the spindle nut to the torque setting given in the Specifications Section, then release the brake lever and fit a new split-pin to secure the spindle nut, spreading correctly the ends of the split-pin. Refit the speedometer drive cable, applying a smear of grease to the metal abutment on the cable lower end to prevent corrosion. Secure the cable with its circlip and adjust the front brake as described in Routine Maintenance. Finally check for free wheel rotation and correct speedometer operation, and that the front brake works properly.

3.2a Slacken adjuster locknut to release brake cable

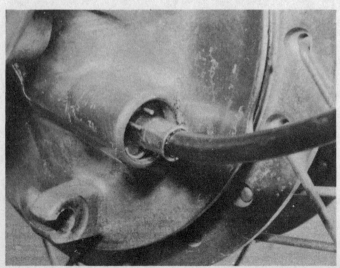

3.2b Speedometer cable bottom end is retained by a circlip

3.3a Tabs on speedometer drive gear must align with slots in hub boss

3.3b Do not omit either the two plain washers ...

3.3c ... or the hub right-hand spacer

3.3d Lug on fork lower leg must engage in brake backplate slot, as shown

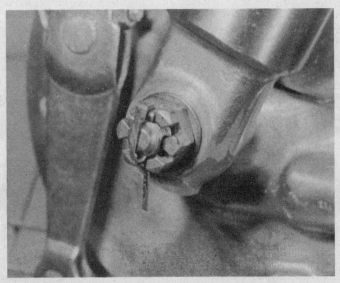

3.3e Always fit a new split-pin, spreading its ends as shown

4　Front wheel bearings: removal, examination and refitting

1　Remove the front wheel as described in the previous Section. Withdraw the brake backplate, then invert the wheel and remove the hub right-hand spacer and, on XT125 models only, the dust cover.

2　Position the wheel on a work surface with its hub well supported by wooden blocks so that enough clearance is left beneath the wheel to drive out the left-hand bearing. Ensure the blocks are placed as close to the bearing as possible, to lessen the risk of distortion of the hub casting whilst the bearings are being removed or fitted.

3　Place the end of a long-handled drift against the upper face of the left-hand bearing and tap the bearing downwards out of the wheel hub. The spacer located between the two bearings may be moved sideways slightly in order to allow the drift to be positioned against the face of the bearing. Move the drift around the face of the bearing whilst drifting it out of position, so that the bearing leaves the hub squarely.

4　With the one bearing removed, the wheel may be lifted and the spacer withdrawn from the hub. Invert the wheel and remove the second bearing, using a similar procedure. The dust seal which fits against the right-hand bearing will be driven out as the bearing is removed. This seal should be closely inspected for any indication of damage, hardening or perishing and renewed if necessary. It is advisable to renew this seal as a matter of course if the bearings are found to be defective.

5　Remove all the old grease from the hub and bearings, giving the latter a final wash in petrol. Check the bearings for signs of play or roughness when they are turned. If there is any doubt about the condition of a bearing, it should be renewed.

6　If the original bearings are to be refitted, they should be repacked with the recommended grease before being fitted into the hub. New bearings must also be packed with the recommended grease. Ensure that the bearing recesses in the hub are clean and both bearings and recess mating surfaces lightly greased to aid fitting. Check the condition of the hub recesses for evidence of abnormal wear which may have been caused by the outer race of a bearing spinning. If evidence of this happening is found, and the bearing is a loose fit in the hub, it is best to seek advice from a Yamaha Service Agent or a competent motorcycle engineer. Alternatively a proprietary product such as Loctite Bearing Fit may be used to retain the bearing outer race; this will mean, however, that the bearing housing must be carefully cleaned and degreased before the locking compound can be used.

7　With the wheel hub and bearing thus prepared, fit the bearings and central spacer as follows. With the hub again well supported by the wooden blocks, drift the first of the two bearings into position. Use a soft-faced hammer in conjunction with a socket or length of metal tube which has an overall diameter which is slightly less than that of the outer race of the bearing, but which does not bear at any point on the bearing sealed surface or inner race. Tap the bearing into place against the locating shoulder machined in the hub, remembering that the sealed surface of the bearing must always face outwards. With the first bearing in place, invert the wheel, insert the central spacer and pack the hub centre no more than $\frac{2}{3}$ full with high-melting point grease. Fit the second bearing, using the same procedure. Take great care to ensure that each of the bearings enters its housing correctly, that is, square to the housing, otherwise the housing surface may be broached.

8　Use the same method to refit the seal against the right-hand bearing. Refit the wheel to the machine as described in Section 3 of this Chapter.

4.7a Spacer flange must fit on hub right-hand side – pack cavity with grease

4.7b Bearing sealed surface must face outwards

4.7c Drift must bear on outer race only, as shown

Tyre changing sequence - tubed tyres

 A Deflate tyre. After pushing tyre beads away from rim flanges push tyre bead into well of rim at point opposite valve. Insert tyre lever adjacent to valve and work bead over edge of rim.

Use two levers to work bead over edge of rim. Note use of rim protectors **B**

 C Remove inner tube from tyre

When first bead is clear, remove tyre as shown  **D**

 E When fitting, partially inflate inner tube and insert in tyre

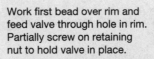

Work first bead over rim and feed valve through hole in rim. Partially screw on retaining nut to hold valve in place.  **F**

 G Check that inner tube is positioned correctly and work second bead over rim using tyre levers. Start at a point opposite valve.

Work final area of bead over rim whilst pushing valve inwards to ensure that inner tube is not trapped **H**

5 Front brake: examination and renovation

1 The brake assembly can be withdrawn from its hub after removal of the wheel from the machine.

2 Examine the condition of the brake linings. If they are worn beyond the specified limit the brake shoes should be renewed. The linings are bonded on and cannot be supplied separately.

3 If oil or grease from the wheel bearings has badly contaminated the linings, the brake shoes should be renewed. There is no satisfactory way of degreasing the lining material. Any surface dirt on the linings can be removed with a stiff-bristled brush. High spots on the linings should be carefully eased down with emery cloth.

4 Examine the drum surface for signs of scoring, wear beyond the service limit or oil contamination. All of these conditions will impair braking efficiency. Remove all traces of dust, preferably using a brass wire brush, taking care not to inhale any of it as it is of an asbestos nature, and consequently harmful. Remove oil or grease deposits, using a petrol soaked rag.

5 If deep scoring is evident, due to the linings having worn through to the shoe at some time, the drum must be skimmed on a lathe, or renewed. Whilst there are firms who will undertake to skim the drum without dismantling the wheel, it should be borne in mind that excessive skimming will change the radius of the drum in relation to the brake shoes, thereby reducing the friction area until extensive bedding in has taken place. Also full adjustment of the shoes may not be possible. If in doubt about this point, the advice of one of the specialist engineering firms who undertake this work should be sought.

6 It is a false economy to try to cut corners with brake components; the whole safety of both machine and rider being dependent on their good condition.

7 Removal of the brake shoes is accomplished by folding the shoes together so that they form a 'V'. With the spring tension relaxed, both shoes and springs may be removed from the brake backplates as an assembly. Detach the springs from the shoes and carefully inspect them for any signs of fatigue or failure. If in doubt, compare them with a new set of springs.

8 Before fitting the brake shoes, check that the brake operating cam is working smoothly and is not binding in its pivot. The cam can be removed by withdrawing the retaining bolt on the operating arm and pulling the arm off the shaft. Before removing the arm, it is advisable to mark its position in relation to the shaft, so that it can be relocated correctly, with the wear indicator pointer.

9 Remove any deposits of hardened grease or corrosion from the bearing surface of the brake cam and shoe by rubbing it lightly with a strip of fine emery paper or by applying solvent with a piece of rag. Lightly grease the length of the shaft and the face of the operating cam prior to reassembly. Clean and grease the pivot stub which is set in the backplate.

10 Check the condition of the O-ring which prevents the escape of grease from the end of the camshaft. If it is in any way damaged or perished, then it must be renewed before the shaft is relocated in the backplate. Relocate the camshaft and align and fit the operating arm with the O-ring and wear indicator pointer. Tighten securely the pinch bolt.

11 Before refitting existing shoes, roughen the lining surface sufficiently to break the glaze which will have formed in use. Glasspaper or emery cloth is ideal for this purpose but take care not to inhale any of the asbestos dust that may come from the lining surface.

12 Fitting the brake shoes and springs to the brake backplate is a reversal of the removal procedure. Some patience will be needed to align the assembly with the pivot and operating cam whilst still retaining the spring in position; once they are correctly aligned, they can be pushed back into position by pressing downwards to snap them into position. Do not use excessive force, as there is risk of distorting the brake shoes permanently.

6 Rear wheel: examination and renovation

The rear wheel is identical in design and construction to the front; refer to Section 2 of this Chapter.

5.7 Fold brake shoes together as shown to remove

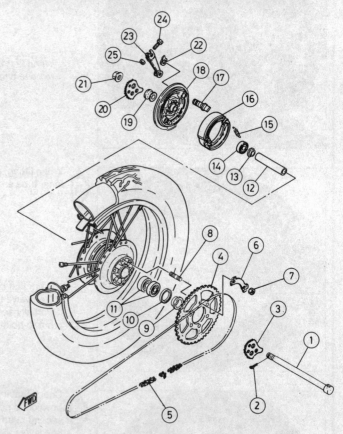

Fig. 5.2 Rear wheel and brake assembly – XT125

1	Wheel spindle	14	Right-hand bearing
2	Split pin	15	Return spring – 2 off
3	Left-hand snail cam	16	Brake shoe – 2 off
4	Sprocket	17	Brake operating cam
5	Final drive chain	18	Brake backplate
6	Tab washer – 3 off	19	Right-hand spacer
7	Nut – 6 off	20	Right-hand snail cam
8	Stud – 6 off	21	Nut
9	Left-hand spacer	22	Wear indicator pointer
10	Oil seal	23	Brake operating lever
11	Left-hand bearing – 2 off	24	Bolt
12	Spacer	25	Nut
13	Spacer flange		

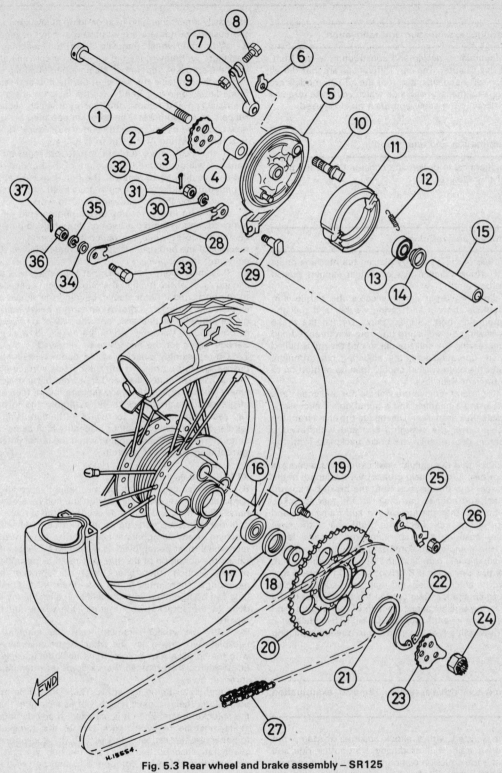

Fig. 5.3 Rear wheel and brake assembly – SR125

1	Wheel spindle	11	Brake shoe – 2 off	21	Spacer ring	30	Spring washer
2	Split pin	12	Return spring – 2 off	22	Circlip	31	Nut
3	Right-hand snail cam	13	Right-hand bearing	23	Left-hand snail cam	32	Split pin
4	Right-hand spacer	14	Spacer flange	24	Nut	33	Bolt
5	Brake backplate	15	Spacer	25	Tab washer – 2 off	34	Washer
6	Wear indicator pointer	16	Left-hand bearing	26	Nut – 4 off	35	Spring washer
7	Brake operating lever	17	Oil seal	27	Final drive chain	36	Nut
8	Bolt	18	Left-hand spacer	28	Brake torque arm	37	Split pin
9	Nut	19	Cush drive bush – 4 off	29	Bolt		
10	Brake operating cam	20	Sprocket				

7 Rear wheel bearings: examination and renovation

The rear hub is identical in design and construction to the front; refer to Section 4 of this Chapter. The only differences are that the oil seal is now on the hub left-hand side, and that the XT125 models are fitted with two bearings on the left-hand side which will make removal rather more difficult. Exactly the same approach must be used.

8 Rear brake: examination and renovation

The rear brake is identical in design and construction to the front; refer to Section 5 of this Chapter.

9 Rear wheel: removal and refitting

1   Raise the wheel clear of the ground by placing the machine on its centre stand or on a strong wooden box or similar support placed under the engine/gearbox unit.
2   Remove the R-clip or split-pin which secures the torque arm retaining nut, then remove the nut and spring washer and pull the torque arm off its mounting bolt, (SR125 only). Detach the brake operating rod by unscrewing the adjusting nut from the threaded end of the rod and then depressing the brake pedal so that the rod is pulled clear of the brake cam operating arm; the adjusting nut, trunnion, brake return spring and the plain washer should then be refitted on to the operating rod to prevent their loss.
3   Withdraw the split pin and remove the spindle nut and snail cam. Withdraw the spindle, using a hammer and a metal drift if necessary, and catch the spacers as they drop clear. Disengage the chain from the sprocket, loop the chain over the swinging arm and withdraw the wheel from the machine, then remove the brake backplate from the hub.
4   On reassembly, check that the spindle, snail cams and spacers are clean and free from corrosion, then smear grease over the length of the spindle. Insert the spacer into the oil seal. Refit the brake backplate.
5   Offer up the wheel and engage the chain on the rear sprocket, ensuring on XT125 models that the lug on the sub-frame fork end engages with the slot in the brake backplate. Refit one of the snail cams to the spindle, ensuring that its numbered surface faces outwards, then refit the spindle, not forgetting the hub right-hand spacer. Refit the second snail cam and the spindle retaining nut, connect the brake torque arm again (SR125 only), and the brake rod.
6   Check and adjust the chain tension and rear brake adjustment as described in Routine Maintenance, then tighten the spindle nut to the torque setting given in the Specifications Section of this Chapter and fit a new split pin, spreading its ends securely. On SR125 models only, do not forget to fit a new split pin or R-clip to the torque arm retaining nut.

10 Rear sprocket and cush drive assembly: removal, examination and refitting

SR125 models

1   The transmission is fitted with a shock absorber to damp out shock loads in the drive train, thus producing a smoother ride and extending the life of the transmission components. While the components can be examined when in place on the machine, and the sprocket mounting nuts tightened in this position, if any components are found to be in need of renewal, the rear wheel must be removed to gain access to them.
2   Examine the teeth of the rear sprocket. If these are hooked, chipped, or otherwise damaged, the sprocket must be renewed. It is considered bad practice to renew just one sprocket or the chain alone; both front and rear sprockets and the chain should be renewed together at all times. When the sprocket has been checked, lock the wheel by applying hard the back brake, and attempt to rotate the sprocket backwards and forwards. While some movement should be evident due to the damping action of the cush drive, excessive movement, which is normally revealed by a rough and jerky ride

especially when changing gear or riding at low speed, will indicate that the cush drive rubbers are worn and in need of renewal.
3   With the wheel removed from the machine and the brake backplate withdrawn, lay the wheel on a convenient working surface with the sprocket uppermost. Using a pair of circlip pliers, remove the circlip which retains the sprocket on the hub and lift away the spacer immediately below it. Bend back the locking tabs of the tab washers, then slacken and remove the four nuts which secure the cush drive rubbers to the sprocket. The sprocket can then be lifted clear and the new one fitted by reversing the above procedure. Tighten the four nuts to a torque setting of 2.5 kgf m (18 lb ft).
4   If the cush drive rubbers are to be renewed, some skill and patience will be required as they are of the bonded rubber type which are always difficult to remove. The first step is to apply a liberal dose of penetrating fluid to each cush drive bush, and to leave the wheel for as long as possible to allow the fluid to work.
5   As shown in the accompanying photograph, refit the sprocket (if removed) and assemble a two- or three-legged puller to pull upwards on the sprocket while the puller centre bears, via a spacer, on the material of the hub itself. If one is extremely lucky, all four bushes will come out in one piece.
6   It is more likely, however, that the rubber will distort and shear, leaving most of the bush in the hub. In such a case, apply a pin punch to the bush metal outer sleeve, bending the sleeve inwards so that it is loosened and can be drawn out with a heavy pair of pliers. In view of the difficulty of this task, and the risk of damage to the hub, it is recommended that the wheel be taken to a competent Yamaha Service Agent for the bushes to be renewed.
7   On reassembly, check that the hub recesses into which the new bushes are to be pressed, and the outside surface of the new bushes themselves are quite clean and free from burrs or scratches. Use fine emery cloth to polish away any that are found, then apply a thin smear of grease to each surface to aid assembly and to prevent corrosion. Tap each bush firmly into its recess in the hub using a hammer and a tubular drift (a socket spanner is ideal) which bears only on the metal outer of the bush. Cease tapping when the metal outer is flush with the surrounding surface of the hub.

XT125 models

8   The transmission of these machines has no shock absorber, the sprocket being mounted directly on the hub by six studs and retaining nuts. While the condition and security of the sprocket can be checked, and the sprocket nuts tightened with the wheel installed in the machine, if any components are found to be in need of attention the rear wheel must be removed as described in Section 9 of this Chapter. Check the condition of the sprocket teeth as described in paragraph 2 of this Section, then check that the sprocket is secure on its mountings. There must be no movement in any direction. While the nuts can be tightened with the wheel in place, if any damage has been done to the sprocket or the studs, the wheel must be removed for repairs.
9   With the wheel removed from the machine and the brake backplate withdrawn, lay the wheel on a convenient working surface with the sprocket uppermost. Bend back the locking tabs of the three tab washers, then remove the six sprocket retaining nuts and lift the sprocket away.
10 Carefully examine the studs. There should be no damage at any point along their exposed length, but especially at that point on which the sprocket bears when it is installed. If any damage is revealed, the studs must be renewed. Lock two of the sprocket mounting nuts together on the exposed thread and, by applying a spanner to the lower nut, unscrew the stud from the hub. On refitting, apply a few drops of thread locking compound to that part of the stud which will screw into the hub, lock the two nuts together on that part which will be exposed, and screw the stud into the hub. By applying a spanner to the upper of the two nuts, tighten the stud securely. Release and remove the two nuts.
11 When the studs have been examined and renewed, check that both faces of the sprocket are absolutely clean and dry, and check that the mating surface of the hub is flat and clean. Refit the sprocket over the studs, press it down to rest on the hub, and check that it cannot move backwards or forwards in the direction of rotation. Refit the tab washers and retaining nuts, tightening the nuts securely to a torque setting of 3.0 kgf m (22 lbf ft) and locking each one by bending an unused portion of the tab washer against one of its flats. The wheel can then be refitted to the machine.

9.5 Note snail cam numbered surface must face outwards

9.6a Do not forget to check brake adjustment ...

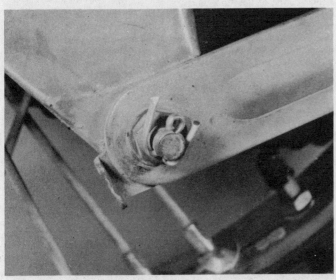

9.6b ... or to secure torque arm nut with a new split-pin, as shown

10.3a To remove rear sprocket (SR125) — withdraw circlip ...

10.3b ... followed by spacer ...

10.3c ... then remove sprocket retaining nuts

10.5 Assemble extractor as shown, in attempt to remove cush drive rubbers

11 Tyres: removal, repair and refitting

1   To remove the tyre from either wheel, first detach the wheel from the machine. Deflate the tyre by removing the valve core, and when the tyre is fully deflated, push the bead away from the wheel rim on both sides so that the bead enters the centre well of the rim. Remove the locking ring and push the tyre valve into the tyre itself.

2   Insert a tyre lever close to the valve and lever the edge of the tyre over the outside of the rim. Very little force should be necessary; if resistance is encountered it is probably due to the fact that the tyre beads have not entered the well of the rim all the way round. If aluminium rims are fitted, damage to the soft alloy by tyre levers can be prevented by the use of plastic rim protectors.

3   Once the tyre has been edged over the wheel rim, it is easy to work round the wheel rim so that the tyre is completely free from one side. At this stage the inner tube can be removed.

4   Now working from the other side of the wheel, ease the other edge of the tyre over the outside of the wheel rim that is furthest away. Continue to work around the rim until the tyre is completely free from the rim.

5   If a puncture has necessitated the removal of the tyre, reinflate the inner tube and immerse it in a bowl of water to trace the source of the leak. Mark the position of the leak, and deflate the tube. Dry the tube, and clean the area around the puncture with a petrol soaked rag. When the surface has dried, apply rubber solution and allow this to dry before removing the backing from the patch, and applying the patch to the surface.

6   It is best to use a patch of self vulcanizing type, which will form a permanent repair. Note that it may be necessary to remove a protective covering from the top surface of the patch after it has sealed into position. Inner tubes made from a special synthetic rubber may require a special type of patch and adhesive, if a satisfactory bond is to be achieved.

7   Before replacing the tyre, check the inside to make sure that the article that caused the puncture is not still trapped inside the tyre. Check the outside of the tyre, particularly the tread area, to make sure nothing is trapped that may cause a further puncture.

8   If the inner tube has been patched on a number of past occasions, or if there is a tear or large hole, it is preferable to discard it and fit a replacement. Sudden deflation may cause an accident, particularly if it occurs with the rear wheel.

9   To replace the tyre, inflate the inner tube for it just to assume a circular shape but only to that amount, and then push the tube into the tyre so that it is enclosed completely. Lay the tyre on the wheel at an angle, and insert the valve through the hole in the wheel rim. Attach the locking ring on the first few threads, sufficient to hold the valve captive in its correct location.

10 Starting at the point furthest from the valve, push the tyre bead over the edge of the wheel rim until it is located in the central well. Continue to work around the tyre in this fashion until the whole of one side of the tyre is on the rim. It may be necessary to use a tyre lever during the final stages.

11 Make sure there is no pull on the tyre valve and again commencing with the area furthest from the valve, ease the other bead of the tyre over the edge of the rim. Finish with the area close to the valve, pushing the valve up into the tyre to ensure that the inner tube is not trapped when the last section of bead is edged over the rim with a tyre lever.

12 Check that the inner tube is not trapped at any point. Reinflate the inner tube, and check that the tyre is seating correctly around the wheel rim. There should be a thin rib moulded around the wall of the tyre on both sides, which should be an equal distance from the wheel rim at all points. If the tyre is unevenly located on the rim, try bouncing the wheel when the tyre is at the recommended pressure. It is probable that one of the beads has not pulled clear of the centre well.

13 Always run the tyres at the recommended pressures and never under or over inflate. The correct pressures are given in the Specifications Section of this Chapter.

14 Tyre replacement is aided by dusting the side walls, particularly in the vicinity of the beads, with a liberal coating of french chalk. Washing up liquid can also be used to good effect, but this has the disadvantage, where steel rims are used, of causing the inner surface of the wheel rim to rust.

15 Never replace the inner tube and tyre without the rim tape in position. If this precaution is overlooked there is a good chance of the ends of the spoke nipples chafing the inner tube and causing a crop of punctures.

16 Never fit a tyre that has a damaged tread or sidewalls. Apart from legal aspects, there is a very great risk of blowout, which can have very serious consequences on a two wheeled vehicle.

17 Tyre valves rarely give trouble, but it is always advisable to check whether the valve itself is leaking before removing the tyre. Do not forget to fit the dust cap, which forms an effective extra seal.

12 Valve cores and caps: general

1   Valve cores seldom give trouble, but do not last indefinitely. Dirt under the seating will cause a puzzling 'slow-puncture'. Check that they are not leaking by applying spittle to the end of the valve and watching for air bubbles.

2   A valve cap is a safety device, and should always be fitted. Apart from keeping dirt out of the valve, it provides a second seal in case of valve failure, and may prevent an accident resulting from sudden deflation.

13 Wheel balancing

1   It is customary on all high performance machines to balance the wheels complete with tyre and tube. The out of balance forces which exist are eliminated and the handling of the machine is improved in consequence. A wheel which is badly out of balance produces through the steering a most unpleasant hammering effect at high speeds.

2   Some tyres have a balance mark on the sidewall, usually in the form of a coloured spot. This mark must be in line with tyre valve, when the tyre is fitted to the inner tube. Even then the wheel may require the addition of balance weights, to offset the weight of the tyre valve itself.

3   If the wheel is raised clear of the ground and is spun, it will probably come to rest with the tyre valve or the heaviest part downward and will always come to rest in the same position. Balance weights must be added to a point diametrically opposite this heavy spot until the wheel will come to rest in ANY position after it is spun.

4   Weights which can be clamped around a convenient spoke nipple will be available in a wide range of sizes from any good motorcycle dealer or tyre centre.

Chapter 6 Electrical system

Refer to Chapter 7 for information relating to the 1991-on SR125 models

Contents

Specifications

Electrical system	SR125	XT125
Voltage	12	6
Earth	Negative	Negative
Flywheel generator		
Charging output	9.0A @ 5000 rpm	at least 1.2A @ 4100 rpm
		no more than 3.0A @ 8000 rpm
Lighting output	14-15V @ 5000 rpm	at least 7.1V @ 3200 rpm
Coil resistance	White-White 0.52 ohm ± 10%	Yellow-Black 0.21 ohm ± 10%
Battery		
Make	GS	FB
Type	12N7-3B	6N4A-4D
Capacity	7Ah	4Ah
Fuse rating	20A	10A
Starter motor		
Make	Mitsuba	N/App
Type	SM-7252	N/App
Output	0.4 kW	N/App
Armature coil resistance	0.023 ohm ± 10%	N/App
Brush length	10.5 mm (0.41 in)	N/App
Service limit	5 mm (0.20 in)	N/App
Brush spring pressure	540-660g (19.1-23.3oz)	N/app
Commutator diameter	23 mm (0.91 in)	N/App
Service limit	22 mm (0.87 in)	N/App
Mica undercut	0.55 mm (0.022 in)	N/App
Groove width	1.8 mm (0.071 in)	N/App
Bulbs		
Headlamp	12V, 35/35W	6V, 35/35W
Parking lamp	12V, 3.4W	6V, 3W
Stop/tail lamp	12V, 21/5W	6V, 21/5W
Turn signal lamp	12V, 21W	6V, 21W
Instrument/warning lamps	12V, 3.4W	6V, 3W

1 General description

The system is powered by a crankshaft-mounted generator located behind the crankcase left-hand cover. On SR125 models the generator output is fed to a combined rectifier/regulator unit where it is converted from alternating current (ac) to direct current (dc) by the rectifier section, and the system voltage is regulated by the electronic voltage regulator. On XT125 models a simple rectifier converts a proportion of the generator output to dc, this being used to charge the battery which powers the horn, stop lamp, turn signals and warning lamps. The remainder is fed directly to the lights, a voltage regulator being fitted to soak up the excess current generated when the lights are switched to the 'Off' or 'P' positions.

2 Testing the electrical system

1 Simple continuity checks, can be carried out using a battery and bulb arrangment to provide a test circuit. For most tests described in this Chapter, however, a pocket multimeter is essential. A basic multimeter capable of measuring volts and ohms can be bought for a very reasonable sum and will provide an invaluable tool. Separate volt and ohm meters may be used in place of a multimeter, provided those with the correct operating ranges are available. In addition, if the generator output is to be checked, an ammeter of 0 – 5 amperes range will be required.
2 Care must be taken when performing any electrical test, because some of the electrical components can be damaged if they are incorrectly connected or inadvertently shorted to earth. This is particularly so in the case of electronic components, instructions regarding meter probe connections are given for each test, and these should be read carefully to prevent accidental damage occurring.
3 Where test equipment is not available, or the owner feels unsure of the procedure described, it is strongly recommended that professional assistance is sought. Errors made through carelessness or lack of experience can so easily lead to damage and need for expensive replacement parts.
4 A certain amount of preliminary dismantling will be necessary to gain access to the components to be tested. Normally, removal of the seat and side panels will be required, with the possible addition of the fuel tank and headlamp unit to expose the remaining components.

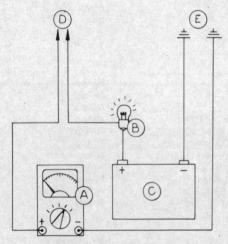

Fig. 6.1 Continuity test circuits

A	Multimeter	D	Positive probe
B	Bulb	E	Negative probe
C	Battery		

3 Wiring: layout and examination

1 The wiring harness is colour-coded and will correspond with the accompanying wiring diagram. When socket connectors are used, they are designed so that reconnection can be made in the correct position only.

2 Visual inspection will usually show whether there are any breaks or frayed outer coverings which will give rise to short circuits. Occasionally a wire may become trapped between two components, breaking the inner core but leaving the more resilient outer cover intact. This can give rise to mysterious intermittent or total circuit failure. Another source of trouble may be the snap connectors and sockets, where the connector has not been pushed fully home in the outer housing, or where corrosion has occurred.
3 Intermittent short circuits can often be traced to a chafed wire that passes through or is close to a metal component such as a frame member. Avoid tight bends in the lead or situations where a lead can become trapped between casings.

4 Charging system: checking the output

1 If the charging system appears to be over or under-charging the battery, the output should be checked first, a task which will require the use of a multimeter or other testing equipment.

SR125 model
2 Remove both side panels to gain access to the battery terminals and, using a dc voltmeter or a multimeter set to the 0 - 20 volts dc scale, measure the battery voltage. A reading of 11 - 12 volts should be obtained when the ignition switch is in the 'On' position. If not, the battery must be examined and re-charged or renewed, as described in the relevant Sections of this Chapter. It must be stressed that the battery must be in peak condition if the test is to be at all accurate and that the battery leads must not be disconnected during the test. **Note:** If the machine is run with the battery disconnected, the increased voltage across the alternator terminals will rise, causing damage to the regulator/rectifier unit or to the alternator windings.
3 Connect the positive (red) probe lead to the positive (+) battery terminal and the negative (black) probe lead to the negative (—) battery terminal. Start the engine and note the voltage reading at 2000 rpm. This should be 14.5 ± 0.5 volts if the system is operating correctly.
4 If the readings obtained do not correspond with those given, first check the wiring, switches and connections, then the battery; if no faults are found, proceed to test the alternator coils and the rectifier as described in the subsequent Sections of this Chapter. If these prove to be in good condition the regulator side of the regulator/rectifier unit must be at fault, but this can only be confirmed by the substitution of a new unit.

XT125 model – charging system
5 If symptoms arise which indicate a fault in the charging or lighting systems, the two must be checked in separate tests. In both cases, the battery must be in good condition and fully charged, as described in the relevant Sections of this Chapter, and the engine must be warmed up to normal operating temperature. To check the charging system, remove the right-hand sidepanel and start the engine. Allow it to idle, and disconnect the battery red wire at the snap connector between the battery positive (+) terminal and the fuse. Connect a dc ammeter, or multimeter set to the appropriate scale, between the two connector terminals, the meter positive (+) lead to the fuse terminal and its negative (—) lead to the battery terminal. Set the meter to the 0 - 5 amp scale, then check that the lights are switched off and increase engine speed as specified.
6 The readings obtained at the engine speeds specified should be as follows:

Charging rate – daytime
   1.2A minimum @ 4100 rpm
   3.0A maximum @ 8000 rpm

Switch the lights to the 'On' position and the dipswitch to the 'Hi' position and repeat the test. The readings obtained should be the same. As soon as the test is finished, allow the engine to idle, disconnect the meter and re-connect the battery red wire. Stop the engine. If the results obtained were satisfactory, the generator is functioning correctly and the fault lies in the rectifier, the battery, or the wiring. If the test indicates a fault in the generator, the condition of its coils must be checked, as described in the next Section.

XT125 model – lighting system
7 If the lights appear to be dim, or if constant bulb-blowing is experienced, and the bulb filaments appear to have melted, the lighting

system must be checked to ensure that the correct voltage is being applied. Remove the headlamp unit as described in Section 11 of this Chapter and disconnect the bulb wires. Switch the lights to the 'On' position and the dipswitch to the 'Hi' position. Using an ac voltmeter or a multimeter set to the 0 - 10 volts ac scale, connect the meter positive (+) lead to the yellow headlamp wire terminal and the meter negative (−) lead to the black headlamp wire terminal. Start the engine and increase engine speed as specified. The readings obtained should be as follows:

Lighting voltage
    7.1V minimum @ 3200 rpm

8   If the readings obtained are satisfactory, the system is functioning correctly and the bulb wattage should be checked to ensure that the correct items are fitted. Also check that there is no intermittent fault such as a dirty or loose connection, or a faulty switch. If the readings are not satisfactory, the condition of the stator coils should be checked, as described in the next Section, and then the voltage regulator, the switches, and the wiring between them.

---

5   Generator coils: resistance tests

1   On both models, if the tests described in Section 4 have revealed a fault in the alternator or generator itself, the condition of the individual coils can be checked by measuring their respective resistances.

SR125 model
2   Using an ohmmeter or a multimeter set to the x1 ohms scale, measure the resistance between each of the three white wires leading from the alternator. The readings obtained should be 0.52 ohm ± 10% at 20°C (68°F) in each case.

XT125 models
3   Remove the left-hand sidepanel, then identify and disconnect the wires mentioned in the tests below. The connectors are in the form of a multi-pin block connector and are to be found running up the frame downtube. Using an ohmmeter or a multimeter set to the x1 ohms scale, measure the resistances between the pair of wires shown. The reading obtained should be as follows:

Lighting coil resistance:
    Yellow to Black 0.21 ohm ± 10% at 20°C (68°F)

All models
4   With either machine, if any of the tests described above show one or more stator coils to be faulty, the complete machine should be

taken to an authorised Yamaha agent for accurate testing as the only solution is to renew the coil concerned. While an experienced auto-electrician may be able to repair or rewind a faulty coil, this is a task for the expert.

---

6   Regulator/rectifier unit: location and testing – SR125

1   The combined regulator/rectifier unit fitted to the SR125 models is a heavily finned, sealed metal unit secured behind the left-hand sidepanel by two screws. It should be noted at the outset that the unit cannot be repaired if found faulty, renewal is the only possible solution.
2   The condition of the rectifier can be checked using a multimeter, set on its resistance scale, as a continuity tester. Each of the diodes acts as a one-way valve, allowing current to flow in one direction, but blocking it if the polarity is reversed. Perform the resistance check by following the table accompanying Fig. 6.2. If any one test produces the wrong reading the rectifier will have to be renewed.
3   As previously mentioned, if the regulator is suspected of being faulty by the elimination of all other possibilities, it can only be tested by the substitution of a new unit. It is recommended that the machine be taken to a competent Yamaha Service Agent for accurate testing before this is done.

6.1 Rectifier/regulator unit – SR125

1. B (Red)
2. U (White)
3. V (White)
4. W (White)
5. E (Black)
6. I.C. regulator
7. L (Brown)

Checking element	Pocket test connecting point		Good	Replace (element shorted)	Replace (element opened)
	(+) (red)	(−) (black)			
D₁	B	U	O	O	×
	U	B	×	O	×
D₂	B	V	O	O	×
	V	B	×	O	×
D₃	B	W	O	O	×
	W	B	×	O	×
D₄	U	E	O	O	×
	E	U	×	O	×
D₅	V	E	O	O	×
	E	V	×	O	×
D₆	W	E	O	O	×
	E	W	×	O	×

O ..... Continuity
× ..... Discontinuity

Fig. 6.2 Rectifier resistance test – SR125

7 Regulator and rectifier units – location and testing: XT125

1   The voltage regulator unit is a heavily-finned, silver, sealed metal unit fastened to the left-hand side of the frame down tubes immediately behind the engine/gearbox unit. It requires no maintenance except for a periodic check that it is clean and free from dirt and corrosion and that its two retaining screws are securely fastened.

2   The regulator unit operates on the same principle as a Zener diode, diverting excess lighting voltage away from the bulbs and disposing of it in the form of heat through its finned cover. In this way the varying demands of the bulbs are met, and the risk of bulbs blowing due to voltage surge is reduced greatly.

3   Unfortunately the unit can be tested only with a special test meter, no other data being provided. If the condition of the unit is suspect after the test of the lighting voltage described in Section 4, and other possibilities such as the bulbs, switches and wiring have been eliminated, it must be returned to a Yamaha dealer to be checked. If found to be faulty, it must be renewed as repairs are not possible.

4   The silicon diode rectifier fitted to these machines is a small rectangular black plastic block with two male spade terminals projecting from its underside, which is retained by a single screw to the right-hand side of the frame top tubes, immediately behind the steering head. It requires no maintenance at all, save a periodic check that it is clean, and that both it and its connections are securely fastened.

5   The rectifier consists of a small diode and serves to convert the ac output of the flywheel generator into dc to charge the battery. It should be thought of as a one-way valve, in that it will allow the current to flow in one direction only, thus blocking half of the output wave from the generator.

6   Before removing the unit, identify the polarity of the two terminals by the colour of the wire leading to each one. The red wire leads to the positive (+) terminal and the white wire to the negative (–) or ac terminal.

7   Using a multimeter set to the resistance mode, check for continuity between the two terminals. There should only be continuity from the negative (–) to the positive (+) terminal. This direction of flow may be shown by an arrow on the surface of the unit. If there is continuity in the reverse direction, or if resistance is measured in both directions, the rectifier is faulty and must be renewed. No repair is possible.

8 Battery: examination and maintenance

1   On SR125 models the battery is housed in a tray behind the right-hand sidepanel and is retained in position by a bracket that is locked by a single screw. On XT125 models it is held in a plastic casing that is secured by two bolts to the frame between the rear of the engine/gearbox unit and the sub-frame pivot. To remove the battery, disconnect its terminal leads, remove the two bolts and lower the complete casing to the ground. The casing top can then be unclipped, after its retaining screw has been removed, so that the battery can be extracted. A small panel can be removed from the casing so that the electrolyte level can be checked.

2   The transparent plastic case of the battery permits the upper and lower levels of the electrolyte to be observed without disturbing the battery. Maintenance is normally limited to keeping the electrolyte level between the prescribed upper and lower limits and making sure that the vent tube is not blocked. The lead plates and their separators are also visible through the transparent case, a further guide to the general condition of the battery. If electrolyte level drops rapidly, suspect over-charging and check the system.

3   Unless acid is spilt, as may occur if the machine falls over, the electrolyte should always be topped up with distilled water to restore the correct level. If acid is spilt onto any part of the machine, it should be neutralised with an alkali such as washing soda or baking powder and washed away with plenty of water, otherwise serious corrosion will occur. Top up with sulphuric acid of the correct specific gravity (1.260 to 1.280) only when spillage has occurred. Check that the vent pipe is well clear of the frame or any of the other cycle parts.

4   It is seldom practicable to repair a cracked battery case because the acid present in the joint will prevent the formation of an effective seal. It is always best to renew a cracked battery, especially in view of the corrosion which will be caused if the acid continues to leak.

5   If the machine is not used for a period of time, it is advisable to remove the battery and give it a 'refresher' charge every six weeks or so from a battery charger. The battery will require recharging when the specific gravity falls below 1.260 (at 20°C/68°F). The hydrometer reading should be taken at the top of the meniscus with the hydrometer vertical. If the battery is left discharged for too long, the plates will sulphate. This is a grey deposit which will appear on the surface of the plates, and will inhibit recharging. If there is sediment on the bottom of the battery case, which touches the plates, the battery needs to be renewed. Prior to charging the battery, refer to the following Section for correct charging rate and procedure. If charging from an external source with the battery on the machine, disconnect the leads, or the rectifier will be damaged.

6   Note that when moving or charging the battery it is essential that the following basic safety precautions are taken:

(a)   Before charging, check that the battery vent is clear or, where no vent is fitted, remove the combined vent/filler caps. If this precaution is not taken, the gas pressure generated during charging may be sufficient to burst the battery case, with disastrous consequences

(b)   Never expose a battery on charge to naked flames or sparks. The gas given off by the battery is highly explosive

(c)   If charging the battery in an enclosed area, ensure that the area is well ventilated

(d)   Always take great care to protect yourself against accidental spillage of the sulphuric acid contained within the battery. Eyeshields should be worn at all times. If the eyes become contaminated with acid they must be flushed with fresh water immediately and examined by a doctor as soon as possible. Similar attention should be given to a spillage of acid on the skin.

Note also that although, should an emergency arise, it is possible to charge the battery at a more rapid rate than that stated in the following Section, this will shorten the life of the battery and should therefore be avoided if at all possible.

7   Occasionally, check the condition of the battery terminals to ensure that corrosion is not taking place, and that the electrical connections are tight. If corrosion has occurred, it should be cleaned away by scraping with a knife and then using emery cloth to remove the final traces. Remake the electrical connections whilst the joint is still clean, then smear the assembly with petroleum jelly (NOT grease) to prevent recurrence of the corrosion. Badly corroded connections can have a high electrical resistance and may give the impression of complete battery failure.

7.1 Voltage regulator – XT125

7.4 Rectifier – XT125

8.1a Battery is retained as shown – SR125

8.1b XT125 – remove top mounting bolt and ...

8.1c ... bottom mounting bolt to release battery casing

8.1d Small panel can be removed to inspect electrolyte level

9 Battery: charging procedure

1   Whilst the machine is used on the road it is unlikely that the battery will require attention other than routine maintenance because the generator will keep it fully charged. However, if the machine is used for a succession of short journeys only, mainly during the hours of darkness when the lights are in full use, it is possible that the output from the generator may fail to keep pace with the heavy electrical demand, especially if the machine is parked with the lights switched on. Under these circumstances it will be necessary to remove the battery from time to time to have it charged independently.

2   The normal maximum charging rate for any battery is 1/10 the rated capacity. Hence the charging rate for the battery fitted to SR125 models is 0.7 amp, while that of the 4 Ah battery fitted to XT125 models if 0.4 amp. A slightly higher charge rate may be used in emergencies only, but this should never exceed 1 amp.

3   Ensure that the battery/charger connections are properly made, ie the charger positive (usually coloured red) lead to the battery positive (the red wire) lead, and the charger negative (usually coloured black or blue) lead to the battery negative (the black/white wire) lead. Refer to the previous Section for precautions to be taken during charging. It is especially important that the battery cell cover plugs are removed to

eliminate any possibility of pressure building up in the battery and cracking its casing. Switch off the charger if the cells become overheated, ie over 45°C (117°F).

4   Charging is complete when the specific gravity of the electrolyte rises to 1.260 - 1.280 at 20°C (68°F). A rough guide to this state is when all cells are gassing freely. At the normal (slow) rate of charge this will take between 3 - 15 hours, depending on the original state of charge of the battery.

5   If the higher rate of charge is used, never leave the battery charging for more than 1 hour as overheating and buckling of the plates will inevitably occur.

10 Fuse: location and renewal

1   The electrical system is protected by a single fuse of 20 or 10 amp rating, as appropriate. It is retained in a plastic casing set in the battery positive (+) terminal lead, and is clipped to a holder behind the left-hand side panel. If the spare fuse is ever used, replace it with one of the correct rating as soon as possible.

2   Before renewing a fuse that has blown, check that no obvious short circuit has occurred, otherwise the replacement fuse will blow immediately it is inserted. It is always wise to check the electrical circuit thoroughly, to trace the fault and eliminate it.

3   When a fuse blows while the machine is running and no spare is available, a 'get you home' remedy is to remove the blown fuse and wrap it in silver paper before replacing it in the fuse holder. The silver paper will restore the electrical continuity by bridging the broken fuse wire. This expedient should never be used if there is evidence of short circuit or other major electrical faults, otherwise more serious damage will be caused. Replace the 'doctored' fuse at the earliest possible opportunity, to restore full circuit protection.

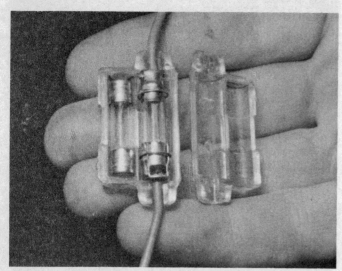

10.1 Fuse and spare are retained in plastic casing behind left-hand side panel

11 Switches: general

1   While the switches should give little trouble, they can be tested using a multimeter set to the resistance function or a battery and bulb test circuit. Using the information given in the wiring diagram at the end of this Manual, check that full continuity exists in all switch positions and between the relevant pairs of wires. When checking a particular circuit follow a logical sequence to eliminate the switch concerned.

2   As a simple precaution always disconnect the battery before removing any of the switches, to prevent the possibility of a short circuit. Most troubles are caused by dirty contacts, but in the event of the breakage of some internal part, it will be necessary to renew the complete switch.

3   If a switch is tested and found to be faulty, there is nothing to be lost by attempting a repair. It may be that worn contacts can be built up with solder, or that a broken wire terminal can be repaired, again using a soldering iron. The handlebar switches can all be dismantled to a greater or lesser extent. It is, however, up to the owner to decide if he has the skill to carry out this sort of work.

4   While none of the switches require routine maintenance of any sort, some regular attention will prolong their life a great deal. In the author's experience, the regular and constant application of WD40 or a similar water-dispersant spray not only prevents problems occurring due to waterlogged switches and the resulting corrosion, but also makes the switches much easier and more positive to use. Alternatively, the switch may be packed with a silicone-based grease to achieve the same result.

12 Starter motor: examination and renovation

1   Although the starter motor is mounted on the front of the engine and is retained by two screws, it cannot be removed until the crankcase right-hand cover has been withdrawn first. Refer to the relevant Sections of Chapter 1 for details of removal and refitting. Note that the battery should be disconnected first to prevent the possibility of short circuits. It is advisable, on refitting. to smear petroleum jelly or silicone grease over the starter motor terminal before refitting the rubber grommet.

2   The end covers are secured to the motor body by two long screws which pass through the length of the motor. With these screws removed, the right-hand end cover can be separated form the motor body and the brush retaining plate exposed.

3   With the flat of a small screwdriver, lift the end of the spring clip bearing on the end of each brush and draw the brushes from their holders. Measure the length of each brush; if it is less than the service limit of 5.0 mm (0.2 in), renew the brush.

4   Before fitting the brushes, make sure that the commutator is clean, using a strip of glass paper. Never use emery cloth or wet-and-dry as the small abrasive fragments may embed themselves in the soft copper of the commutator and cause excessive wear of the brushes. Finish off the commutator with metal polish to give a smooth surface and finally wipe the segments over with a methylated spirit soaked rag to ensure a grease free surface. Check that the mica insulators, which lie between the segments of the commutator, are undercut. If the amount of undercut is seen to be less than the service limit of 0.55 mm (0.022 in), then the armature should be withdrawn from the motor body and returned to an official Yamaha service agent or an experienced auto-electrician for recutting.

5   Fit the brushes in their holders and check that they slide quite freely. If the original brushes are being refitted, make sure they are fitted in their original positions as they will have worn to the profile of the commutator.

6   If the motor has given indications of a more serious fault, withdraw the armature from the motor body, set a multimeter to its resistance function and carry out a check for equal resistance between the commutator segments and for good insulation between each commutator segment and the armature core. A fault in insulation or continuity will require renewal of the armature.

7   Before commencing reassembly of the motor, check the condition of the O-ring which forms a seal between the flanged end cap and the motor body and the condition of both the oil seal and O-ring located in the opposite end cap. If any of these items are seen to be damaged or deteriorating then they must be renewed. The seal can be removed from its location within the end cap by carefully easing it from position with the flat of a small screwdriver whilst taking care to avoid causing damage to the soft alloy mating surfaces of the cap. Ensure that, when fitting the new seal, the seal enters the end cap squarely. Lubricate the outer surface of the seal with a small amount of oil around the seal lip before reassembling the motor.

8   Check the condition of the shims, located one at either end of the armature, and commence reassembly of the starter motor whilst referring to the figure accompanying this text for the fitted positions of the components. It will be found that some difficulty will be experienced when refitting the right-hand end cap and brush holder assembly. Care must be taken to locate the brushes correctly on the commutator and to align the notch in the motor body with the corresponding notch in the end cap. A similar method of alignment is used for the opposing cap.

12.1 Crankcase right-hand cover must be removed before starter can be withdrawn

12.2 Long bolts secure motor end caps – do not omit washers and seals

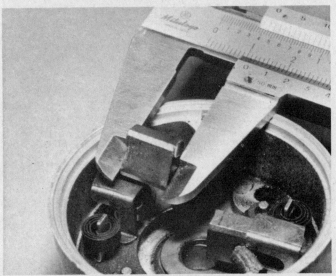

12.3 Measuring brush length

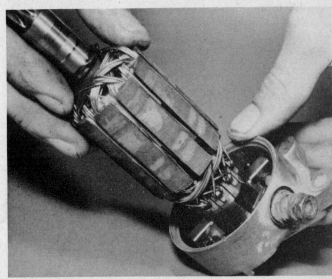

12.8a Be careful when refitting brushes – they are easily damaged

12.8b Check condition of shims ...

12.8c ... before refitting end cap

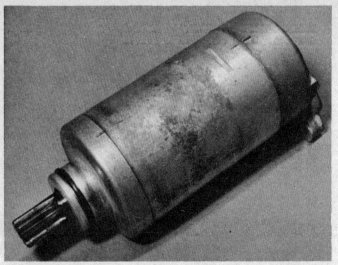

12.8d Align notches in end caps with those on body before tightening bolts

Fig. 6.3 Starter motor – SR125

1 Armature
2 O-ring
3 O-ring – 2 off
4 Brush
5 Brush
6 Shims
7 Bolt – 2 off
8 Starter motor lead
9 Rubber grommet – 2 off
10 Terminal – 2 off
11 Screw
12 Motor body
13 Circlip
14 Oil seal
15 Needle roller bearing
16 End cap
17 Spring – 2 off
18 Pin
19 Bush
20 Washer – 2 off
21 Washer – 2 off
22 Seal – 2 off

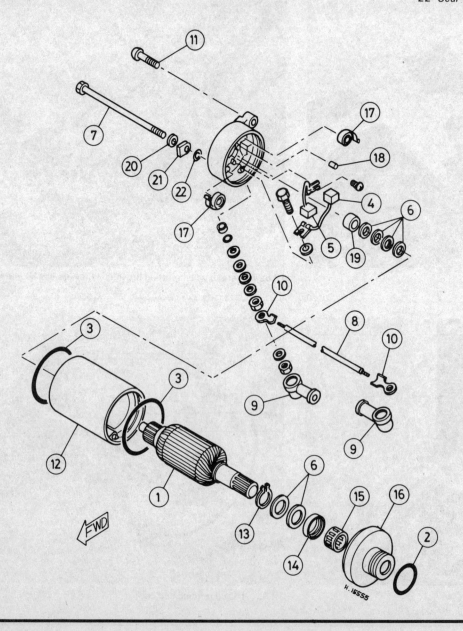

13 Starter solenoid switch (relay) and circuit cut-off relay: location and testing

1   If the starter will not operate, first suspect a discharged battery. This can be checked by trying the horn or switching on the lights. If this check shows the battery to be in good shape, suspect the starter solenoid which should come into action with a pronounced click. It is located close to the battery, to which it is connected by a heavy duty cable. Before condemning the starter solenoid, carry out the following tests.

2   Disconnect the earth lead from the negative (–) terminal of the battery and move it well clear of the terminal. Remove the rubber cover from the starter solenoid and disconnect the low tension lead at the connector. Unscrew and remove the two nuts from the solenoid and disconnect the leads from the threaded terminals. Remove the starter solenoid from its retainer by sliding it out of position.

3   The solenoid coil should be tested by connecting a battery across its terminals. The low tension wire runs to one terminal, the second terminal is that to which the heavy duty cable from the battery is connected. On connecting the battery, a pronounced click should be heard as the contacts close. Maintain the power so that the contacts remain closed, and check for continuity across the two heavy duty terminals. This should be done with a multimeter set to the resistance

function. If continuity does not exist, there is evidence that the starter relay has failed.

4   Alternatively, connect a multimeter set to the x1 ohm range between the low tension wire and the switch mounting bracket or a similar good earth point. If a reading of 3-4 ohms is obtained, the switch is in good condition. If not, the switch is faulty and must be renewed.

5   The starter motor circuit cut-off relay is mounted behind the right-hand side-panel, below the air filter casing and next to the battery. It is removed by unplugging the multi-pin block connector and withdrawing the relay from its mountings. Its function is to cut-off power to the starter relay unless the transmission is in neutral or the clutch lever is pulled into the handlebar. In addition, if one is attempting to start the engine with the headlamp switched on, the relay will temporarily cut off the power to the headlamp, thus minimising the load on the battery.

6   The cut-off relay can be tested using a good quality multimeter, making the connections as shown in the accompanying illustrations. Note that the second test requires the use of a 12 volt battery; this must be fully charged if the test is to be effective.

7   If the relay is found to be faulty it must be renewed as repairs are not possible, but owners should note that faults are far more likely to occur in the system's wiring, connections or in one of the switches; these should be tested first, as described elsewhere in this Chapter, before the relay is suspected.

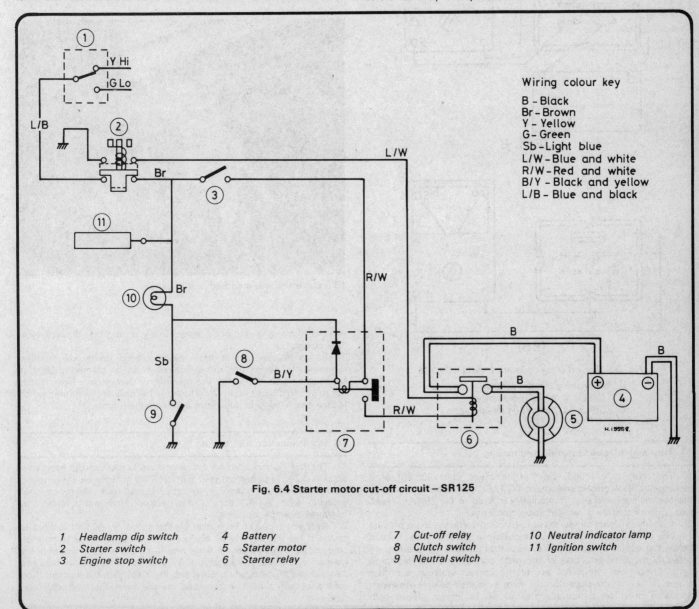

Fig. 6.4 Starter motor cut-off circuit – SR125

1 *Headlamp dip switch*	4 *Battery*	7 *Cut-off relay*
2 *Starter switch*	5 *Starter motor*	8 *Clutch switch*
3 *Engine stop switch*	6 *Starter relay*	9 *Neutral switch*
		10 *Neutral indicator lamp*
		11 *Ignition switch*

Wiring colour key

B – Black
Br – Brown
Y – Yellow
G – Green
Sb – Light blue
L/W – Blue and white
R/W – Red and white
B/Y – Black and yellow
L/B – Blue and black

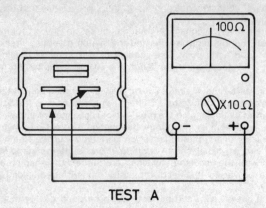

TEST A

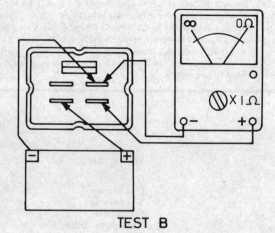

TEST B

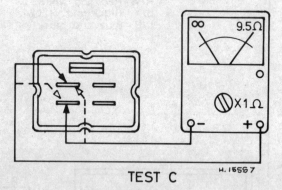

TEST C

H. 16597

Fig. 6.5 Cut-off relay resistance tests – SR125

A   *Measuring the coil winding resistance*
B   *Checking the relay operation*
C   *Checking the relay diode operation*

13.1 Starter relay is located behind left-hand sidepanel – SR125

13.5 Cut-off relay is mounted next to battery

and that the wiring is in good order. Finally, ensure that the battery is fully charged.

3   Faults in any one or more of the above items will produce symptoms for which the turn signal relay may be blamed unfairly. If the fault persists even after the preliminary checks have been made, the relay must be at fault. Unfortunately the only practical method of testing the relay is to substitute a known good one.

14 Turn signal relay: location and testing

1   The relay is a round silver sealed metal unit (SR125) or a rectangular black plastic sealed unit (XT125); it is rubber mounted at the rear of the headlamp, immediately in front of the steering head, and is connected by a two-pin connector block.

2   If the turn signal lamps cease to function correctly, there may be any one of several possible faults responsible which should be checked before the relay is suspected. First check that the turn signal lamps are correctly mounted and that all the earth connections are clean and tight. Check that the bulbs are of the correct wattage and that corrosion has not developed on the bulbs or in their holders. Any such corrosion must be thoroughly cleaned off to ensure proper bulb contact. Also check that the turn signal switch is functioning correctly

15 Horn: location and testing

1   The horn is mounted on a flexible steel bracket to the headlamp bracket (XT125) or bottom yoke (SR125). No maintenance is required other than regular cleaning to remove road dirt and occasional spraying with WD40 or a similar water dispersant lubricant to minimise internal corrosion.

2   Different types of horn may be fitted; if a screw and locknut is provided on the outside of the horn, the internal contacts may be adjusted to compensate for wear and to cure a weak or intermittent horn note. Slacken the locknut and rotate slowly the screw until the clearest and loudest note is obtained, then retighten the locknut. If no means of adjustment is provided on the horn fitted, it must be renewed.

3   If the horn fails to work, first check that the power is reaching it

by disconnecting the wires. Substitute a 6 or 12 volt bulb, switch on the ignition and press the horn button. If the bulb lights, the circuit is proved good and the horn is at fault; if the bulb does not light, there is a fault in the circuit which must be found and rectified.
4   To test the horn itself, connect a fully-charged 6 or 12 volt battery directly to the horn. If it does not sound, a gentle tap on the outside may free the internal contacts. If this fails, the horn must be renewed as repairs are not possible.

16 Headlamp: bulb renewal and beam alignment

1   The headlamp reflector unit and rim are retained by one bolt on XT125 models and by two screws on SR125 models; remove the bolt or screws and withdraw the rim and reflector unit.
2   Twist the bulb holder anti-clockwise and withdraw it, complete with the bulb. To separate the two, press the bulb in and twist anti-clockwise to release. Refitting is a straightforward reversal of the above.
3   The parking lamp bulb is a conventional bayonet fitting in a bulb holder that is pressed into a rubber grommet set in the rear of the reflector unit.
4   On XT125 models beam height is adjusted by slackening the mounting bolts and tilting the headlamp shell for vertical adjustment and by slackening the single bolt and rotating the reflector unit for horizontal adjustment. On SR125 models, two spring loaded screws are set in the bottom and side of the rim to serve the same respective functions.
5   In the UK, regulations stipulate that the headlamp must be arranged so that the light will not dazzle a person standing at a distance greater than 25 feet from the lamp, whose eye level is not less than 3 feet 6 inches above that plane. It is easy to approximate this setting by placing the machine 25 feet away from a wall, on a level road, and setting the dip beam height so that it is concentrated at the same height as the distance of the centre of the headlamp from the ground. The rider must be seated normally during this operation and also the pillion passenger, if one is carried regularly.

17 Instrument panel: bulb renewal

Follow the instructions given in Section 12 of Chapter 4 to release the instruments and unplug the bulb holders. Each instrument or warning lamp bulb is a conventional bayonet fitting in its holder.

18 Turn signal and stop/tail lamps: bulb renewal

1   With the exception of the turn signal lamps fitted to SR125 models, all stop/tail and turn signal lamp lenses are retained by two screws. Remove these screws and withdraw the lens, taking care not to tear the sealing gasket. On SR125 turn signal lamps, insert a coin or screwdriver into the slot in the lamp body and twist carefully to unclip the lens.
2   All bulbs are of the conventional bayonet fitting ie press in and twist anti-clockwise to release. Refitting is the reverse of the above, but note that stop/tail lamp bulbs have offset pins so that the bulb can be fitted one way only. Do not overtighten lens retaining screws (where applicable) or the lens may crack.
3   Remove all traces of moisture and corrosion from the lamp interior and renew the sealing gasket if it is found to be torn or compressed. Turn signal lamps with black plastic interiors can be improved by lining with cooking foil; this will greatly improve their visibility in bright sunlight.

14.1a Turn signal relay – XT125

14.1b Turn signal relay – SR125

15.1 Horn is bolted to bottom fork yoke – SR125

16.1 Remove two screws to release headlamp rim

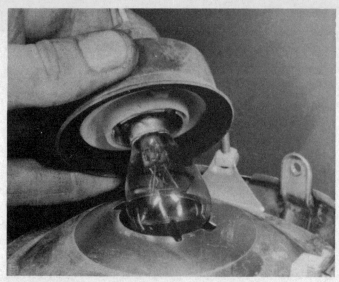

16.2 Bulb is a bayonet fitting in holder

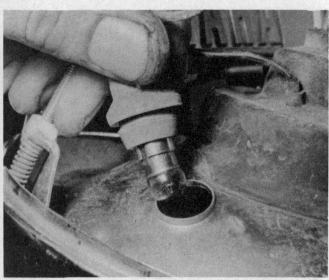

16.3 Parking lamp bulb is pressed into rubber grommet in reflector

18.1a Turn signal and stop/tail lamp lenses are retained by screws ...

18.1b ... or clipped in place

18.2 All bulbs are bayonet fitting

Wiring diagram colour key — both diagrams

R	Red	Sb	Light blue
B	Black	Dg	Dark green
Y	Yellow	G/Y	Green and yellow
L	Blue	R/W	Red and white
P	Pink	L/W	Blue and white
W	White	L/B	Blue and black
G	Green	L/R	Blue and red
O	Orange	Br/W	Brown and white
Br	Brown	B/Y	Black and yellow
Ch	Chocolate	B/W	Black and white

Wiring diagram component key — XT125

1	Right-hand handlebar switch	17	Left-hand handlebar switch
2	Engine kill switch	18	Horn switch
3	Front brake stop lamp switch	19	Indicator switch
4	Ignition coil	20	Headlamp dip switch
5	CDI unit	21	Lighting switch
6	Rectifier	22	Left-hand front indicator
7	Fuse	23	Horn
8	Battery	24	Speedometer lamp
9	Right-hand rear indicator	25	Parking lamp
10	Tail/stop lamp	26	Headlamp
11	Left-hand rear indicator	27	Ignition switch
12	Rear brake stop lamp switch	28	Indicator warning lamp
13	Voltage regulator	29	High beam lamp
14	Indicator relay	30	Neutral indicator lamp
15	Neutral indicator switch	31	Right-hand front indicator
16	Generator	32	Tachometer lamp — 1983/84 models

Wiring diagram component key — SR125 (1982 to 1985 models)

1	TCI unit	19	Tail/stop lamp
2	Ignition coil	20	Parking lamp
3	Spark plug	21	Headlamp dip switch
4	Engine kill switch	22	Front brake stop lamp switch
5	Starter button	23	Rear brake stop lamp switch
6	Indicator relay	24	Neutral indicator switch
7	Indicator switch	25	Lighting switch
8	Right-hand front indicator	26	Ignition switch
9	Right-hand rear indicator	27	Neutral indicator light
10	Right-hand indicator warning lamp	28	Clutch switch
11	Left-hand front indicator	29	Starting circuit cut-off relay
12	Left-hand rear indicator	30	Starter motor
13	Left-hand indicator warning lamp	31	Starter motor solenoid
14	Horn	32	Battery
15	Horn switch	33	Fuse
16	Headlamp	34	Alternator
17	High beam lamp	35	Voltage regulator and rectifier
18	Speedometer light		

154

Wiring diagram – SR125 (1982 to 1985 models)

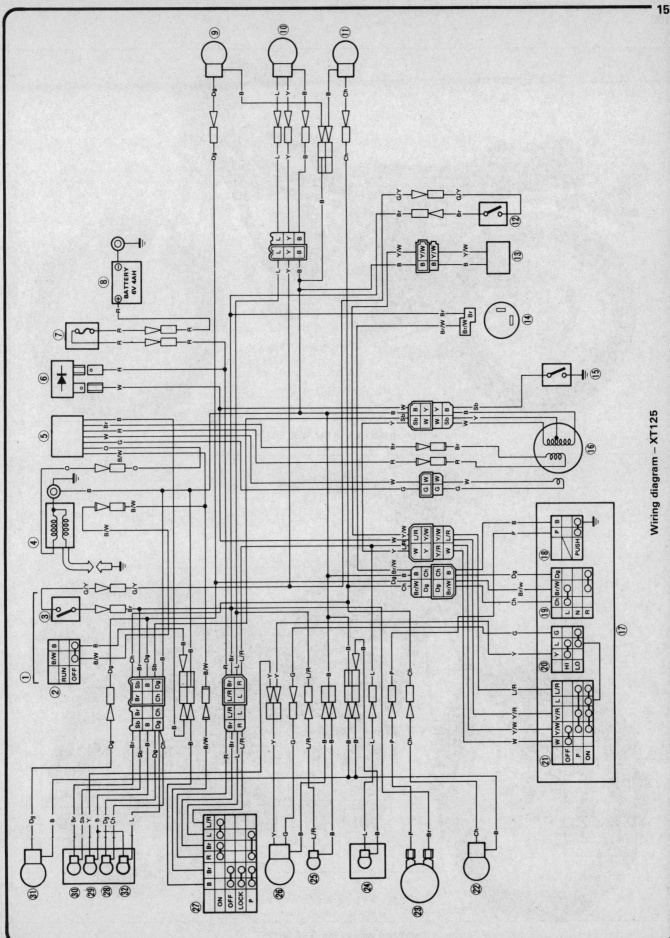

Wiring diagram – XT125

Right-hand view of the 1996 SR125

Left-hand view of the 1996 SR125

Chapter 7 The 1991-on SR125 models

Contents

Specifications

Model dimensions and weights – 1992-on models

Overall length	1915 mm (75.4 in)
Overall width	
1992 to 1996 models	765 mm (30.1 in)
1997-on models	775 mm (30.5 in)
Overall height	
1992 to 1998 models	1080 mm (42.5 in)
1999-on models	1100 mm (43.3 in)
Seat height	
1992 to 1996 models	740 mm (29.1 in)
1997-on models	745 mm (29.4 in)
Wheelbase	1280 mm (50.4 in)
Ground clearance	
1992 to 1996 models	160 mm (6.3 in)
1997-on models	155 mm (6.1 in)
Kerb weight (with oil and full fuel tank)	113 kg (249 lb)

Idle speed

1999-on models	1300 – 1400 rpm

Ignition system – 1997-on models

System type	Capacitor discharge (CDI)
Source coil resistance	Brown-Green 624 – 936 ohm @ 20°C
Pulser coil resistance	Red-White 656 – 984 ohm @ 20°C
1997 and 1998 models	
HT coil primary winding resistance	0.32 – 0.48 ohm @ 20°C
HT coil secondary winding resistance	5.68 – 8.52 K ohm @ 20°C
1999-on models	
HT coil primary winding resistance	0.18 – 0.28 ohm @ 20°C
HT coil secondary winding resistance	6.32 – 9.48 K ohm @ 20°C

Front forks – 1992-on models

Spring free length	
1992 to 1998 models	326 mm (12.83 in)
1999-on models	353 mm (13.90 in)
Service limit (1992-on models)	321 mm (12.64 in)
Oil capacity (per leg)	
1992 to 1996 models	184 cc
1997 models	177 cc
1998 models	184 cc
1999-on models	187 cc

Front forks – 1992-on models (continued)

Oil level
1992 to 1996 models	149 mm (5.9 in)
1997 models	135 mm (5.31 in)
1998 models	140 mm (5.51 in)
1999-on models	138 mm (5.43 in)

Recommended fork oil
1992 to 1996 models	SAE 10W fork oil
1997 and 1998 models	SAE 15W fork oil
1999-on models	SAE 10W fork oil

Front brake – 1992-on models

Front brake lever freeplay	2 – 5 mm (0.08 – 0.20 in)
Fluid specification	DOT 4 or DOT 3
Pad friction material wear limit	0.8 mm (0.03 in)
Master cylinder bore diameter	12.7 mm (0.50 in)

Caliper bore diameter
1992 to 1996 models	38.10 mm (1.50 in)
1997-on models (upper bore)	30.16 mm (1.19 in)
1997-on models (lower bore)	25.40 mm (1.00 in)

Disc thickness
1992 to 1996 models	5.0 mm (0.20 in)
1997-on models	4.0 mm (0.16 in)

Disc service limit
1992 to 1996 models	4.5 mm (0.18 in)
1997-on models	3.5 mm (0.14 in)
Disc runout	0.5 mm (0.02 in)

Tyre pressures – 1992-on models

	Front	Rear
Up to 198 lb (90 kg) load	25 psi (1.8 kg/cm^2)	28 psi (2.0 kg/cm^2)
Over 198 lb (90 kg) load	25 psi (1.8 kg/cm^2)	32 psi (2.3 kg/cm^2)

Bulbs – 1999-on models

Headlamp	12V, 60/55W
Parking lamp	12V, 3.4W
Stop/tail lamp	12V, 21/5W
Turn signal lamp	12V, 21W
Instrument lamp	12V, 3W
Warning lamps	12V, 1.7W

Torque settings – 1992-on models

	kgf m	lbf ft
Cam chain tensioner mounting bolts	1.0	7.2
Cam chain tensioner cap bolt	1.0	7.2
Side stand pivot bolt	1.9	13.7
Side stand pivot bolt locknut	1.6	11
Handlebar clamp bolts	2.0	14
Steering stem crown bolt (1992 to 1998 models)	4.0	29
Steering stem crown nut (1999-on models)	11.0	79.5
Front fork bottom yoke pinch bolts	3.0	22
Front fork top yoke pinch bolts (1999-on models)	1.9	13.7
Fork cap bolt (1999-on models)	1.9	13.7
Rear suspension unit upper bolt	4.0	29
Rear suspension unit lower bolt	3.0	22
Brake caliper mounting bolts (1992 to 1996 models)	3.5	25
Brake pad retaining pin (1992 to 1996 models)	2.3	17
Brake caliper bracket bolts (1997-on models)	4.0	29
Brake caliper fixing bolt (1997-on models)	2.3	17
Brake disc mounting bolts		
1992 to 1996 models	2.0	14
1997-on models	2.3	17
Brake hose banjo union bolts	3.0	22
Master cylinder clamp bolts	0.9	6.5
Front wheel spindle		
1992 to 1996 models	5.8	42
1997-on models	5.9	43
Front wheel spindle pinch bolt		
1992 to 1996 models	1.9	13.7
1997-on models	2.0	14
Rear wheel spindle nut (1997-on models)	6.5	47
Rear sprocket retaining nuts (1997-on models)	4.0	29

1 Introduction

The SR125 was reintroduced into the UK market in February 1991. The only difference from the previous model was in the use of square-bodied indicators rather than the original round units, and the inclusion of a side stand switch.

1992-on models were fitted with an hydraulic disc front brake in place of the original drum unit, and braking efficiency was uprated with a two-piston caliper mounted on the left-hand fork leg in 1997.

1997-on models featured a CDI electronic ignition system, a modified alternator and starter motor, and the carburettor was fitted with an electric heater to prevent icing.

1999-on models were fitted with a new front fork top yoke and steering head bearing adjuster and the original style headlamp and instrument panel were replaced by a separate chrome headlamp assembly and speedometer. The only change to the engine was the fitting of an automatic cam chain tensioner.

When working on a 1991 or later SR125 models, refer first to this Chapter for the information required. If no mention is made, the task will be the same as for the SR125 models covered in the preceding Chapters of this manual.

2 Routine maintenance: intervals – 1992-on models

Note: *Refer to the information in parentheses for location of the supporting text.*

Daily (pre-ride) checks

Check the engine/transmission oil level (Routine maintenance)
Check the final drive chain tension (Routine maintenance)
Check the front brake fluid level and brake operation (Section 3 of this Chapter)
Check the rear brake operation (Routine maintenance)
Check the tyre pressures (Routine maintenance)
Check the operation of the controls and steering (Routine maintenance)
Check the operation of the lights, indicators, horn and speedometer
Ensure you have enough fuel to complete your journey

Every 300 miles (500 km)

Check, adjust and lubricate the final drive chain (Routine maintenance)

Six monthly or every 4000 miles (6000 km)

Check the battery electrolyte level and vent tube (Routine maintenance)
Check, clean and regap the spark plug (Routine maintenance)
Check and adjust the valve clearances (Routine maintenance)
Adjust the cam chain – 1992 to 1998 models only (Routine maintenance)
Clean the air filter (Routine maintenance)
Check the carburettor, throttle cable and fuel pipe (Routine maintenance)
Change the engine/transmission oil (Routine maintenance)
Check and adjust the clutch (Routine maintenance)
Check the front brake pad wear, lever freeplay and hose condition (Section 3 of this Chapter)
Check and adjust the rear brake (Routine maintenance)
Check the wheels and tyres (Routine maintenance)
Check the wheel bearings (Chapter 5)
Check the front and rear suspension operation (Routine maintenance)
Check the steering head bearings for freeplay (Routine maintenance – 1992 to 1998 models, Section 3 of this Chapter – 1999-on models)
Check that the sidestand mounting is secure and the pivot properly lubricated (Section 3 of this Chapter)
Check that operation of the sidestand switch (Section 3)
Check all fasteners for tightness (Routine maintenance)

Annually or every 8000 miles (12 000 km)

Change the engine/transmission oil filter (Routine maintenance)
Check the swinging arm bearings for freeplay (Routine maintenance)
Overhaul the rear brake (Chapter 5)

Every 16 000 miles (24 000 km)

Regrease the swinging arm bearings (Routine maintenance)
Regrease the steering head bearings (Chapter 4 and Section 10 of this Chapter)

Every two years

Renew the front brake caliper piston seals (Section 16 or 17 of this Chapter)
Renew the front brake master cylinder piston assembly (Section 19 of this Chapter)

Every four years

Renew the front brake hydraulic hose (Section 20 of this Chapter)

Additional maintenance items

Note: *The following tasks are not included in the maintenance schedule for the 1992-on SR125 models, but will require attention at higher mileages.*

Clean the fuel tap filter (Routine maintenance – 1992 to 1998, Section 5 of this Chapter – 1999-on models)
Change the front fork oil (Routine maintenance)
Renew the spark plug (Routine maintenance)

3 Routine maintenance: additional operations

Front brake fluid level check

1 The brake fluid level can be viewed through the sightglass in the front of the master cylinder reservoir. Position the bike on its centre stand and if necessary, turn the handlebars so that the master cylinder is level. Check that the fluid is level with or above the LOWER mark line on the reservoir body.

2 If the fluid requires topping up, remove the two screws and free the reservoir cover. Lift the cover and diaphragm away. Cover the area around the reservoir with a cloth to protect from brake fluid spills, and top up the reservoir with the specified fluid so that it is just above the LOWER mark line. **Note:** *Never use old brake fluid or fluid from a*

3.1 Check that fluid level is above LOWER line (arrowed) on reservoir body

3.2a Reservoir cover is retained by two screws

3.2b Ensure that the diaphragm is folded correctly before refitting the cover

3.5a On 1992 to 1996 models, with the brake applied check that the wear indicator (arrowed) on each pad does not contact the disc

3.5b Measuring brake pad friction material thickness

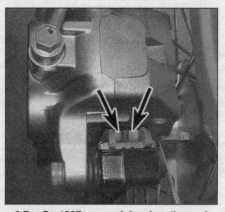

3.7a On 1997-on models, view the pad material (arrowed) from the rear of the caliper or . . .

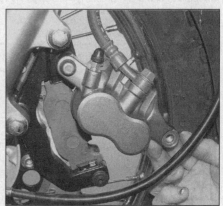

3.7b . . . displace the caliper to check the pads

container which has not been resealed after use. Make sure the diaphragm is correctly folded and refit the reservoir cover.
3 If there is a rapid fall in the fluid level suspect a leak in the system. Inspect the brake hose and its connections, and the caliper and master cylinder seals and rectify the problem immediately.

Front brake pad wear check – 1992 to 1996 models

4 View the caliper from the rear to check the amount of pad wear.
5 Have an assistant hold the front brake on and check the pad wear indicators (small raised tangs extending from each pad's backing plate) in relation to the disc surface. If they are close to the disc surface, fit new pads. If it is impossible to view the pads due to a build-up of road dirt, or there is some doubt about the amount of friction material remaining, remove the pads (see Section 14) and measure the thickness of the friction material. Renew the pads if they are worn to the service limit or fouled with oil or grease.
6 Do not allow the pads to wear down so far that the wear indicators contact the disc. A pronounced squeal will be produced, braking efficiency will be reduced and the disc surface will be scored.

Front brake pad wear check – 1997-on models

7 View the caliper from the rear to check the amount of pad wear. Alternatively, unscrew and remove the caliper fixing bolt and pivot the caliper upwards clear of the brake pads. Do not operate the brake while the caliper is off the disc.
8 Remove the pads from the caliper bracket, noting the position of the upper and lower pad springs, then measure the thickness of the friction

material (see Step 5). Renew the pads if they are worn to the service limit or fouled with oil or grease.

Front brake lever freeplay

9 Measure the amount of freeplay at the end of the brake lever before the brake comes into effect. If necessary, adjust the freeplay using the screw at the lever stock. Slacken the locknut and rotate the adjuster clockwise to reduce freeplay, or anticlockwise to increase it.

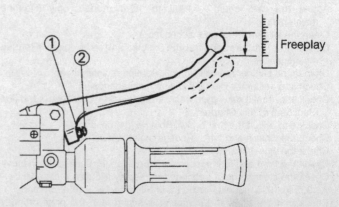

Fig. 7.1 Brake lever freeplay measurement (Sec 3)

1 Locknut   2 Adjuster screw

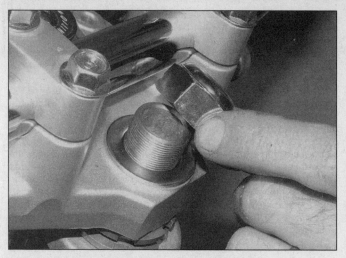

3.14a Remove the steering stem nut . . .

3.14b . . . and loosen the clamp bolts

Note: *It is important to have a small amount of freeplay to prevent brake drag.*

10 Operate the brake lever and check that the movement becomes hard as the lever nears the handlebar grip. If the lever action feels spongy, there is air in the hydraulic system. Bleed the brake as described in Section 21.

Front brake hose examination

11 Inspect the entire length of hose for signs or cracks, splitting or abrasion. Dark stains on the rubber indicate fluid leakage. Check also that there is no sign of damage where the hose joins the banjo union at each end. If the hose is defective it must be renewed (see Section 20).

12 Check that the hose is secured by the clamps on the fork lower leg and bottom yoke.

Check and adjust the steering head bearings – 1999-on models

13 Position the bike on its centre stand. Check the bearings as described in Routine maintenance.

14 To adjust the bearings, first undo and remove the steering stem nut and washer and loosen the top yoke clamp bolts.

15 Undo and remove the two nuts securing the speedometer bracket and headlamp assembly bracket to the underside of the top yoke, then gently ease the top yoke and handlebar assembly upwards off the fork tubes and position it clear of the steering head. Secure the assembly with cable ties to ensure no strain is placed on the brake hydraulic hose and wiring.

16 Lift the tab washer out of the notches in the locknut, then undo and remove the locknut and the rubber washer.

17 Adjust the bearings with a C-spanner as described in Routine maintenance.

18 When the bearings are correctly adjusted, install the rubber washer and tighten the locknut finger-tight. Hold the adjuster ring to prevent it turning, then tighten the locknut to align the notches in the nut and the adjuster ring and install the tab washer.

3.16a Lift off the tab washer . . .

3.16b . . . then remove the locknut and rubber washer

3.17 Adjust the bearings with a C-spanner

19 Install the remaining components in the reverse order of disassembly, noting the torque settings at the beginning of this Chapter.

Sidestand and sidestand switch checks

20 Check the security of the sidestand pivot bolt and its locknut. If they are loose, tighten them to the specified torque setting. Apply a few drops of motor oil to the pivot. Check that the return spring holds the stand securely in the up (retracted) position; if not, renew the spring.
21 The sidestand switch prevents the motorcycle being started if the transmission is in gear and the stand is down, and cuts the engine if the stand is put down while the engine is running and in gear.
22 Check the operation of the switch by shifting the transmission into neutral, retracting the stand and starting the engine. Pull in the clutch lever and select a gear. Extend the sidestand. The engine should stop as the sidestand is extended. If the sidestand switch does not operate as described, check its circuit (see Section 29).

---

4 Cylinder head and cam chain tensioner: removal and refitting – 1997-on models

Cylinder head – 1997-on models

1 Refer to Chapter 2, Section 41 for the cylinder head refitting procedure, noting the revised tightening sequence shown in Fig. 7.2 for the cylinder head bolts.

Cylinder head and cam chain tensioner – 1999-on models

2 These models are fitted with an automatic cam chain tensioner. Follow the procedure in Chapter 2, Section 6 for removing the cylinder head, noting the different procedure for removing the cam chain tensioner in paragraph 3.
3 Slacken evenly the two bolts which retain the tensioner to the back of the cylinder barrel. With the bolts removed the tensioner can be withdrawn, complete with its extended plunger. The remainder of the procedure is as described in Chapter 2, Section 6.
4 The cam chain , its sprockets, the chain guide and tensioner blade can be examined for wear as described in Chapter 2, Section 24. The operation of the tensioner can be checked by removing the cap bolt from the end of the tensioner body, then inserting a small flat-bladed screwdriver into the tensioner so that it engages the slot in the end of the plunger. Rotate the screwdriver clockwise as the head of the plunger is pressed into the body. Remove the screwdriver and slowly release the head of the plunger, checking that it extends smoothly and

without binding. If the tensioner doesn't operate smoothly or shows obvious signs of wear it must be renewed – individual parts are not available.
5 Refer to Chapter 2, Section 41 for the cylinder head refitting procedure, noting the revised tightening sequence shown in Fig. 7.2, then tighten the two cylinder barrel Allen screws.
6 When refitting the cam chain tensioner, locate a flat-bladed screwdriver into the head of the tensioner plunger and rotate the screwdriver clockwise whilst pressing the head of the plunger into the tensioner body. Install a new gasket on the tensioner face, then install the tensioner on the cylinder barrel with the screwdriver still held in place. Install the two bolts to retain the tensioner body, then release the screwdriver – the tensioner plunger should be heard to extend inwards into contact with the back of the tensioner blade. Install the cap bolt in the end of the tensioner body, then tighten this and the two retaining bolts to the specified torque setting (see the beginning of this Chapter).
7 Continue the remainder of the rebuild sequence as described in Chapter 2, Section 41.

---

5 Fuel tap and filter: removal, examination and refitting – 1999-on models

Note: *The filter bowl and filter fitted to the underside of the fuel tap are omitted on 1999-on models.*

1 The fuel tap is secured to the underside of the tank by two screws (see Chapter 2). The fuel filter is integral with the fuel tap. Take care when withdrawing the tap from the tank to avoid damaging the filter gauze.
2 Cleaning the fuel filter is advised after a particularly high mileage has been covered. It is also necessary if fuel starvation is suspected.
3 Allow the filter to dry, then clean the gauze with a soft brush or low pressure compressed air to remove all traces of dirt and fuel sediment. Check the gauze for holes. If any are found, a new tap should be fitted. A damaged filter will allow dirt particles to enter the tap body.
4 If fuel flow problems are experienced which are not due to a blocked filter, or if fuel leaks from the tap body, remove the tap from the tank and undo the screw retaining the tap lever, then undo the screws retaining the tap cover. Remove the cover, then remove the tap internal components, noting the order in which they are fitted.
5 Clean and inspect all the tap components, renewing any parts which are worn or damaged – if fuel flow problems have been experienced the rubber valve in the back of the tap should be renewed. When reassembling the tap, always fit a new internal O-ring. Tighten the cover screws securely and check the operation of the tap.
6 Fit a new O-ring to the tap-to-tank mounting flange and ensure the fuel hose is secured to the tap by its retaining clip.

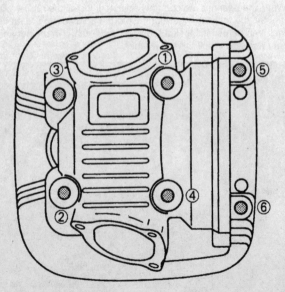

Fig. 7.2 1997-on cylinder head tightening sequence (Sec 4)

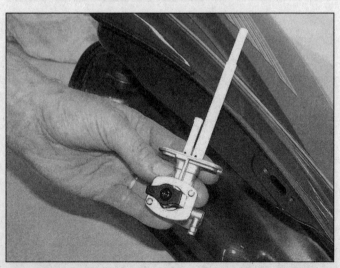

5.1 Fuel filter is integral with the tap on 1999-on models

6.1a Carburettor heater . . .

6.1b . . . is controlled by the thermo-switch

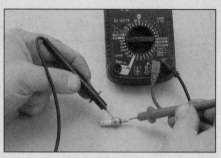

6.5 Heater resistance test

6   Carburettor heater: check, removal, and refitting – 1997-on models

1 The carburettor heater is fitted to the right-hand side of the carburettor body and is controlled by a thermo-switch mounted behind the left-hand side panel. At low ambient temperatures the thermo-switch will be closed, allowing power to pass to the heater unit, thus preventing icing of the carburettor. If carburettor icing is experienced, the thermo-switch and heater unit can be tested as follows.

2 Remove the left-hand side panel to access the thermo-switch. Disconnect the two wire connectors to the switch and prise the thermo-switch from its rubber mounting.

3 The thermo-switch is tested by immersing it in water and checking for continuity at specific temperatures. You will need a vessel to hold the water, a heat source, a thermometer and a multimeter. Connect the meter probes to the thermo-switch wires and immerse the switch in the water. Place a thermometer in the water so that its bulb is close to the switch and not touching the sides of the vessel.

4 Continuity should be shown with the water cold. Gently heat the water and note the temperature at which the switch indicates no continuity (switch opens); this should occur at 16°C ± 5°C. After this point, turn off the heat source and as the water cools note the temperature at which the meter indicates continuity (switch closes); this should be 8°C ± 3°C. If the thermo-switch does not function as described in must be renewed.

5 If the thermo-switch is operating correctly, the heater unit could be at fault. Disconnect the wire connector from the heater unit and the earth wire connector from the bracket. Unscrew the heater unit from the carburettor. Measure the resistance of the unit by connecting the probes of a multimeter between the two wire terminals of the switch. If the reading differs widely from the specified value of 6 to 10 ohms, the switch must be renewed.

6 When installing the heater unit, remember to position the washer between the bracket and carburettor body. Securely reconnect the wiring connectors.

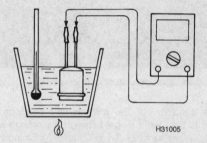

Fig. 7.3 Thermo-switch test set-up (Sec 6)

7   Throttle twistgrip: removal and refitting – 1997-on models

1 The twistgrip is separate from the right-hand switch housing. To remove the twistgrip and gain access to the throttle cable, undo the twistgrip housing screws and remove the top half of the housing. The twistgrip can now be pulled off the end of the handlebar.

2 To remove the cable from the twistgrip, unscrew the locking ring securing the cable elbow in the lower half of the housing, then disconnect the cable nipple from the twistgrip pulley and withdraw the cable.

3 Refit the components in the reverse order of removal and adjust the throttle cable freeplay (see Routine maintenance).

8   Ignition system: component location and testing – 1997-on models

HT coil

1 The HT coil is mounted on the frame top tube behind the steering head. Remove the fuel tank to access the coil (see Chapter 2). Disconnect the HT lead from the spark plug and the wires from the HT coil, then unbolt the coil from the frame.

7.1 Undo the twistgrip housing screws to access the throttle cable

8.1 Location of the HT coil (arrowed)

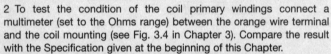

8.5a Ignition pulser coil (arrowed) . . .

8.5b . . . and alternator stator inside the crankcase cover

2 To test the condition of the coil primary windings connect a multimeter (set to the Ohms range) between the orange wire terminal and the coil mounting (see Fig. 3.4 in Chapter 3). Compare the result with the Specification given at the beginning of this Chapter.
3 To test the condition of the coil secondary windings, first unscrew the spark plug cap from the end of the HT lead, then connect a multimeter (set to the K ohms range) between the HT lead end and the coil mounting. Compare the resistance reading with the Specification given at the beginning of this Chapter.
4 If either of the readings is appreciably different from the specified figure, it is likely that the coil is faulty and should be checked by a Yamaha Service Agent.

Pulser coil and source coil

5 The ignition pulser coil and the source coil, which is integral with the alternator stator, are mounted inside the crankcase left-hand cover.
6 To test the condition of the pulser coil, remove the seat, then trace the wiring from the back of the crankcase cover and disconnect it at the multi-pin connector. Use a multimeter to check the resistance between the red and white wire terminals on the coil side of the connector. To test the source coil, connect a multimeter between the brown and green wire terminals on the coil side of the connector.
7 If either of the readings differ greatly from the Specifications at the beginning of this Chapter it is likely that the appropriate coil is faulty and should be checked by a Yamaha Service Agent.

9.5 Brake caliper bracket mounting bolts (arrowed)

8 To remove either the pulser coil or the source coil, first remove the crankcase left-hand cover (see Chapter 1). Note the position of the wiring guide and the location of the wiring grommets inside the cover.
9 On installation of the alternator stator, ensure the wiring is correctly routed before installing the fixing screws.

CDI unit

10 The CDI unit is a small square sealed unit bolted to the frame underneath the seat. No details are available for checking the unit on home workshop equipment, so if tests on other ignition system components fail to isolate the cause of an ignition fault, have the unit tested by a Yamaha Service Agent.

9 Front fork legs: removal and refitting – 1999-on models

1 Place the machine on its centre stand and remove the front wheel (see Section 12).
2 Undo the mounting bolts and remove the front mudguard.
3 To remove the right-hand fork leg, first loosen, but do not remove, the fork pinch bolt in the top yoke. If the fork leg is going to be disassembled or the fork oil is going to be changed, slacken the fork top bolt while the leg is still clamped in the bottom yoke.
4 Loosen but do not remove the fork pinch bolt in the bottom yoke and remove the fork leg by twisting it and pulling it downwards.
5 To remove the left-hand fork leg, undo the bolts securing the front brake caliper bracket to the fork lower leg and detach the bracket and caliper. Secure the caliper to the bike with a cable tie to ensure no strain is placed on the hydraulic hose, then follow Steps 3 and 4.
6 Installation is the reverse of removal. Slide the leg up through the bottom yoke into the top yoke until the top edge of the fork tube is level with the top edge of the yoke. Tighten the fork pinch bolt in the bottom yoke to the torque setting specified at the beginning of this Chapter. If required, tighten the fork top bolt to the specified torque setting, and then tighten the fork pinch bolt in the top yoke to the specified torque setting. Ensure that the brake pads align correctly on each side of the brake disc when the caliper is fitted.

10 Steering head assembly: removal and refitting – 1999-on models

1 Remove the front fork legs (see Section 9).
2 Remove the top yoke and handlebar assembly (see Section 3, Steps 14 and 15).
3 Release the wiring loom and front brake hydraulic hose from the clamps securing them to the bottom yoke.

11.2 Speedometer bracket is secured by nuts (arrowed) on the underside of the top yoke

12.2 Unscrew the knurled ring to disconnect the cable

12.3a Remove the pinch bolt from the right-hand fork leg . . .

12.3b . . . then unscrew wheel spindle to free the wheel

12.4a Fit the headed spacer in the hub right-hand side . . .

12.4b . . . and the speedometer drive unit in the left-hand side – make sure the cutouts and driveplate tangs align (arrowed)

4 Undo and remove the two bolts securing the headlamp assembly bracket to the bottom yoke.

5 Lift the tab washer out of the notches in the steering head bearing locknut, then undo and remove the locknut and the rubber washer (see Section 3, Step 16). Support the weight of the bottom yoke and undo the bearing adjuster ring, then lower the bottom yoke out of the steering head (see also Chapter 4, Section 5).

6 Refitting is the reverse of disassembly. Check the steering head bearings as described in Section 3 of this Chapter.

11 Speedometer head: removal and refitting – 1999-on models

1 Unscrew the knurled ring securing the speedometer cable to the underside of the speedometer and disconnect the cable. Trace the wiring from the speedometer and disconnect it at the connector.

2 Undo and remove the two nuts securing the speedometer bracket and headlamp assembly bracket to the underside of the top yoke, then lift the speedometer off the machine.

3 Undo the screw securing the speedometer cover and remove the cover. If required, undo the two nuts securing the speedometer to the bracket and the two screws securing the bracket cover to the bracket.

4 Refitting is the reverse of removal.

12 Front wheel: removal and refitting – 1992-on models

1 Place the machine on its centre stand, then place a support under the engine/transmission unit so that the front wheel is raised off the ground.

2 Unscrew the speedometer cable retaining ring and pull the cable clear.

3 Slacken the pinch bolt in the right-hand fork lower leg, then unscrew and withdraw the wheel spindle. Lower the wheel from the forks. Remove the spacer from the right-hand side of the hub and the speedometer drive unit from the left-hand side. Do not operate the front brake with the wheel removed.

4 Clean all old grease and any corrosion off the wheel spindle, then smear it with new grease. Apply a smear of grease to the hub seals, then install the spacer in the hub right-hand side and the speedometer drive unit in the left-hand side, aligning its cutouts with the driveplate tangs in the hub.

5 Lift the wheel into the forks, being careful to slot the brake disc between the caliper pads and position the speedometer drive unit so that its slot engages the lug on the fork lower leg. Slide the wheel spindle through from the right-hand side and screw it into the left-hand fork leg. Tighten the spindle, followed by the pinch bolt, both to the specified torque setting.

6 Check that the speedometer cable is routed through the guide on the mudguard. Insert the cable into the drive unit on the wheel and tighten the knurled ring to secure it.

7 Check that the wheel rotates freely and the brake works properly.

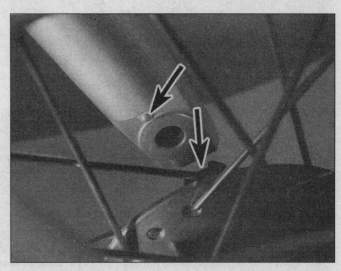

12.5 Slot in speedometer drive unit must engage lug on fork leg (arrowed) as wheel is refitted

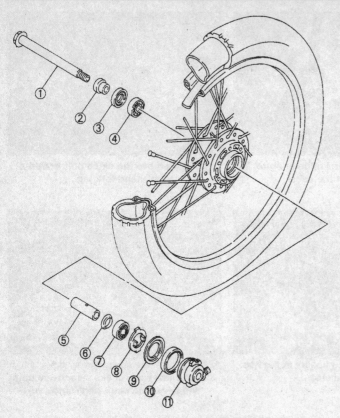

Fig. 7.4 Front wheel assembly (Sec 13)

1	Wheel spindle	7	Bearing
2	Spacer	8	Driveplate
3	Seal	9	Driveplate retainer
4	Bearing	10	Seal
5	Spacer	11	Speedometer drive unit
6	Spacer flange		

13 Front wheel bearings: removal, examination and refitting – 1992-on models

1 Remove the front wheel (see Section 12).

2 Using a large flat-bladed screwdriver, lever the seal from each side of the hub. Where fitted, lift the speedometer driveplate retainer and the driveplate itself out of the hub left-hand side.

3 Remove, examine and install the bearings as described in Chapter 5, Section 4. Refer to Fig. 7.4 and note the fitting of the bearing spacer and, if fitted, spacer flange.

4 Where fitted, install the speedometer driveplate in the hub left-hand side so that its projections engage the slots in the hub, then fit the driveplate retainer.

5 Press new seals into the left and right-hand sides of the hub, then install the wheel (see Section 12).

14 Front brake pads: renewal – 1992 to 1996 models

1 Slacken the pad retaining pin, but don't remove it yet. Remove the two caliper mounting bolts and slip the caliper off the disc. There is no need to disconnect the brake hose, just make sure that it is not strained while the caliper is detached. Do not operate the brake while the caliper is off the disc.

2 Remove the pad retaining pin and withdraw the brake pads, anti-squeal shim (on piston side pad) and anti-rattle spring. Clean these components and inside the caliper with brake system cleaner to remove all traces of road dirt.

3 Push the piston back into the caliper to accommodate the increased thickness of the new pads. If the piston is difficult to press back, attach a piece of tubing to the bleed valve and place the other end of the tubing in a jar. Open the bleed valve a half turn to allow the escape of fluid as the piston is pushed back. Tighten the bleed valve and remove the tube when this has been done.

4 Before installing the pads, check that the caliper body is free to slide on the mounting bracket slider pins. If the pins are corroded, the brake will not work correctly (see Section 16).

5 Push the mounting bracket against the caliper body and locate the anti-rattle spring in the caliper body. The spring has a chamfer on one

14.1a Slacken the pad retaining pin (arrowed) and remove the two bolts . . .

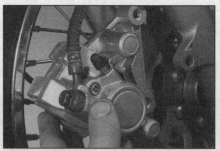

14.1b . . . then slip the caliper off the disc

14.2 Remove the pad retaining pin to free the brake pads

14.5 Ensure the anti-rattle spring is fitted the correct way around - note the chamfers (arrowed)

14.7a Ensure the anti-squeal shim is in place and fit the piston side pad . . .

14.7b . . . then install the fixed pad

14.7c Slip the pad retaining pin through the pad holes and screw it into the thread in the caliper

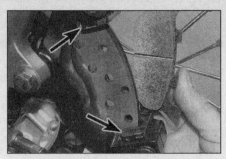

15.2a Remove the pads and the pad plates (arrowed)

15.2b Remove the anti-rattle spring (arrowed)

side and will only fit one way around in the caliper. **Note:** *If new pads are being fitted, renew the anti-rattle spring and pad anti-squeal shim.*

6 Apply a smear of copper-based grease to the shank of the pad retaining pin and to the back of the pad which locates against the piston. **Note:** *Only a smear of grease is required otherwise there is a danger of it getting onto the friction material or disc.*

7 Ensure the anti-squeal shim is located on the back of the piston side pad, and locate both pads in the caliper so that their friction material faces inwards (towards the disc). Insert the pad retaining pin into the caliper body and through the hole in each brake pad. Screw the pad retaining pin in by hand, leaving final tightening until the caliper is mounted on the fork leg.

8 Mount the caliper back on the fork leg, making sure that the disc fits between the pads. Tighten the caliper mounting bolts and pad retaining pin to their specified torque settings.

9 Pump the brake lever to bring the pads back into contact with the disc and check the fluid level in the master cylinder (see Section 3). Check that the brake works correctly before riding the motorcycle.

15 Front brake pads: renewal – 1997-on models

1 Unscrew and remove the caliper fixing bolt, then pivot the caliper upwards clear of the disc and pull the caliper off the bracket (see Section 3, Step 7). There is no need to disconnect the brake hose, just make sure that it is not strained while the caliper is detached. Do not operate the brake while the caliper is off the disc.

2 Remove the pads from the caliper bracket, then unclip the upper and lower pad plates from the bracket and remove the anti-rattle spring from inside the caliper. Renew the plates if they are worn or damaged, otherwise clean them and the inside of the caliper with brake system cleaner to remove all traces of road dirt.

3 Check that the pads have worn evenly at each end. If they have worn unevenly, one of the pistons is probably sticking in the caliper, in which case the caliper must be overhauled (see Section 17).

4 Remove all traces of corrosion from the slider pin and caliper fixing bolt.

5 Push the pistons back into the caliper to accommodate the increased thickness of the new pads. If the pistons are difficult to press back, attach a piece of tubing to the bleed valve and place the other end of the tubing in a jar. Open the bleed valve a half turn to allow the escape of fluid as the pistons are pushed back. Tighten the bleed valve and remove the tube when this has been done.

6 Install the anti-rattle spring in the caliper. Clip the upper and lower pad plates onto the caliper bracket.

7 Apply a smear of copper-based grease to the slider pin, the shank of the caliper fixing bolt and to the back of the pad which locates against the pistons. **Note:** *Only a smear of grease is required otherwise there is a danger of it getting onto the friction material or disc.*

8 Install both pads in the caliper bracket so that the friction material faces towards the disc, then locate the end of the slider pin in the bracket and push it all the way into the bracket. Pivot the caliper down over the pads, ensuring the pads remain in position in the bracket, then install the caliper fixing bolt and tighten it to the specified torque setting.

9 Pump the brake lever to bring the pads back into contact with the disc and check the fluid level in the master cylinder. Check that the brake works correctly before riding the motorcycle.

16 Front brake caliper: overhaul – 1992 to 1996 models

1 Remove the brake pads and anti-rattle spring (see Section 14).

2 Using pointed-nose pliers, unhook the coil spring from the mounting bracket and withdraw it from the caliper body.

16.2a Unhook the coil spring from the caliper bracket . . .

16.2b . . . and withdraw the spring from the caliper body

16.3 Slide the mounting bracket out of the caliper body

16.4 The mounting bracket plate (arrowed) should be clipped in place

16.12 Position the brake hose banjo union neck as shown

3 Slide the mounting bracket out of the caliper body and clean the bracket and caliper with brake system cleaner. Use steel wool to clean any corrosion off the mounting bracket slider pins and lubricate them with a smear of copper-based grease.

4 Inspect the slider pin dust seals set in the caliper body; if they are split, water and dirt will cause recurring problems for the sliding action of the caliper. Renew the dust seals if necessary. Check that the mounting bracket plate is securely clipped to the bracket.

5 To displace the piston from the caliper, first place the caliper in a clean plastic bag and tape the neck of the bag around the brake hose. Carefully pump the brake lever to force the piston out by hydraulic pressure; any spilled brake fluid will be contained by the bag.

6 Undo the banjo union bolt to free the hydraulic hose from the caliper body, then wrap the end of the hose in a plastic bag to prevent dirt entering the system.

7 Inspect the caliper piston and bore. If they are corroded or scored they should be renewed. If the caliper is in good condition, remove the seals from their grooves with a wooden or plastic tool to avoid damaging the bore surface. Use steel wool to polish away any corrosion from the end of piston which extends beyond the dust seal.

8 Clean the caliper internals with new hydraulic fluid – the use of petroleum-based agents will cause the seals to swell and degrade.

9 Always use new seals when overhauling the caliper. Lubricate the new piston seal with brake fluid and insert it into the inner groove in the caliper bore. Do the same with the new dust seal, inserting it in the outer groove in the caliper bore. Lubricate the piston surface with brake fluid, then press it fully into the caliper bore, closed side first.

10 Slide the mounting bracket fully back into the caliper. Make sure the sleeve is in place on the coil spring and hook it through the hole in the caliper. Hook the other end of the spring over the caliper bracket.

11 Install the brake pads and caliper as described in Section 14.

12 Connect the brake hose to the caliper using a new sealing washer on each side of the banjo union. Position the union so that its neck abuts the projection on the caliper, then install and tighten the union bolt to the specified torque setting.

13 Refill the system with new hydraulic fluid and bleed out any air (see Section 21).

17 Front brake caliper: overhaul – 1997-on models

1 Unscrew and remove the caliper fixing bolt, then pivot the caliper upwards clear of the brake pads and pull the caliper off the bracket. Remove the anti-rattle spring from inside the caliper and clean the caliper with brake system cleaner.

2 Use steel wool to clean any corrosion off the slider pin and the shank of the caliper fixing bolt.

3 Inspect the dust seals set in the caliper bracket; if they are split, water and dirt will cause recurring problems for the sliding action of the caliper. Renew the dust seals if necessary.

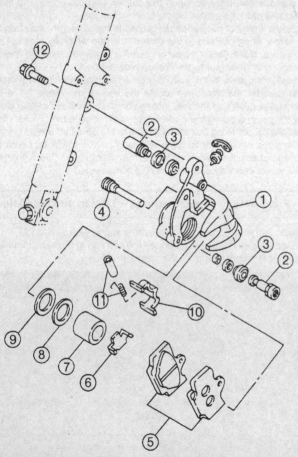

Fig. 7.5 Front brake caliper – 1992 to 1996 models (Sec 16)

1	Caliper and mounting bracket	7	Piston
2	Slider pins	8	Dust seal
3	Slider pin dust seals	9	Fluid seal
4	Pad retaining pin	10	Anti-rattle spring
5	Brake pads	11	Coil spring and sleeve
6	Pad anti-squeal shim	12	Caliper mounting bolt

17.3 Caliper bracket dust seals

18.2 Using a dial gauge to measure brake disc runout

18.3 Using a micrometer to measure disc thickness

18.5 Brake disc is retained to wheel by six bolts

4 Follow Steps 5 and 6 in Section 16 to displace the pistons and separate the caliper from the brake hose. Note that the upper piston is a larger diameter than the lower piston.

5 Follow Steps 7 to 9 in Section 16 to clean and inspect the caliper and pistons and install new piston seals and dust seals. Note that the seals in the upper piston bore are a larger diameter than the seals in the lower piston bore.

6 If removed, install the brake pad springs and pads in the caliper bracket (see Section 3), then install the caliper and check the operation of the brake (see Steps 7 and 8, Section 15).

7 Connect the brake hose to the caliper using a new sealing washer on each side of the banjo union. Position the union so that its neck abuts the projection on the caliper, then install and tighten the union bolt to the specified torque setting.

8 Refill the system with new hydraulic fluid and bleed out any air (see Section 21).

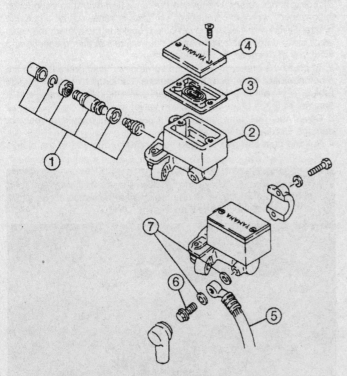

Fig. 7.6 Front brake master cylinder (Sec 19)

1 *Piston assembly*	4 *Cover*
2 *Master cylinder*	5 *Hydraulic hose*
body/reservoir	6 *Banjo union bolt*
3 *Diaphragm*	7 *Sealing washers*

18 Front brake disc: examination, removal and refitting – 1992-on models

Examination

1 Visually inspect the surface of the disc for score marks and other damage. Light scratches are normal after use and won't affect brake operation, but deep grooves and heavy score marks will reduce braking efficiency and accelerate pad wear. If the disc is badly grooved it must be machined or renewed.

2 To check disc runout, position the machine on its centre stand with the front wheel off the ground. Mount a dial gauge to the fork leg, with the plunger on the gauge touching the surface of the disc about 10 mm (1/2 in) from the outer edge. Rotate the wheel and watch the gauge needle, comparing your reading with the limit listed in this Chapter's Specifications. If the runout is greater than the service limit, check the wheel bearings for play. If the bearings are worn, renew them and repeat this check. If the disc runout is still excessive, machining by a competent engineering shop may be possible, otherwise fit a new disc.

3 The disc must not be machined or allowed to wear down to a thickness less than the service limit listed in this Chapter's Specifications. Check the thickness of the disc with a micrometer; if less than the service limit, renew the disc.

Removal and refitting

4 Remove the wheel as described in Section 12.

5 Mark the relationship of the disc to the wheel, so it can be installed in the same position. Unscrew the disc retaining bolts and remove the disc from the wheel. Loosen the bolts a little at a time, in a criss-cross pattern, to avoid distorting the disc.

6 When refitting the disc on the wheel, align the previously applied matchmarks (if you're reinstalling the original disc). Make sure the arrow stamped on the disc marking the normal direction of rotation is pointing in the direction of wheel rotation.

7 Apply a drop of thread-locking compound to the bolt threads and tighten them in a criss-cross pattern evenly and progressively to the torque setting specified at the beginning of this Chapter. Clean the disc with brake system cleaner. If a new disc has been installed, remove any protective coating from its working surfaces.

8 Refit the wheel as described in Section 12.

9 Operate the brake lever several times to bring the pads into contact with the disc. Check the operation of the brake carefully before riding the bike.

19 Front brake master cylinder: overhaul – 1992-on models

1 Slacken the mirror retaining locknut and unscrew the mirror from the master cylinder body.

2 Remove the locknut from the underside of the brake lever, and unscrew the lever pivot bolt. As the brake lever is withdrawn, take care not to loose the small coil spring.

19.3a Depress the tab on the underside of the master cylinder body . . .

19.3b . . . and withdraw the brake light switch

19.10 Master cylinder clamp markings

3 Depress the tab on the underside of the master cylinder and pull the brake light switch out of the master cylinder body.

4 Displace the rubber cover and loosen the brake hose banjo union bolt on the master cylinder, then undo the two bolts which clamp the master cylinder to the handlebar and remove the master cylinder. Position a drain tray beneath the master cylinder, then remove the reservoir cover and diaphragm and empty the fluid from the reservoir.

5 Remove the banjo union bolt and allow any fluid to drain, then tie a polythene bag over the brake hose end to prevent the loss of fluid and ingress of dirt.

6 Pull the dust boot off the end of the master cylinder piston bore to expose the piston end and the circlip which retains it. Remove the circlip and pull the piston and its seals out of the bore, followed by the spring.

7 Inspect the master cylinder piston and bore. If they are corroded or scored they must be renewed. Note that the piston, its seals, spring, circlip and dust seal are only available as a complete set.

8 Clean the master cylinder internals with new hydraulic fluid. **Note:** *Don't use petroleum-based agents because they will cause the seals to swell and degrade.* Make sure that the fluid ports in the reservoir are clear.

9 Insert the spring in the bore so that its tapered end faces the piston. Lubricate the piston seals with new hydraulic fluid and insert the piston assembly in the bore. Hold the piston depressed whilst the circlip is located in its groove. Install the dust seal in the end of the master cylinder bore.

10 Position the master cylinder on the handlebar so that it is upright and install the clamp with the UP mark and arrowhead facing upwards. Install the two clamp bolts; tighten the top bolt fully to the specified torque setting, then do the same with the other bolt.

11 Using a new sealing washer on each side of the banjo union, reconnect the brake hose to the master cylinder. Tighten the banjo union bolt to the specified torque setting and slip the rubber cover back into place.

12 Clip the brake light switch into the master cylinder. Install the brake lever, making sure that the coil spring is correctly positioned. Apply a smear of grease to the lever pivot bolt and slip it into place. Install the nut on its underside and tighten it securely. Install the mirror and make sure it is angled correctly.

13 Fill the reservoir with new brake fluid and bleed the brake of air as described in Section 21. Check the fluid level when finished, and install the diaphragm and reservoir cover (see Section 3).

14 Check the brake lever freeplay (see Section 3, paragraph 9) and make sure the brake operates correctly before riding the machine. Check that the stop light comes on when the brake lever is operated.

20 Front brake hose: renewal – 1992-on models

1 Attach a length of clear tubing to the bleed valve on the caliper and insert the other end of the pipe into a jar. Open the bleed valve one turn and pump the front brake lever repeatedly to expel the hydraulic fluid from the system. Remove the reservoir cover and diaphragm to check that all fluid has drained from the reservoir. Tighten the bleed valve.

2 Unscrew the banjo union bolt from the caliper and place a polythene bag around the hose to catch any residual fluid. Take note of the hose routing as a guide to installation of the new hose, then free the hose from its clamps on the fork lower leg and bottom yoke. Finally unscrew the banjo union bolt to free the hose from the master cylinder.

3 Route the new hose in exactly the same way as the original, ensuring that it is neither twisted nor trapped by the steering components. Use a new sealing washer on each side of the banjo unions and reconnect the hose to the master cylinder and caliper. Tighten the banjo union bolts to the specified torque setting.

4 Secure the hose with the two clamps.

5 Refill the system with new brake fluid. Bleed the brake as described in Section 21. Check the fluid level when finished, and install the diaphragm and reservoir cover (see Section 3).

6 Check that there is no sign of fluid leakage from the hose or its connections and check the operation of the brake before riding the machine.

21 Front brake: bleeding – 1992-on models

1 Bleeding the brake is simply the process of removing all the air bubbles from the master cylinder reservoir, the hose and the caliper. Bleeding is necessary whenever a brake system hydraulic connection is loosened, when a component or hose is renewed, or when the master cylinder or caliper is overhauled. Leaks in the system may also allow air to enter, but leaking brake fluid will reveal their presence and warn you of the need for attention.

2 To bleed the brake, you will need some new, clean brake fluid of the recommended type (see Specifications), a length of clear plastic tubing, a jar partially filled with clean brake fluid, some rags and a spanner to fit the brake caliper bleed valve.

3 Cover the fuel tank and other painted components to prevent damage if brake fluid is spilled.

4 Pull the dust cap off the bleed valve. Attach one end of the plastic

21.4 Brake bleeding equipment in use

22.2 A self-locking rear wheel spindle nut (arrowed) and sprocket nuts are fitted to 1997-on models

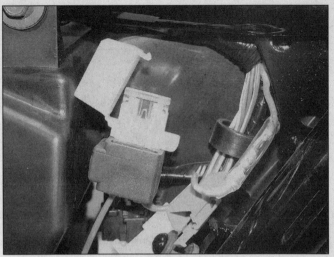

23.1 Unclip the fuse casing to check the fuse on 1998-on models

tubing to the bleed valve and submerge the other end in the brake fluid in the jar. If the system has been drained, refill the reservoir with new brake fluid and refit the reservoir diaphragm and cover.

5 Open the bleed valve one turn and pump the brake lever until fluid is seen to issue from the plastic tubing, then tighten the bleed valve. **Note:** *Keep a close watch on the fluid level in the reservoir during the bleeding process and top it up before it reaches the LOWER line.*

6 Remove the reservoir cover and diaphragm and slowly pump the brake lever a few times, until no air bubbles can be seen floating up from the holes in the bottom of the reservoir. Doing this bleeds the air from the master cylinder end of the hose. Refit the diaphragm and cover.

7 Carefully pump the brake lever three or four times then hold it in while opening the bleed valve. When the valve is opened, brake fluid will flow out of the caliper into the tubing and the lever will move toward the handlebar.

8 Retighten the bleed valve, then release the brake lever gradually. Repeat the process until no air bubbles are visible in the brake fluid leaving the caliper and the lever is firm when applied.

9 Disconnect the bleeding equipment and install the dust cap on the bleed valve.

10 Check the fluid level in the reservoir, wipe up any spilled brake fluid and check the entire system for leaks. **Note:** *If it's not possible to produce a firm feel to the lever the fluid my be aerated – let the brake fluid in the system stabilise for a few hours and then repeat the procedure.*

22 Rear wheel and rear sprocket: removal and refitting – 1997-on models

1 Refer to Chapter 5, Section 9, noting the following.

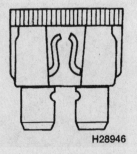

H28946

Fig. 7.7 A break in the element of a blown fuse (Sec 23)

2 The rear wheel spindle nut and the rear sprocket retaining nuts are of the self-locking type. After the components have been disassembled several times the locking device will no longer be effective and new nuts should be fitted. Always tighten the nuts to the specified torque setting.

23 Fuse: location and renewal – 1998-on models

1 The electrical system is protected by a single 20 amp plug-in type fuse in a casing located behind the left-hand side panel. Unclip the top of the casing and pull the fuse out to check it visually. The fuse is clearly marked with its rating and must only be replaced by a fuse of the correct rating.

2 A blown fuse is easily identified by a break in the element. If the fuse blows, be sure to check the wiring circuit very carefully for evidence of a short-circuit. Look for bare wires and chafed, melted or burned insulation. **Note:** *If the fuse is replaced before the cause is located, the new fuse will blow immediately.*

3 A spare fuse can be clipped in the holder alongside the casing. It is advisable to carry a spare fuse on the machine at all times.

4 Periodically spray the fuse ends and fuseholder terminals with electrical contact cleaner to prevent corrosion.

24 Starter motor: examination and renovation – 1997-on models

1 Disconnect the battery negative (-ve) lead then remove the starter motor (see Chapter 1, Section 7).

2 Undo the two long bolts that secure the end covers to the motor body and carefully separate the components (see Chapter 6, Section 12). Make a careful note of the order in which the shims and washers are fitted to the armature shaft.

3 The brushes are located in holders on a brushplate which fits inside the right-hand end cover. If either of the brushes is worn below the service limit of 3.5 mm, fit a new brushplate assembly.

4 Clean the commutator and test for continuity between the commutator bars, then reassemble the starter motor (see Chapter 6, Section 12).

25 Turn signal relay: location and testing – 1998-on models

1 The relay is mounted on the right-hand side of the frame top tube alongside the carburettor. If the turn signals cease to function, first

25.1 Location of turn signal relay (arrowed) on 1998-on models

check the sockets and bulbs and the signal wiring (see Chapter 6, Section 14).

26 Turn signal: bulb renewal – 1997-on models

1 Remove the screw on the back of the turn signal body, then squeeze the sides of the signal lens and unclip it from the body. Push the bulb into the socket and twist it anti-clockwise to remove it.
2 Check that the contacts inside the socket are clean and free from corrosion before installing the new bulb. Ensure that the screw location in the lens aligns with the signal body before clipping the lens in place. Take care not to overtighten the fixing screw.

27 Headlamp: bulb renewal and beam alignment – 1999-on models

Note: *The headlamp bulb is of the quartz halogen type. Do not touch the bulb glass as skin acids will shorten the bulb's service life. If the bulb* is accidentally touched, it should be wiped carefully when cold with a rag soaked in methylated spirit and dried before fitting.

1 Undo the two screws retaining the headlamp rim and reflector unit and pull the unit out of the shell. Disconnect the wiring connector from the back of the headlamp bulb and turn the sidelight bulbholder anti-clockwise to remove it. The sidelight bulb is a conventional bayonet fitting in the holder.
2 Remove the rubber cover from the back of the headlamp bulb, then release the bulb retaining ring and lift the bulb out, noting how it fits. Refitting is the reverse of removal.
3 Headlamp beam alignment is adjusted by the two spring-loaded screws in the upper edge of the rim.

28 Speedometer and warning lights: bulb renewal – 1999-on models

1 Undo the three bolts securing the headlamp to its bracket and lower the headlamp to gain access to the screw on the underside of the speedometer. Undo the screw and remove the cover.
2 The speedometer light and warning light bulbholders are a push fit in the speedometer casing and the bulbs are a push fit in the bulbholders. Ensure the bulbholder contacts are clean before installing a new bulb.

29 Sidestand switch: testing, removal and refitting

Testing

1 The sidestand switch is part of the safety circuit which prevents the engine from starting with the transmission in gear unless the clutch lever is pulled in and the sidestand is up, and prevents the engine from running with the sidestand down unless the transmission is in neutral.
2 To test the switch, trace the wiring from the switch and disconnect it at the connector. Attach the probes of a multimeter (set to the ohms scale) across the terminals on the switch side of the connector. Continuity should be indicated with the sidestand in the up (retracted) position, and no continuity (open-circuit) with the stand down (extended). If the switch doesn't operate as indicated it is faulty and should be renewed.
3 If the switch is OK, yet the problem still exists, refer to the wiring

26.1 Removing the turn signal lens

27.2a Detach the sidelight bulbholder and remove the rubber cover (arrowed) . . .

27.2b . . . then unscrew the headlamp bulb retaining ring (arrowed)

27.3 Headlamp beam adjuster screw (arrowed)

28.1 Undo the screw to remove the speedometer cover

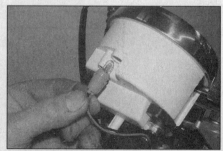

28.2 Bulbholders are a push fit in the casing

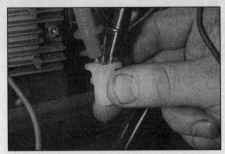

29.2 Make the continuity test on the switch side of the sidestand switch connector

29.3a Diode is taped into the wiring harness next to the ignitor on 1991 to 1996 models

29.3b Starter cut-off relay is located under the right-hand side cover on 1991 to 1996 models

29.3c Sidestand relay is located under the left-hand side cover on 1991 to 1996 models . . .

29.3d . . . and under the right-hand side cover on 1997-on models

29.5 Sidestand switch is secured to its bracket by two screws

diagram at the end of this Chapter and check all wires and connections in the circuit for continuity. On 1992 to 1996 models, check the wiring between the sidestand relay, diode, neutral switch, stater cut-off relay and ignitor. On 1997-on models, check the wiring between the sidestand relay, neutral switch, clutch switch and CDI unit (diode is integral with CDI unit). No test details are available for the system components – refer to a Yamaha Service Agent for advice.

Removal and refitting

4 Disconnect the sidestand switch wiring at the connector.

5 Remove the two screws to free the switch from the stand bracket. Withdraw the wiring, taking note of its routing and freeing it from any cable ties.

6 The switch cannot be dismantled for repair, but note that there is nothing to be lost by spraying it with a water dispersant aerosol. Road dirt can work its way past the rubber gaiter and cause the switch to stick.

7 Refit in a reverse of the removal procedure. Check the operation of the switch.

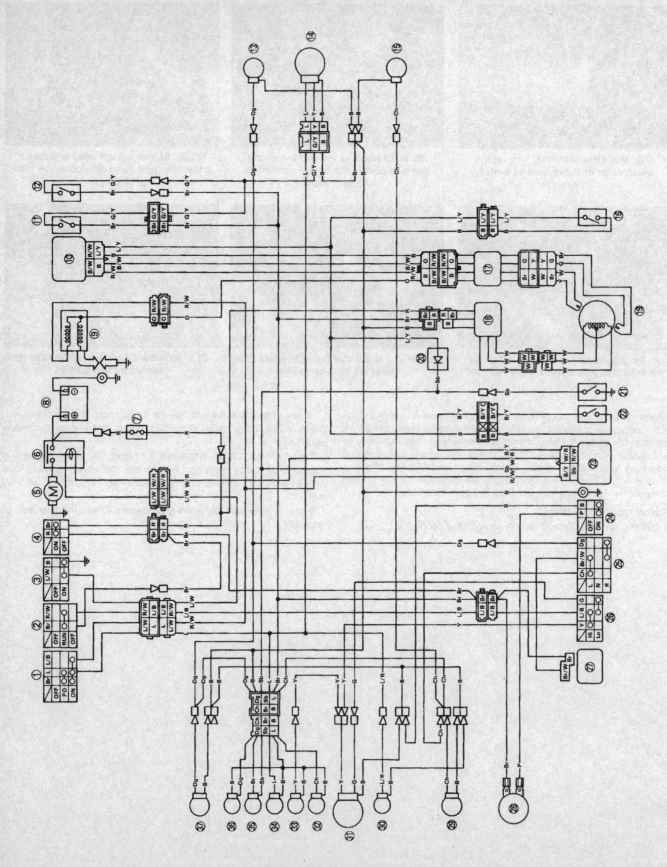

Wiring diagram – 1991 to 1996 models

see page 175 for key

Wiring diagram component key – 1991 to 1996 models

Component key
1 Lighting switch
2 Engine kill switch
3 Starter button
4 Ignition switch
5 Starter motor
6 Starter motor solenoid
7 Fuse
8 Battery
9 Ignition HT coil
10 Sidestand relay
11 Front brake stop lamp switch
12 Rear brake stop lamp switch
13 Right-hand rear turn signal
14 Tail/stop lamp
15 Left-hand rear turn signal
16 Sidestand switch
17 Ignitor
18 Voltage regulator and rectifier
19 Alternator
20 Diode
21 Neutral switch
22 Clutch switch
23 Starting circuit cut-off relay
24 Horn switch
25 Turn signal switch
26 Headlamp dip switch
27 Turn signal relay
28 Horn
29 Left-hand front turn signal
30 Parking lamp
31 Headlamp
32 Left-hand turn signal warning light
33 High beam lamp
34 Speedometer light
35 Neutral indicator light
36 Right-hand turn signal warning light
37 Right-hand front turn signal

Wire colour key
R   Red
B   Black
Y   Yellow
L   Blue
P   Pink
W   White
G   Green
O   Orange
Br Brown
Ch Chocolate
Sb Light blue
Dg Dark green
G/Y Green and yellow
R/W Red and white
L/W Blue and white
L/B Blue and black
L/R Blue and red
L/Y Blue and yellow
Br/W Brown and white
B/Y Black and yellow
B/W Black and white
W/R White and red

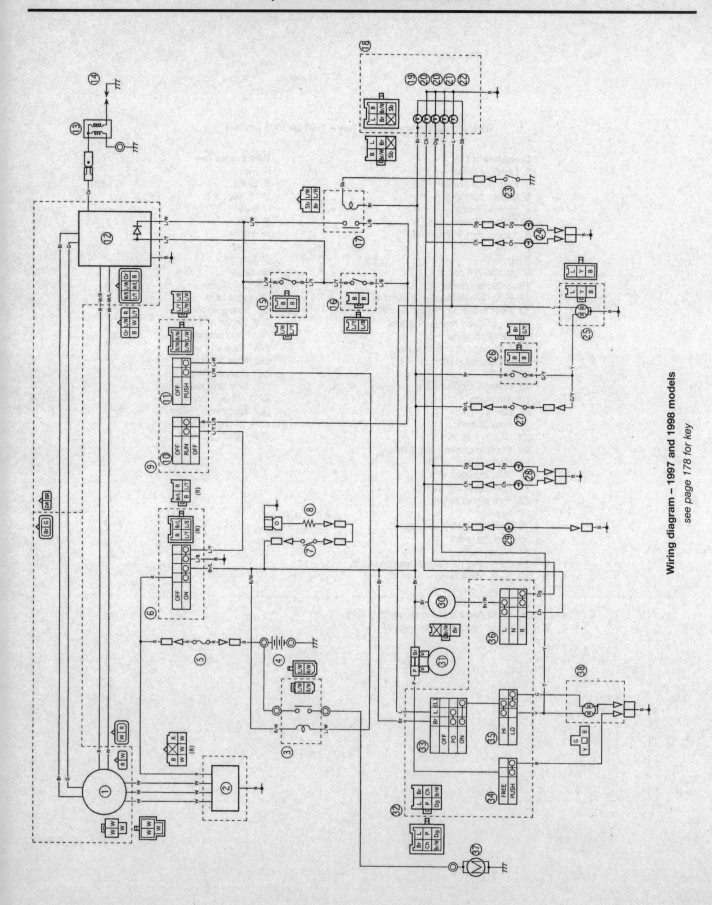

Wiring diagram – 1997 and 1998 models
see page 178 for key

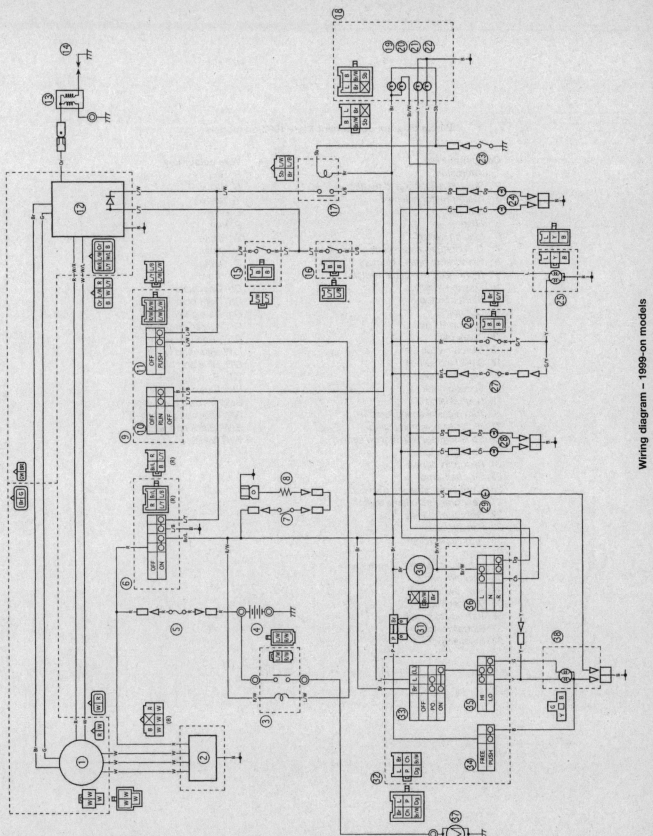

Wiring diagram – 1999-on models
see page 178 for key

Wiring diagram component key – 1997-on models

Component key

1   Alternator
2   Voltage regulator and rectifier
3   Starter motor solenoid
4   Battery
5   Fuse
6   Ignition switch
7   Carburettor heater thermo-switch
8   Carburettor heater element
9   Right-hand handlebar switch
10   Engine kill switch
11   Starter button
12   CDI unit
13   Ignition HT coil
14   Spark plug
15   Clutch switch
16   Sidestand switch
17   Sidestand relay
18   Speedometer
19   Neutral lamp
20   Turn signal warning lamp
21   High beam warning lamp
22   Speedometer illumination lamp
23   Neutral switch
24   Rear turn signals
25   Stop/tail lamp
26   Front brake stop lamp switch
27   Rear brake stop lamp switch
28   Front turn signals
29   Parking lamp
30   Turn signal relay
31   Horn
32   Left-hand handlebar switches
33   Lighting switch
34   Horn switch
35   Dimmer switch
36   Turn signal switch
37   Starter motor
38   Headlamp

Wire colour key

R   Red
B   Black
Y   Yellow
L   Blue
P   Pink
W   White
G   Green
O   Orange
Br   Brown
Ch   Chocolate
Sb   Light blue
Dg   Dark green
G/Y   Green and yellow
R/W   Red and white
L/W   Blue and white
L/B   Blue and black
L/R   Blue and red
L/Y   Blue and yellow
Br/W   Brown and white
B/Y   Black and yellow
B/W   Black and white
W/R   White and red

Index

A

About this manual 2
Accessories 12
Acknowledgements 2
Adjustments:-
   brakes 28, 160
   cam chain 31
   carburettor 100
   clutch 30
   final drive chain 26
   steering head bearings 30
   valve clearances 31
Air filter element 29

B

Balancer drive gears:-
   examination and renovation 64
   refitting 78
   removing 49
Balancing shaft 53
Battery:-
   charging procedure 145
   check 28
   examination and maintenance 144

Bearings:-
   engine 53, 54
   rear suspension pivot 36
   steering head 30, 36, 118, 161
   wheel 36, 134, 138, 166
Bleeding – disc brake 170
Brakes:-
   adjusting 28, 160
   bleeding 170
   caliper 167, 168
   checking 26, 28, 159, 160
   disc 169
   drum brake examining and renovation 136, 138
   fault diagnosis 22
   fluid level check 159
   hose 161, 170
   master cylinder 169
   overhaul 36, 163
   pads 160, 166, 167
   specifications 130, 158

C

Caliper – front brake 167, 168
Cam chain 31, 46, 63, 84
Cam chain tensioner 31, 44, 57, 63, 88, 162
Camshaft and rocker gear 54

Haynes Motorcycle Manuals – The Complete List

Title	Book No
APRILIA RSV1000 Mille (98 - 03)	4255
BMW 2-valve Twins (70 - 96)	◆ 0249
BMW K100 & 75 2-valve Models (83 - 96)	◆ 1373
BMW R850, 1100 & 1150 4-valve Twins (93 - 04)	◆ 3466
BSA Bantam (48 - 71)	0117
BSA Unit Singles (58 - 72)	0127
BSA Pre-unit Singles (54 - 61)	0326
BSA A7 & A10 Twins (47 - 62)	0121
BSA A50 & A65 Twins (62 - 73)	0155
DUCATI 600, 750 & 900 2-valve V-Twins (91 - 96)	◆ 3290
Ducati MK III & Desmo Singles (69 - 76)	◇ 0445
Ducati 748, 916 & 996 4-valve V-Twins (94 - 01)	◆ 3756
GILERA Runner, DNA, Stalker & Ice (97 - 04)	4163
HARLEY-DAVIDSON Sportsters (70 - 03)	◆ 2534
Harley-Davidson Shovelhead and Evolution Big Twins (70 - 99)	2536
Harley-Davidson Twin Cam 88 (99 - 03)	◆ 2478
HONDA NB, ND, NP & NS50 Melody (81 - 85)	◇ 0622
Honda NE/NB50 Vision & SA50 Vision Met-in (85 - 95)	◇ 1278
Honda MB, MBX, MT & MTX50 (80 - 93)	0731
Honda C50, C70 & C90 (67 - 99)	0324
Honda XR80R & XR100R (85 - 04)	2218
Honda XL/XR 80, 100, 125, 185 & 200 2-valve Models (78 - 87)	0566
Honda H100 & H100S Singles (80 - 92)	◇ 0734
Honda CB/CD125T & CM125C Twins (77 - 88)	◇ 0571
Honda CG125 (76 - 00)	◇ 0433
Honda NS125 (86 - 93)	◇ 3056
Honda MBX/MTX125 & MTX200 (83 - 93)	◇ 1132
Honda CD/CM185 200T & CM250C 2-valve Twins (77 - 85)	0572
Honda XL/XR 250 & 500 (78 - 84)	0567
Honda XR250L, XR250R & XR400R (86 - 03)	2219
Honda CB250 & CB400N Super Dreams (78 - 84)	◇ 0540
Honda CR Motocross Bikes (86 - 01)	2222
Honda CBR400RR Fours (88 - 99)	◇ ◆ 3552
Honda VFR400 (NC30) & RVF400 (NC35) V-Fours (89 - 98)	◇ ◆ 3496
Honda CB500 (93 - 01)	◇ ◆ 3753
Honda CB400 & CB550 Fours (73 - 77)	0262
Honda CX/GL500 & 650 V-Twins (78 - 86)	0442
Honda CBX550 Four (82 - 86)	◇ 0940
Honda XL600R & XR600R (83 - 00)	2183
Honda XL600/650V Transalp & XRV750 Africa Twin (87 - 02)	◇ 3919
Honda CBR600F1 & 1000F Fours (87 - 96)	◆ 1730
Honda CBR600F2 & F3 Fours (91 - 98)	◆ 2070
Honda CBR600F4 (99 - 02)	◆ 3911
Honda CB600F Hornet (98 - 02)	◇ ◆ 3915
Honda CB650 sohc Fours (78 - 84)	0665
Honda NTV600 Revere, NTV650 & NT650V Deauville (88 - 01)	◇ ◆ 3243
Honda Shadow VT600 & 750 (USA) (88 - 03)	2312
Honda CB750 sohc Four (69 - 79)	0131
Honda V45/65 Sabre & Magna (82 - 88)	0820
Honda VFR750 & 700 V-Fours (86 - 97)	◆ 2101
Honda VFR800 V-Fours (97 - 01)	◆ 3703
Honda VFR800 V-Tec V-Fours (02 - 05)	◆ 4196
Honda CB750 & CB900 dohc Fours (78 - 84)	0535
Honda VTR1000 (FireStorm, Super Hawk) & XL1000V (Varadero) (97 - 00)	◆ 3744
Honda CBR900RR FireBlade (92 - 99)	◆ 2161
Honda CBR900RR FireBlade (00 - 03)	◆ 4060
Honda CBR1100XX Super Blackbird (97 - 02)	◆ 3901
Honda ST1100 Pan European V-Fours (90 - 01)	◆ 3384
Honda Shadow VT1100 (USA) (85 - 98)	2313

Title	Book No
Honda GL1000 Gold Wing (75 - 79)	0309
Honda GL1100 Gold Wing (79 - 81)	0669
Honda Gold Wing 1200 (USA) (84 - 87)	2199
Honda Gold Wing 1500 (USA) (88 - 00)	2225
KAWASAKI AE/AR 50 & 80 (81 - 95)	1007
Kawasaki KC, KE & KH100 (75 - 99)	1371
Kawasaki KMX125 & 200 (86 - 02)	◇ 3046
Kawasaki 250, 350 & 400 Triples (72 - 79)	0134
Kawasaki 400 & 440 Twins (74 - 81)	0281
Kawasaki 400, 500 & 550 Fours (79 - 91)	0910
Kawasaki EN450 & 500 Twins (Ltd/Vulcan) (85 - 04)	2053
Kawasaki EX & ER500 (GPZ500S & ER-5) Twins (87 - 99)	◆ 2052
Kawasaki ZX600 (Ninja ZX-6, ZZ-R600) Fours (90 - 00)	◆ 2146
Kawasaki ZX-6R Ninja Fours (95 - 02)	◆ 3541
Kawasaki ZX600 (GPZ600R, GPX600R, Ninja 600R & RX) & ZX750 (GPX750R, Ninja 750R) Fours (85 - 97)	◆ 1780
Kawasaki 650 Four (76 - 78)	0373
Kawasaki Vulcan 700/750 & 800 (85 - 04)	◆ 2457
Kawasaki 750 Air-cooled Fours (80 - 91)	0574
Kawasaki ZR550 & 750 Zephyr Fours (90 - 97)	◆ 3382
Kawasaki ZX750 (Ninja ZX-7 & ZXR750) Fours (89 - 96)	◆ 2054
Kawasaki Ninja ZX-7R & ZX-9R (94 - 04)	◆ 3721
Kawasaki 900 & 1000 Fours (73 - 77)	0222
Kawasaki ZX900, 1000 & 1100 Liquid-cooled Fours (83 - 97)	◆ 1681
MOTO GUZZI 750, 850 & 1000 V-Twins (74 - 78)	0339
MZ ETZ Models (81 - 95)	◇ 1680
NORTON 500, 600, 650 & 750 Twins (57 - 70)	0187
Norton Commando (68 - 77)	0125
PEUGEOT Speedfight, Trekker & Vivacity (96 - 02)	◇ 3920
PIAGGIO (Vespa) Scooters (91 - 03)	◇ 3492
SUZUKI GT, ZR & TS50 (77 - 90)	◇ 0799
Suzuki TS50X (84 - 00)	◇ 1599
Suzuki 100, 125, 185 & 250 Air-cooled Trail bikes (79 - 89)	0797
Suzuki GP100 & 125 Singles (78 - 93)	◇ 0576
Suzuki GS, GN, GZ & DR125 Singles (82 - 99)	◇ 0888
Suzuki 250 & 350 Twins (68 - 78)	0120
Suzuki GT250X7, GT200X5 & SB200 Twins (78 - 83)	◇ 0469
Suzuki GS/GSX250, 400 & 450 Twins (79 - 85)	0736
Suzuki GS500 Twin (89 - 02)	◆ 3238
Suzuki GS550 (77 - 82) & GS750 Fours (76 - 79)	0363
Suzuki GS/GSX550 4-valve Fours (83 - 88)	1133
Suzuki SV650 (99 - 02)	◆ 3912
Suzuki GSX-R600 & 750 (96 - 00)	◆ 3553
Suzuki GSX-R600 (01 - 02), GSX-R750 (00 - 02) & GSX-R1000 (01 - 02)	◆ 3986
Suzuki GSF600 & 1200 Bandit Fours (95 - 04)	◆ 3367
Suzuki GS850 Fours (78 - 88)	0536
Suzuki GS1000 Four (77 - 79)	0484
Suzuki GSX-R750, GSX-R1100 (85 - 92), GSX600F, GSX750F, GSX1100F (Katana) Fours (88 - 96)	◆ 2055
Suzuki GSX600/750F & GSX750 (98 - 02)	◆ 3987
Suzuki GS/GSX1000, 1100 & 1150 4-valve Fours (79 - 88)	0737
Suzuki TL1000S/R & DL1000 V-Strom (97 - 04)	◆ 4083
Suzuki GSX1300R Hayabusa (99 - 04)	◆ 4184
TRIUMPH Tiger Cub & Terrier (52 - 68)	0414
Triumph 350 & 500 Unit Twins (58 - 73)	0137
Triumph Pre-Unit Twins (47 - 62)	0251
Triumph 650 & 750 2-valve Unit Twins (63 - 83)	0122
Triumph Trident & BSA Rocket 3 (69 - 75)	0136
Triumph Fuel Injected Triples (97 - 00)	◆ 3755
Triumph Triples & Fours (carburettor engines) (91 - 99)	◆ 2162
VESPA P/PX125, 150 & 200 Scooters (78 - 03)	0707
Vespa Scooters (59 - 78)	0126
YAMAHA DT50 & 80 Trail Bikes (78 - 95)	◇ 0800

Title	Book No
Yamaha T50 & 80 Townmate (83 - 95)	◇ 1247
Yamaha YB100 Singles (73 - 91)	◇ 0474
Yamaha RS/RXS100 & 125 Singles (74 - 95)	◇ 0331
Yamaha RD & DT125LC (82 - 87)	◇ 0887
Yamaha TZR125 (87 - 93) & DT125R (88 - 02)	◇ 1655
Yamaha TY50, 80, 125 & 175 (74 - 84)	◇ 0464
Yamaha XT & SR125 (82 - 02)	◇ 1021
Yamaha Trail Bikes (81 - 00)	2350
Yamaha 250 & 350 Twins (70 - 79)	0040
Yamaha XS250, 360 & 400 sohc Twins (75 - 84)	0378
Yamaha RD250 & 350LC Twins (80 - 82)	0803
Yamaha RD350 YPVS Twins (83 - 95)	1158
Yamaha RD400 Twin (75 - 79)	0333
Yamaha XT, TT & SR500 Singles (75 - 83)	0342
Yamaha XZ550 Vision V-Twins (82 - 85)	0821
Yamaha FJ, FZ, XJ & YX600 Radian (84 - 92)	2100
Yamaha XJ600S (Diversion, Seca II) & XJ600N Fours (92 - 03)	◆ 2145
Yamaha YZF600R Thundercat & FZS600 Fazer (96 - 03)	◆ 3702
Yamaha YZF-R6 (98 - 02)	◆ 3900
Yamaha 650 Twins (70 - 83)	0341
Yamaha XJ650 & 750 Fours (80 - 84)	0738
Yamaha XS750 & 850 Triples (76 - 85)	0340
Yamaha TDM850, TRX850 & XTZ750 (89 - 99)	◇ ◆ 3540
Yamaha YZF750R & YZF1000R Thunderace (93 - 00)	◆ 3720
Yamaha FZR600, 750 & 1000 Fours (87 - 96)	◆ 2056
Yamaha XV (Virago) V-Twins (81 - 03)	◆ 0802
Yamaha XVS650 & 1100 Dragstar/V-Star (97 - 05)	◆ 4195
Yamaha XJ900F Fours (83 - 94)	◆ 3239
Yamaha XJ900S Diversion (94 - 01)	◆ 3739
Yamaha YZF-R1 (98 - 03)	◆ 3754
Yamaha FJ1100 & 1200 Fours (84 - 96)	◆ 2057
Yamaha XJR1200 & 1300 (95 - 03)	◆ 3981
Yamaha V-Max (85 - 03)	◆ 4072
ATVs	
Honda ATC70, 90, 110, 185 & 200 (71 - 85)	0565
Honda TRX300 Shaft Drive ATVs (88 - 00)	2125
Honda TRX300EX & TRX400EX ATVs (93 - 04)	2318
Honda Foreman 400 and 450 ATVs (95 - 02)	2465
Kawasaki Bayou 220/250/300 & Prairie 300 ATVs (86 - 03)	2351
Polaris ATVs (85 - 97)	2302
Polaris ATVs (98 - 03)	2508
Yamaha YFS200 Blaster ATV (88 - 02)	2317
Yamaha YFB250 Timberwolf ATVs (92 - 00)	2217
Yamaha YFM350 & YFM400 (ER and Big Bear) ATVs (87 - 03)	2126
Yamaha Banshee and Warrior ATVs (87 - 03)	2314
ATV Basics	10450
TECHBOOK SERIES	
Motorcycle Basics TechBook (2nd Edition)	3515
Motorcycle Electrical TechBook (3rd Edition)	3471
Motorcycle Fuel Systems TechBook	3514
Motorcycle Maintenance TechBook	4071
Motorcycle Workshop Practice TechBook (2nd Edition)	3470
GENERAL MANUALS	
Twist and Go (automatic transmission) Scooters Service and Repair Manual	4082

◇ = not available in the USA   ◆ = Superbike

The manuals on this page are available through good motorcycle dealers and accessory shops. In case of difficulty, contact: **Haynes Publishing** (UK) +44 1963 442030   (USA) +1 805 498 6703 (FR) +33 1 47 17 66 29   (SV) +46 18 124016 (Australia/New Zealand) +61 3 9763 8100

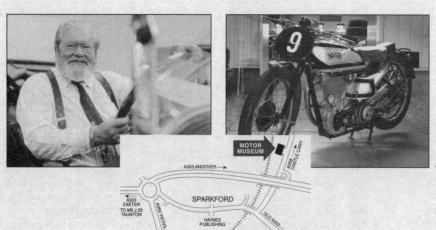